DILEMMAS OF INDEPENDENCE

DILEMMAS OF INDEPENDENCE

Ukraine After Totalitarianism

Alexander J. Motyl

COUNCIL ON FOREIGN RELATIONS PRESS

NEW YORK

COUNCIL ON FOREIGN RELATIONS BOOKS

The Council on Foreign Relations, Inc., is a nonprofit and non-partisan organization devoted to promoting improved understanding of international affairs through the free exchange of ideas. The Council does not take any position on questions of foreign policy and has no affiliation with, and receives no funding from, the United States government.

From time to time, books and monographs written by members of the Council's research staff or visiting fellows, or commissioned by the Council, or written by an independent author with critical review contributed by a Council study or working group are published with the designation "Council on Foreign Relations Book." Any book or monograph bearing that designation is, in the judgment of the Committee on Studies of the Council's Board of Directors, a responsible treatment of a significant international topic worthy of presentation to the public. All statements of fact and expressions of opinion contained in Council books are, however, the sole responsibility of the author.

If you would like more information on Council publications, please write the Council on Foreign Relations, 58 East 68th Street, New York, NY 10021, or call the Publications Office at (212)734-0400.

Library of Congress Cataloging-in-Publication Data

Motyl, Alexander J.
    Dilemmas of independence : Ukraine after totalitarianism / by Alexander J. Motyl.
        p.   cm.
    Includes bibliographical references and index.
    ISBN 0-87609-131-1 : $17.95
    1. Ukraine—Politics and government—1991–   I. Title.
DK508.846.M68   1993
947'.710854—dc20

                                                        93-16966
                                                        CIP

94   95   96   97   EB   10   9   8   7   6   5   4   3   2

Cover design: Michael Storrings

"Some products are beginning to reappear in the stores, but the prices are astronomical, not yet appropriate for our pockets. But I don't mind. Let me eat only potatoes, as long as it's in our own state. I thank the Almightly for letting us attain a Ukraine so easily, without any loss of life or bloodshed. True, we lost millions during the seventy-year existence of the Soviet state, but that's probably why the Lord had pity on us now. I fear only that our people won't maintain our state with dignity, that they'll begin fighting over positions again. There must be unity, and together we must rebuild our unhappy and ruined Ukraine."

—M. V., Letter from Lviv,
February 26, 1992

Ukraine will return to the civilized world hand in hand with Russia—virtually no one doubts that now. But what expression it will have on its face as it does so is another question. If the parliament of its partner state periodically takes the liberty of making "friendly reproaches" and territorial allusions, no matter how solidly based they are on documents of the Soviet era and no matter what results (or, more likely, lack of results) they produce, Ukraine will walk beside Russia with clenched teeth. . . .

—Vitaly Portnikov,
Nezavisimaya gazeta,
December 11, 1992

C O N T E N T S

ACKNOWLEDGMENTS

Postmodernists have proclaimed the death of the author. Perhaps. This one, certainly, would have had far more difficulty hanging onto life without the critical comments, factual corrections, and encouragement of Nadia Diuk of The National Endowment for Democracy, Judson Flanagan, Mark von Hagen of Columbia University, David Haproff of the Council on Foreign Relations, Stanley Heginbotham of the Social Science Research Council, Adrian Karatnycky of the AFL-CIO, G. B. Kej, Allen Lynch of the University of Virginia, Myroslav Prokop of Prolog Research Corporation, Jenik Radon of Radon and Ishizumi, Trudy Rubin of *The Philadelphia Inquirer*, Richard Shriver of *Ukrainian Business Digest*, Sophia Sluzar of the Department of State, Bohdan Vitvitsky of the U.S. Attorney's Office in New Jersey, and Theresa Weber of the International Executive Service Corps. Special thanks are due to Michael Mandelbaum, director of the Council's Project on East-West Relations, who patiently supported this project from beginning to end, and to Charles Furtado of the Harriman Institute, who lost a bet but always gave support.

Some sections of the book have appeared in shorter versions in other publications: "Russian Hegemony and Non-Russian Insecurity: Dilemmas of the USSR's Successor States," *Harriman Institute Forum* (December 1991); "Empire or Stability? The Case for Soviet Dissolution," *World Policy Journal* (Summer 1991); "Totalitarian Collapse, Imperial Disintegration, and the Rise of the Soviet West," in Michael Mandelbaum, ed., *The Rise of Nations in*

x   *the Soviet Union* (New York: Council on Foreign Relations, 1991).
These sections have been thoroughly revised and updated.

Some of the research that went into this book was conducted
on two trips to Ukraine, in January and August 1992. I am greatly
indebted to Ihor Ostash, Director of the International School of
Ukrainian Studies in Kiev, and Zenovy Drevnyak, chief-of-staff of
the Lviv Regional Administration, for their invaluable assistance
during my stays in their cities. My trip to Lviv was funded by a
PepsiCo Summer Travel Fellowship of the Harriman Institute.

This book is part of the Council on Foreign Relations Project
on East-West Relations, which is supported by the Carnegie
Corporation.

PREFACE

Premises, Consequences, Biases

S ince 1991, Ukraine has been an independent state. For several hundred years, however, most of Ukraine was an integral part of first, tsarist Russia and then the Soviet Union. How a colony became one of Europe's largest states and what statehood means for Ukraine and its neighbors are the principal subjects of this book.

Although both the Russian and the Soviet empires left indelible marks on Ukraine and Ukrainians, the Soviet imprint was deeper, because it was more recent and because the USSR represented a historically unique political system—a totalitarian empire. The fall of the Soviet Union has thus bequeathed two legacies to Ukraine and the other successor states: imperial collapse and totalitarian ruin. The legacy of empire encourages the forceful promotion of rapid and fundamental change; the legacy of totalitarianism negates the very possibility of that change. Coping with these contradictory legacies, overcoming their baneful effects, and producing modern, democratic, market-oriented states is the complex challenge facing Ukraine and its neighbors. As I will argue, however, in meeting these challenges, independent Ukraine must come to grips with numerous dilemmas offering equally good or, more typically, equally bad alternatives. And how Ukraine deals with the dilemmas of independence is a question that will affect not only its own future, but also that of surrounding countries and of the West.

This book, then, is about Ukraine, but not just about Ukraine. It is also about the Soviet Union and Russia, which have defined Ukraine as much as Ukraine has defined itself, and about the other post-Communist states, whose recent history is almost identical to Ukraine's. My premise throughout is that Ukraine is not unique. As a former colony, Ukraine is comparable to other postimperial states; as a victim of totalitarianism, Ukraine shares many characteristics with the formerly Soviet republics and the satellite states of Central Europe.

The comparative approach gives this study several distinguishing features. The first is most obvious: in contrast to most books that deal with particular ex-Soviet republics, this one devotes considerable attention to the meanings attached to such concepts as empire, totalitarianism, nationalism, state, civil society, and market, which are necessary for comparison. Second, at the heart of what follows is a theory of how empires rise and fall, especially totalitarian empires, and of the consequences of their collapse for nationalism, civil society, nation-building and state-building, and economic reform. Third, this study purports not only to explain what has happened, but also to suggest what will happen—but only if certain conditions hold. As a result, the book inevitably provides policymakers with advice, even if of the kind that they are likely to reject. Fourth, this work is not so detailed as most accounts of former Soviet republics tend to be. One reason for this decision is unabashedly practical: the rapid pace of change in all of Eastern Europe threatens blow-by-blow accounts with premature obsolescence. Even more important at a time of immense flux, however, is to look at the big picture, rather than focusing on particular details, so as to get a sense of the larger forces pushing countries, leaders, and groups in specific directions.

Finally, readers should know that this study is pessimistic about the future of Ukraine, Russia, and the other successor states. This is the result in part of its analytical emphasis on broad social and institutional forces instead of on personalities. Whereas Boris Yeltsin, Leonid Kravchuk, Václav Havel, and Lech Walesa may give us grounds for hope, the legacies of empire and totalitarianism incline one toward despair. The future for *everyone* concerned—for Ukraine, for Russia, and for the West—is likely to be bleak. History does not end in this book, and the new world order does not begin here. Even if readers remain disinclined to accept this view, at least they will become familiar with the larger picture so as to identify the many constraints that policymakers must overcome.

Regardless of whether one agrees with the policy recommendations made in this book, its pessimistic tone does imply that current American and West European policies toward the USSR's successor states are the worst that one could imagine. Doing little to help the successor states is tantamount to doing nothing, and insisting that the successor states do everything immediately on their own is, I suggest, to court disaster. Radically transformative policies will *not* work, because they *cannot* work under the uniquely post-totalitarian and postimperial conditions characteristic of all the successor states. Yet Western advisers are encouraging the post-Communist states to consider nothing less than such revolutionary change. The new states are supposed to complete transitions to market economies and democracy as quickly as possible, under conditions—the penury and confusion bequeathed to them by the collapse of empire and totalitarianism—that are least conducive to such a transformation. And the new states are never to waver in their commitment to democratic procedures and human rights while depriving their own *demos* of their livelihood. I do not see how Ukraine, Russia, or even Poland can pull it off. If aggressively pursued, policies that promote rapid and radical economic, political, and social change are a surefire way of creating massive political instability, social chaos, and ethnic conflict. The only alternative is an evolutionary set of policies that involve the sequencing of political, social, and economic reform within countries and among countries.

As readers will have noticed from the preceding paragraph, I am skeptical about the efficacy and desirability of revolutionary transformations, even if they go by the name of "radical reform" or "shock therapy" and are promoted by university professors or international civil servants. Virtually all revolutions—rapid and fundamental changes of a polity, economy, and society—have been exceedingly violent undertakings, and they have rarely, if ever, succeeded in attaining their goals more than temporarily.

I have two more biases. Although I see nothing inherently wrong with the separatism of nations and the creation of national states—and that is what nationalism really is about—I cannot agree with the nationalist assumption that nations are immutable, monolithic, and God-given entities. Nations change, they come and go, as do, incidentally, classes, states, and all other social and political groups. This point bears emphasizing because the nationalist reification of nations has begun to penetrate the Western discourse as well. Scholars, policymakers, and journalists talk of "the" Ukrainians and "the" Russians in Ukraine as if their identities, interests, and loyalties were set in stone—which of course is not to say that Ukrainians, Russians, and Jews do not exist as separate nations and that they do not have identities, interests, and loyalties, but that these are of a fluid and variable kind. Worst of all, in talking in this manner we suggest that national identity is determined either by birth or by registration. According to this logic, all individuals with "Ukrainian" or "Russian" or "Jewish" stamped on their passports must remain just that. The Soviet regime may have believed it, and nationalists may believe it, but there is no reason for us to fall into that trap and, as a result, to overlook the fact that the malleability of ethnic identity means that ethnic conflict is neither historically inevitable nor immune to policy solutions.

My final bias concerns human rights. Despite the degree to which discussion of them has become a part of public discourse, the issues raised and the distinctions drawn in these discussions— between the rights of individuals and the rights of groups—will be of minimal relevance to ongoing political, social, and economic processes in Eastern Europe. Human rights certainly are important, but in contrast to the prevailing habit, this book avoids discussion of human rights in general and of the supposed right to national self-determination in particular, and focuses instead on the *real* issues involved—politics, economics, society, and culture.

Underlying such skepticism is my conviction that mystification and simplification have no place in scholarship or in policymaking. Just as we should not mystify the nation, national identity, and the state, we also would do well not to simplify rights, national liberation struggles, and, especially, transitions to democracy and market economies. In this analysis of Ukraine, inside and outside the Russian and Soviet empires, I have attempted to do just that.

A.J.M.
New York City, January 1993

INTRODUCTION

Dilemmas for Ukraine

U nlike most of the other Soviet successor states, Ukraine matters. It is important for a variety of reasons that ensure it a central role in the future of Europe and thus in the foreign policy of the United States. First on the list are Ukraine's impressive physical size, economic potential, and resource endowment. Second is Ukraine's propinquity to—indeed, some might argue that Ukraine is part of—Central Europe in general and to Poland, the Czech Republic, Slovakia, and Hungary in particular. Third is Ukraine's defining impact on Russia. Fourth is Ukraine's resultant importance to the stability and security of Europe as a whole.

WHY UKRAINE MATTERS

Some statistics convey Ukraine's size. Its current population, 52 million, is the fifth largest in Europe, minus Russia—after Germany, Great Britain, Italy, and France, and the latter three outnumber Ukraine by only a few million. Measuring 232,046 square miles, Ukraine's territory is the largest, with France as its closest competitor with 211,207 square miles. Ukraine is about the size of Poland, Hungary, the former Czechoslovakia, and Austria combined.

Ukraine's heavy and light industry, however dilapidated after seven decades of communism, has enormous growth potential.

1

2   Ukraine produced a disproportionately large share of the USSR's metallurgical equipment, heavy electric machines, electric motors, turbines, power transformers, metal-working machine tools, locomotives, freight cars, excavators, bulldozers, coal and grain combines, cars, trucks, buses, tractors, and rolled steel. Ukraine also produced bicycles, washing machines, refrigerators, radios, televisions, and cameras; a variety of construction materials such as cement, reinforced concrete structures and parts, insulating, facing, and wall materials, silicate glass, and ceramics; and basic chemicals, fertilizers, and synthetic fibers. A substantial part of the Soviet military-industrial and space complexes was also located in Ukraine.

Its agriculture probably could, with the appropriate reforms, transform Ukraine into what it was at the beginning of the twentieth century—Europe's "breadbasket." Ukraine accounted for close to a quarter of the USSR's total agricultural output, producing one-fourth of Soviet grain, almost half the corn, and over half the sugar beets. Ukraine also produces in quantity soybeans, tobacco, flax, vegetables, eggs, beef, and other animal products. No less impressive are Ukraine's natural resources, in particular its coal and iron ore deposits, which accounted for about one-fourth and almost one half, respectively, of Soviet production. Ukraine has significant deposits of manganese, potassium, titanium, mercury, magnesium, uranium, graphite, mineral salts, gypsum, and alabaster, as well as substantial reserves of petroleum and natural gas, which together with nuclear power cover more than half its energy needs.[1]

Finally, the quality of Ukraine's human capital is high. The population is fully literate, and close to 90 percent of the employed population has a higher or secondary (complete or incomplete) education. More than 150,000 highly qualified specialists graduate annually from over 150 colleges and universities, which have a total student body of about one million.[2] The scientists employed by the Ukrainian Academy of Sciences are world-class theorists in such fields as mathematics, cybernetics, physics, chemistry, and electronics.

Size and resources make Ukraine the largest and most power- **3**
ful country between Germany and Russia. Although Berlin and
Moscow have historically tended to view East-Central Europe as
lying within their respective spheres of influence, the collapse of
communism and the emergence of independent successor states
will probably transform this former hinterland into a coherent
political-economic space with an authentic identity of its own.
With historical and cultural bonds originating in their association
with the Polish-Lithuanian Commonwealth, the Hapsburg empire, or both, with close economic ties fashioned in the post–
World War II period by the Council on Mutual Economic Assistance, with common fears of domination by Germany and Russia,
and with virtually identical tasks of post-totalitarian reconstruction, Ukraine, Poland, the Czech Republic, Slovakia, Hungary,
Belarus, and the Baltic states should in time come to fashion an
East-Central European subregion of the new Europe. By virtue of
its political, economic, and demographic importance, Ukraine
will play a key role in forming, or blocking, such an association,
and, like Germany in Western Europe, it could even dominate
such a community as well.

The Centrality of Russia

Ukraine also has a critically important role to play in Eastern
Europe, as the leading non-Russian actor in the post-Soviet order,
however it turns out. And that means that the future of the former
USSR is as much in the hands of Kiev as it is in those of Moscow.
Economic reform, transitions to democracy, and the stability and
peace of this part of the world—none of these questions can be
addressed by Moscow or through Moscow alone. Kiev simply
cannot be ignored.

This observation underlines what is central for Ukraine: its
relationship with Russia. Ukraine cannot be understood in isolation from Russia, but, by the same token, Russia cannot be
understood in isolation from Ukraine. The two countries define
each other in a way that few others do. The historical interconnec-
tions between Ukraine and Russia have penetrated every aspect of

4   their current relationship. Their relations are therefore complex and are likely to remain so for the foreseeable future.

As Ukraine and Russia come to define themselves on their own terms, and not exclusively in relation to each other, tensions, disagreements, and perhaps even armed conflicts will arise. That might not matter if both countries were small and geopolitically insignificant. But they are not. As a result, the Russo-Ukrainian relationship will exert a defining influence on events in the Commonwealth of Independent States and Central Europe. And should those relations degenerate into warfare (as they could if the legacies of empire and totalitarianism are not handled with care), the impact on West European security and thus on global stability would be enormous. It is scarcely an exaggeration to say that Moscow and Kiev hold the keys to world peace. It is imperative, therefore, that Russia and Ukraine divorce quickly, if not quietly, and that their subsequent relations remain, if not cordial, at least not overtly hostile. Serbia's relations with Slovenia, Croatia, and Bosnia-Herzegovina dare not serve as a model for Russia's relations with Ukraine.

The Unknown Country

For all of Ukraine's actual and potential importance, the country remains virtually unknown throughout most of the world. One reason is that, as a Soviet republic, Ukraine was presumed, not altogether incorrectly, to be the equivalent of a Canadian province, American state, or German *Land*, meriting relatively little foreign policy attention. No less important was the extreme difficulty Western journalists had in acquiring accurate information about Ukraine. Before the stewardship of Soviet leader Mikhail Gorbachev, travel restrictions generally prevented or dissuaded correspondents from venturing beyond Moscow. Readers of the Western press in the 1970s, for instance, would have been hard-pressed to learn that the dissident movement was actually strongest in Ukraine and Lithuania, not in Moscow, where Western journalists were stationed.

Scholars contributed their share to Ukraine's invisibility. As students of Soviet ethnic relations—the "nationality question"— can attest, most mainstream Sovietologists and Kremlinologists considered their professional interest in non-Russians to be an exotic pursuit. Ukrainian studies, like Armenian studies, were frequently considered irrelevant to "real" politics in the USSR, politically motivated by émigré agendas, and emotionally charged by nationalist perspectives. In a word, it was supposed to be "unscholarly."

Underlying these excessively harsh attitudes was a Ukrainian image problem. All too often, Ukrainians were exclusively associated with the Cold War and allegations of collaboration with the Nazis during World War II—the case of John Demjanjuk comes to mind—and anti-Semitism. To some degree such images were justified; to some degree, obviously not. Ukrainian-Americans have endorsed "Evil Empire" language and policies, but only because their homeland had been seized by an empire that was surely less than morally good. Many Ukrainians did collaborate with the Nazis, but the vast majority did not, and the relative number of collaborationists was lower than that in most European countries. The history of relations between ethnic Ukrainians and ethnic Jews includes some terrible episodes. Ukraine has been the site of many anti-Jewish pogroms, but for long stretches of history the Ukrainian and Jewish populations have lived side by side peacefully. Ukrainian history, like the history of every people, has been far from one-dimensional. Ukrainian nationalists have generally stressed only the positive side; it would be equally erroneous to dwell exclusively on the negative. Neither does justice to a rather more complex picture.

Several years of glasnost and perestroika and the subsequent collapse of the USSR have removed the veil of obscurity from Ukraine. Independent countries, especially important ones such as Ukraine, are always of interest to policymakers. The end of totalitarianism has removed the major barriers to journalistic investigation of Ukraine. The obvious centrality of the nationality question to the collapse of the USSR has transformed a marginal

6   scholarly pursuit into the very core of post-Soviet studies. And the
ability of Ukrainian nationalists in Ukraine to forge and maintain
interethnic coalitions with ethnic Russians and Jews, to talk and
act as democrats, and apparently to forswear nuclear weapons has
substantially corrected Ukraine's image problem. The obstacles to
studying Ukraine are more or less gone, while the need to understand it has correspondingly grown.

Some Basic Data

Ukraine borders the Black Sea and the Sea of Azov to the south,
Russia to the east and northeast, Belarus to the north, Poland and
Slovakia to the northwest and west, and Hungary, Romania, and
Moldova to the west and southwest. Turkey, with which Ukraine
has had complex ties, lies directly across the Black Sea. Administratively, Ukraine is divided into twenty-four provinces (oblasts),
one autonomous republic, the Crimea, and, at last count, some
479 districts (raions). Kiev, the capital, is its largest city (population 2.6 million); four other cities have a population of over one
million; forty-six have a population of over 100,000. Kharkiv,
Dnipropetrovsk, Donetsk, Luhansk, Zaporizhzhia, and Kryvy
Rih, all in the east, are the major industrial centers; Mykolaiv,
Kherson, and Odessa are port cities with shipbuilding facilities;
Sevastopol is the home of the Black Sea Fleet; in the west,
formerly Hapsburg Lviv is Ukraine's most European city.

Most of Ukraine consists of fertile steppelands and forest-
steppes. The predominantly low-lying territory stands in sharp
contrast to the Carpathian Mountains in the west and the
Crimean Mountains in the south. The Dnieper (Dnipro) River,
dividing Ukraine into a Left Bank in the east and a Right Bank in
the west, is the country's major artery as well as a source of poetic
imagery and popular myth. An abundance of black earth soils
make most of Ukraine ideally suited to agriculture; natural resources are concentrated in the Donets Basin or Donbas, the
Dnieper-Kryvy Rih Basin, and in the Carpathian foothills.

Of Ukraine's approximately 52 million people, about 73
percent are identified as "Ukrainian" and 22 percent as "Russian."

The terms are more ambiguous than they might appear since for the most part they refer to designations contained in Soviet passports. (In the new Ukrainian passports ethnicity will no longer be noted.) In general, the Soviet authorities assigned national identity on the basis of parental identity. If both parents were labeled Ukrainian then so were the children, even if they had never spoken a word of Ukrainian all their lives. If the parents were of mixed origin, children could choose one of their identities at the age of sixteen, when they qualified for their own passports—which also meant that, for instance, a Ukrainian-speaking child of "passport" Russian and Jewish parents could never be Ukrainian! In other words, Soviet statistics on national identity have to be taken with a grain of salt. Somewhat more useful are Soviet statistics on language. On that basis some 88 percent of passport Ukrainians considered Ukrainian their "native tongue," while virtually all passport Russians considered Russian theirs. The problem with these figures, however, is that most urban residents of the central, eastern, and southern oblasts of Ukraine speak Russian at work and in the street. Does that make them Russian-speaking Ukrainians, Russified Ukrainians, or bilingual Russians? As I shall suggest in a later chapter, shared belief in certain defining myths may be the best way of coming to terms with what a "Ukrainian" is or is likely to be.

Therefore Ukraine is anything but homogeneous. In addition to the presence of a substantial passport Russian population, the country is also home to passport Jews, Belarusians, Moldovans, Poles, Bulgarians, Hungarians, and Romanians, each numbering at least 100,000. The eastern and southern provinces are most Russian or Russified; the western and central oblasts are most Ukrainian. Compounding the divide is the fact that the western provinces of Volyn (Volhynia), Rivne, Lviv, Ternopil, Ivano-Frankivsk, Zakarpattya (Transcarpathia), and Chernivtsi were annexed by the Soviet Union from 1939 to 1945, and were thus spared twenty years of Soviet rule and the harshest period of Stalinism, the 1930s. Especially distinctive are Lviv, Ternopil, and Ivano-Frankivsk, which comprise eastern Galicia, and Zakar-

8   pattya and Chernivtsi province, the latter also known as Bukovyna. Parts of Austria-Hungary until 1918, they then weathered the interwar period within Poland, Czechoslovakia, and Romania. Unlike the rest of Ukraine, these regions unquestionably belong to Central Europe, as evidenced by their architecture, culture, manners, and economic traditions.

The Religious Divide

One other fault line deserves mention: religion. To the degree that they are religious, most eastern, southern, and central Ukrainians are Orthodox Christians, as are the Russians and the inhabitants of Volyn and Rivne oblasts. In contrast, most Galicians and many Transcarpathians and Bukovynians are members of the Greek Catholic, or Uniate, Church, a branch of Catholicism established during the Counter-Reformation in the late sixteenth century. The distinction is of more than theological interest. For most of the last two centuries, Uniate Catholicism has served as the main prop for Ukrainian national identity in western Ukraine: in its retention of Orthodox rites, Greek Catholicism distinguished Ukrainians from the Poles, and in its subordination to the Pope, it distinguished them from the Orthodox Russians. Indeed, for much of the twentieth century the Greek Catholic Church, especially under the guidance of the charismatic metropolitan Andrei Sheptytsky, also functioned as one of the major supporters of Ukrainian statehood. Although the Soviet regime banned the church at a bogus synod in 1946 and distributed most of its property to the Orthodox, believers and clergy continued to practice their faith "in the catacombs," from which they emerged in 1989–1990.

In contrast, the Orthodox Church rarely played a nationally supportive function in the Ukrainian east. After Ukrainian Orthodoxy was absorbed into the Russian Orthodox Church in the eighteenth century, Orthodox Christianity served largely to blur distinctions between Ukrainians and Russians, to such an extent that Ukrainian nationalists have generally condemned it for "Russifying" the population. Not surprisingly, a Ukrainian Auto-

cephalous Orthodox Church was founded in 1920, during the
nationalist revolution; no less surprisingly, it was liquidated by the
Soviet Union in 1930 for its autonomist leanings. Ukrainian
Autocephaly was reestablished in 1990, and in a sign of the
nationalist times, the local Russian Orthodox Church renamed
itself the "Ukrainian Orthodox Church." In 1992, the Orthodox
metropolitan of Kiev, Filaret, even agreed to a merger of his
church with that of the Autocephalous, the result being the
"Ukrainian Orthodox Church (Kiev Patriarchate)," an institution that claimed complete independence from the Moscow patriarch. Autocephaly, apparently, proved to be Filaret's last refuge
after journalistic accounts of his amorous affairs and long-time
association with the secret police compelled him to seek legitimacy in national symbols.

Even though they share many cultural traditions and myths,
eastern and western Ukrainians are clearly different, but are they
so different as to constitute separate nations? The question is
premised on too rigid an understanding of what nations involve.
Regionalism is fully compatible with nationhood, as are different
religions, different ethnic origins, even different languages. Naturally, differences complicate what scholars call nation-building.
Current tensions between Uniates and Orthodox, concerned almost exclusively with the question of returning confiscated
churches, Orthodox since 1946, to their former Uniate owners,
do not encourage national solidarity. The same may hold true for
ethnic customs and different languages. Nevertheless, it is important to note that many modern nations are not only multilingual
and multiethnic, but also multiconfessional. Homogeneity may
make the life of nation-builders easier, but heterogeneity surely
does not preclude nationhood.

Separatism, on the other hand, does preclude nationhood,
since it is premised on a desire to leave one national state and
either join another or form one's own. But separatism is not
regionalism, and the latter—the self-identification with one's
immediate locale—is a perfectly "normal" phenomenon in every
modern state. Galician regionalism as well as Donbas and Trans-

10   carpathian regionalism are facts of life, and not necessarily problems. As explained below, however, Crimean separatism is as
much a problem for Ukrainian national identity and Ukrainian
statehood as Québécois separatism is for Canadians. By its very
existence, Crimean separatism denies the universalist aspirations
of Ukrainian identity and the territorial integrity of the state.

UKRAINIAN DILEMMAS

The problem of the Crimea deserves closer attention because in so
many ways it typifies the dilemmas confronting Ukraine and other
states in the post-Soviet era. Historically, the Crimea was the
home of the Crimean Tatars, a Turkic people who settled the
peninsula in the thirteenth century. Tsarist Russia conquered the
Crimea five centuries later, and, as a result of especially harsh
colonial policies, the Tatar share of the local population dropped
sharply, from about 83 percent in 1793 to about 60 percent in
1854. By the mid-1920s, Tatars comprised a quarter of the population, Russians under half, and Ukrainians a tenth.[3]

After the creation of the USSR, the Tatar homeland acquired the status of an autonomous republic within the Russian
Federation. In 1944, however, the entire Tatar population was
forcibly resettled to Central Asia for allegedly collaborating with
the Nazis—a charge that was true for some Tatars, but was non-
sense with respect to the vast majority—and the peninsula was
transformed into a mere Russian oblast. Then, in 1954, for reasons
that are still not fully clear, Nikita Khrushchev granted Ukraine
the Crimea as a "gift" from Russia on the occasion of the 300th
anniversary of the Pereyaslav Treaty, according to which, so went
the official version, the Ukrainian Cossack chieftain, Bohdan
Khmelnytsky, and Tsar Alexei bound their countries in perpetu-
ity. Despite the province's formally Ukrainian status, however,
most of the postwar settlers were from Russia proper, with the
result that, at present, Russians comprise two-thirds of the population and Ukrainians one-fourth. After the late 1950s, the
Crimean Tatars actively pressed the Soviet government to be

allowed to return to their ancestral lands, but to no avail. In   **11**
marked contrast to such similarly resettled nations as the Meskhe-
tian Turks, the Chechen, the Ingush, and others who were given
back their homelands, the Tatars had great difficulty in returning
even on an individual basis. The Soviet government stonewalled
them.[4]

Why were the Tatars repeatedly denied their request? One
reason was real estate: the Crimea had become the Soviet elite's
vacation playground, and repatriation would have raised embarrassing and costly questions of ownership rights. The other reason
was the Black Sea Fleet: considered a strategic force by the Soviet
Command, the fleet would have had a decidedly anomalous status
in a Crimea ruled by Tatars. Both reasons also suggest why most
postwar settlers in the Crimea were Russians from Russia. A
pleasant climate would attract all nationalities equally, so the
preponderance of Russians suggests that a government policy was
at work, one intended to populate a region of enormous financial
and strategic importance with reliable supporters of the central
regime.

Three conclusions follow from this historical sketch. First,
the argument that the Crimea is historically Russian is incorrect,
which is not to say that Russians do not believe in it passionately.
If anyone has a legitimate claim to the Crimea, it is surely the
Crimean Tatars. Second, the real issues, strategic importance and
tourist value, are more tangible and, objectively at least, devoid of
emotional content. In other words, the roots of current Russo-
Ukrainian tensions lie not in the issue of self-determination for
Russians but in the conflict over military and economic interests,
the kinds of things that most states quarrel about at most times.
Finally, the history of the Crimea is anything but simple, a fact
suggesting that solutions to present problems also cannot be simple. Bringing back all Tatars and giving them control of the local
government, as some Tatar nationalists recommend, is as impossible as throwing out all Russians; giving the entire fleet to
Ukraine is as muddle-headed as giving it all to Russia; attaching
the Crimea to Russia makes as little sense as forcibly Ukrainizing

12   its Russian population. None of these extremist solutions will untangle the convoluted nature of the Crimean problem.

The Language Problem

The complexity of the Crimean issue is typical of the entire postimperial and post-totalitarian legacy left to Ukraine and the other successor states. Centuries of imperialism and decades of totalitarianism have created conditions that defy easy answers or quick fixes. The current status of the Ukrainian language is another case in point. Banned from use in publications by tsarist edicts in the second half of the nineteenth century and repeatedly denigrated as an inferior, peasant tongue, Ukrainian experienced a renaissance in the 1920s and early 1930s during the relatively liberal conditions prevailing in the USSR before the triumph of Stalin. Thereafter, although the language continued to be taught in Ukraine's schools, writers, artists, poets, and intellectuals who showed particular interest in Ukrainian language, culture, or history were generally prosecuted for "Ukrainian bourgeois nationalism" and banished to Siberian concentration camps. Khrushchev eased the repression, but, by instituting a reform in 1958 that gave parents the choice of sending their children to schools with Russian as the language of instruction, he actually made Ukrainian's social status extremely precarious. What appeared to be a liberal reform in fact had the effect, probably intentional, of driving the Ukrainian language out of public life. Because Russian remained the vehicle of political and economic administration, the medium for the USSR's best theater, prose, and poetry, and the "language of the great Lenin," most urban Ukrainians sent their children to Russian-language schools and most Ukrainian political, economic, and educational institutions adopted Russian as their language of everyday use. The effect was what Ukrainian dissidents came to call "Russification." Urban schools and universities became overwhelmingly Russian in all but the western provinces—at present, some three-fourths of all Ukrainian urban children attend Russian-language schools[5]—the press, publishing, cinema, theater, scholarship, and television became Russified as well, and the Ukrainian language was used **13** largely by peasants and writers. Small wonder that most dissidents opposed to Russification were poets, novelists, literary critics, and journalists.

Ukrainian elites surely are not being extreme in requesting that passport Russians and passport Ukrainians learn and, perhaps, even use Ukrainian in public activities and at the workplace—all the more so since these two Eastern Slavic tongues are sufficiently similar as to make each language comprehensible to speakers of the other. Learning Ukrainian cannot be any harder for Russians than learning Russian is for Ukrainians, which is to say, not hard at all. And just as linguistic similarity encouraged the Russification of Ukrainians, it must surely facilitate the use of Ukrainian by Russians. The argument makes sense, but sensible arguments are not necessarily persuasive for individuals opposed to expanding their linguistic horizons, even if at minimal cost. The vast majority of Ukraine's passport Russians and Russified Ukrainians do not fit into this category, but even they would resent nationalist efforts to remake them completely or too quickly. As with the Crimea, simplistic solutions are not suited to the complexity of the situation. Forced Ukrainization is no better than forced Russification, despite the appeal both might have to national extremists, for dealing with the challenges and opportunities presented by ethnic diversity.

The Famine

Two more examples—the Great Famine of 1932–1933 and the question of free speech—should suffice to convey some of the complexity, this time with regard to morality, of post-Communist Ukrainian affairs. In the winter of 1932–1933, several million Ukrainians (imprecise statistics account for the wide range in estimates, from as low as 2 million to as high as 7 million) died as a result of what was surely a preventable famine. Stalin had embarked on the collectivization of peasant agriculture earlier in the decade; the peasants—Ukrainians, Russians, and all others—resisted. They fought the authorities, sabotaged collective farms,

14   killed party activists, and slaughtered their livestock. As a result, some one to two million Kazakh nomads, who were dependent on livestock for their very survival, perished in 1930–1931.

Two years later it was the turn of the Ukrainians and the residents of the Kuban and the Middle Volga region. This time, however, famine set in not as a result of the actions of peasants, but of the actions and inaction of the authorities. Extortionate amounts of grain were requisitioned; sometimes all of it was simply confiscated. Despite the pleas of local party activists who realized that catastrophe was imminent, nothing was done to alleviate the peasants' hunger. Famine was inevitable. Millions of peasants died, cannibalism broke out, and the peasantry, especially the Ukrainian peasantry, which at that time was the core of the Ukrainian nation, was crushed.

For Ukrainians the famine has assumed mythic proportions. It is *the* defining moment of their recent history, no less traumatic and portentous than the Holocaust is for Jews. The famine symbolizes the horror of the Soviet experience, the curse of Russian domination, and the necessity of Ukrainian liberation. Some revisionist Western scholars claim that Ukrainians are wrong to insist that the famine was intentional; other scholars support the Ukrainian position.[6] But the scholarly debate is beside the point for most Ukrainians, who *perceive* the famine as the culmination of centuries of Russian oppression. Such deeply rooted, almost mythical, convictions transform a symbol into a fact that is equally oblivious of empirical corroboration and refutation.

The famine, which became one of the nationalist movement's major rallying cries in 1988–1991, naturally raises the question of guilt. Who is to be held accountable? The all-too-easy answer is: the Soviet system or Stalinism. But who in particular? Some point a finger at "the Russians," but Ukrainians also took part. A more reasonable reply might be: the secret police and its party henchmen. Many, clearly, must still be alive. Should old wounds therefore be opened in the quest for justice? If the famine constitutes a crime against humanity, similar to those perpetrated by the Nazis, then consistency would demand that the answer be "yes." However, finding the evidence would require opening KGB **15** archives, and attacking yesterday's Soviet secret police might alienate today's Ukrainian Security Service. And if the former KGB turns against Ukrainian statehood, then democracy will be imperiled. Worse still, the NKVD (the precursor to the KGB) employed a disproportionately large number of Jews in the 1930s, and a search for guilty secret policemen could assume anti-Jewish overtones. Ukraine's international image would suffer, and the interethnic coalition that helped the nationalists win power would break down. Morality and practicality appear to be irreconcilable; indeed, even different types of moral imperatives may be in conflict. Once again, no simple obvious solution suggests itself to the moral conundrum facing Ukrainians traumatized by their own past.

The Problem of Free Speech

Equally complex is an issue that emerged with full force only in 1992—the question of limitations on free speech. In the year that followed independence there were virtually no restrictions placed on the expression of opinions in the media and at public events. The climate began to change in mid-1992 with a secret directive from President Leonid Kravchuk: radio and television were encouraged to eschew direct criticism of the government and its policies.[7] An additional twist occurred in August, when Kravchuk issued a decree in which he said, "Attempts to split the population, to sow interethnic or intrasocial hostilities and discord, and to exploit interparty quarrels will be considered" harmful to the "national rebirth of Ukraine. . . . Citizens of any country who take such action will be expelled."[8] The reaction of the democratic opposition, of the Ukrainian diaspora, and of Western observers was virtually unanimous.[9] Kravchuk was evidently exhibiting dictatorial tendencies that, as one Ukrainian journalist suggested, were leading Ukraine back into the times of Leonid Brezhnev. The president and his advisers rushed to emphasize that Ukraine remained committed to the Helsinki principles ensuring respect for

16   human rights, but the damage was done. Ukraine and its president
appeared to be veering to the right.

To some degree, the perception was correct. Restrictions on
freedom of the press are restrictions on freedom, no matter what
government officials say. And Kravchuk's impatience with the
vigorous Ukrainian press was a disturbing—and counterproductive—development. At the same time, the measure that inspired
the most outrage, his August decree, was not so straightforward an
issue of infringement of free speech as it seemed. The decree was
directed primarily at the émigré Ukrainian supporters of the right-
wing nationalist, Stepan Bandera,[10] who, while attending the
World Forum of Ukrainians in Kiev in late August, were publicly
expressing some of the extremist, intolerant, and chauvinist views
that have begun to acquire increasing currency outside western
Ukraine. In general, the "Banderites" insist that Kiev should
adopt hard-line policies with respect to the Crimea and Ukraine's
Russians, who, they believe, must be made to realize that they are
residents of a Ukrainian national state in which the Ukrainian
language and political loyalty are mandatory. The Banderites
surely have the right to say what they think, but the reality is that
such sentiments are virtually certain to inflame ethnic passions,
immeasurably worsen interethnic relations, perhaps produce genuine conflict, and conceivably even lead to the demise of the
Ukrainian state. Who, then, is right? Kravchuk, who may be
genuinely motivated by a desire to forestall the danger of ethnic
violence? Or the émigré chauvinists, whose thuggish behavior and
rabid intolerance are hallmarks of Ukrainian diaspora life?

As I shall argue throughout this book, there are many other
dilemmas, some moral, many practical, facing Ukraine in the
post-Soviet era. They are interconnected, and no single challenge
can be fully resolved in isolation from the others and without
consideration for the effect that one solution will have on solutions
to other problems. The interconnectedness and immensity of
Ukraine's problems thus preclude simple solutions; they also preclude solutions that are either radical or rapid.

SURVEYING THE BOOK

Chapter 1 presents an interpretation of Ukrainian history, setting the stage for the subsequent discussion that comprises the rest of the book. Two overarching concepts, empire and totalitarianism, frame the analysis. It is, as chapters 1 and 2 suggest, useful to conceive of the former Soviet Union as a unique kind of empire, a totalitarian one. A core Russian elite in a distinct metropolitan society, Russia, exerted political domination over peripheral elites and societies in the non-Russian republics and Central European states. Russia also exerted economic control over the periphery, sometimes to the core's detriment, but mostly not. The Soviet state, meanwhile, was wholly totalitarian even as late as 1985, if ineffectively and inefficiently so, by virtue of its complete supervision of all social, economic, and cultural life. The totalitarian state served as the foundation for the empire, as the state's monopoly of resources and of decision-making permitted the imperial Russian elite to exercise political control over the periphery. The stability of the state was thus the precondition for the stability of the empire.

From this perspective, it is Mikhail Gorbachev and his policy of perestroika that pushed the totalitarian state over the edge, thereby precipitating the fall of the empire in Central Europe and the republics and provoking the rise of non-Russian nationalism. In other words, it is not, as most analysts argue, nationalism that destroyed the system, but the destruction of the system that gave birth to nationalism as a largely reactive force concerned with self-preservation in a collapsing political, economic, and social environment.

This perspective also conveys the magnitude of the problems confronting all of the USSR's successor states. They must deal with the legacy of empire and totalitarianism with the minimal resources bequeathed to them by both. And Ukraine, like the other non-Russian successor states, must also cope with these challenges while simultaneously attempting both to wrestle its sovereignty from a Russia reluctant or unable to abandon the

18   Soviet Union's and its own imperial past and to placate the demands of a West frustrated and confused by the emergence of so many new countries.

Among the most serious challenges are building a civil society and a democratic polity and creating a national identity, while preserving civil and minority rights. As chapters 2 and 3 argue, these goals are laudable, but the lack of efficient administrative apparatuses, the potential threat posed by Russia, Ukraine's complex relationship with its powerful northern neighbor, and the presumed imperative of radical economic reform will make such a commitment exceedingly difficult to sustain. Western Europe needed centuries to reach these goals.

An equally pressing problem for Ukraine is its security, one of the subjects of chapter 4. Poland, the Czech Republic, Slovakia, and Hungary, no less than Ukraine, Belarus, and the Baltics, distrust Russia, an enormous country, with a huge army and nuclear weapons arsenal and a history of expansionism. Moreover, as chapter 4 suggests, Russia's transition to democracy and market economics is unlikely to succeed, at least not fully or rapidly. Ukraine's declared intention to build its own armed forces and its truculent behavior regarding nuclear weapons thus stem from fear of Russia, not from a desire to become a militarist state and frighten Western Europe.

Ukraine's third challenge is economic reform, the theme of chapter 5. Gorbachev destroyed the command economy without providing a substitute—in contrast to Communist Hungary, Poland, and China, all of which gradually dismantled parts of their command economies and thereby improved their prospects for a successful transition to a market economy. Neither capitalist nor communist, the post-Soviet republics now have the worst of both worlds. If they do nothing, they can at best hope for continued stagnation. For them to embark on the kind of revolutionary economic transformation insisted on by the West, however, means exposing their populations to full-scale deindustrialization, massive unemployment and inflation, and a drastic decline in living standards, which will invite, if not guarantee, political and social **19** instability.

Last but not least, Ukrainians must build a modern state and fashion an effective political elite, the central topics of chapter 6. Without these, no policy, however wise, can be effective. Colo‑ nialism and totalitarianism left the Ukrainians with administra‑ tive apparatuses capable of executing central orders with some degree of efficiency, but thoroughly incapable of exercising policy initiative, formulating realistic goals, or running a state. And without a state or, better still, without an institutionally strong state, it is hard to imagine how they can defend themselves, restructure their economies, establish rule of law, and introduce democratic orders.

The conclusion then considers some of the dilemmas facing the West. It argues that, like Ukraine, Russia, and the other successor states, the countries of the West face difficult choices of their own. The west must appreciate that post‑Soviet reality is, above all, complex. And complexity in this instance, for reasons to be set out more fully below, demands a recognition that Ukraine and the other non‑Russian states must matter at least as much as Russia, that Ukraine urgently needs Western help, and that sim‑ plistic solutions that ignore complexity must be avoided at all cost.

IMPLICATIONS FOR THE WEST

Western countries certainly cannot afford to do nothing. If noth‑ ing is done to help Ukraine and the USSR's other successor states, the devastation wrought on them by empire and totalitarianism will probably spill over into the countries to the west of Ukraine in a manner that would be destabilizing at best and disastrous at worst. Poland, Hungary, the Czech Republic, Slovakia, Bulgaria, and Romania, which would be hard‑pressed to make successful transitions to democracy and market relations in the best of circumstances, would probably fail to do so. And if, as a result, more or less illegitimate, more or less authoritarian regimes emerge in Central Europe, the temptation for them to resort to maximalist

20   foreign policies, to make irredentist claims, and to prefer bombast to diplomacy may be irresistible.

The many problems confronting Ukraine and the other post-Communist states will be especially destabilizing for a West that does nothing to cushion the shock. Whether Western Europe can survive as a coherent entity when confronted by such pitiable neighbors is a question worth pondering, particularly in light of the proposition that the Cold War division of Europe into two ideologically hostile, economically incompatible, and politically competing halves enjoying the protection of great military powers may have been the necessary condition for the emergence of a unified Western Europe. If so, then the return to multipolarity in a post–Cold War Europe may mean that the self-interest of individual states will take precedence over common interests and that Western Europe's economic and political unification will remain on paper—especially if, as is already happening, turmoil and instability on Germany's eastern border draws it away from its European Community partners and involves it in the affairs of its neighbors to the east.

The transformation of all of Europe into a multipolar system may even incline West Europeans to revert to cold-blooded national policies and to countenance war. But even if we assume that war is impossible among West Europeans because values have changed irreversibly, economic interdependence is enormous, and modern war is simply too destructive to contemplate, this is not the case in the East. There, as in the former Yugoslavia, common values have yet to emerge, interdependence either has broken down or is resented, and primitive armies reduce the destructiveness of war. Democratic regimes may not initiate preventive wars or engage one another in military conflicts, but Eastern Europe may not become democratic. Obviously, the worst scenario would involve Ukraine and Russia in such a conflict.

Security will pose the greatest challenge for the United States. With the end of the Cold War, the United States has emerged as the only genuine world power, a role for which the country is, understandably, unprepared. As the American involvement in Iraq suggests, the logic of "unipolarity" may force the **21** United States into becoming the world's sole policeman. Political instability or war in the USSR's successor states might require the United States not only to expend scarce resources in Western and Eastern Europe, but also to involve itself even more deeply in the precarious politics of the region just south of the Caucasus and Central Asia—the Middle East. The "peace dividend" is unlikely to be sizable in an increasingly anarchic world dominated by one genuinely great power.

THE IMPORTANCE OF MODERNITY

Were proximity the only reason for the East's impact on the West, Western Europe and the United States might be able to construct more or less effective moats around themselves. But modernity— the set of political, economic, social, and cultural conditions that distinguish contemporary states from their historical prede- cessors—precludes such a response. Thus, immigration from the East is sure to be an issue because West European prosperity is the product of modern welfare states embedded in a communications network facilitating travel from East to West. Environmental pollution will also be a concern because the quality of life in Western Europe is inextricably bound to that of Eastern Europe as a result of the emergence of a pan-European identity and the revival of capitalist relations in the East. Instability will be a problem because the logic of international relations in a seamless system of states confronts all units with security dilemmas that they have to address. It is modernity—the modern state, the developed economy, the educated population, and the all-perva- sive technology—that will force whatever remains of the unified West to cope more actively and less simplistically with the ongoing transformations in the East.

In this sense, Ukraine already *is* a part of Europe. The real task, therefore, is to make it a stable, secure, and prosperous part—and that can be done only if the complexity of its condition is realized and radical solutions are eschewed. The point, then, is

22   not to prevent Ukraine's—or Russia's—transformation into Weimar-type states. After all, Weimar Germany, for all its many faults, was a democracy with a healthy and creative civil society. It is *post*-Weimar Ukraine and *post*-Weimar Russia that must be avoided at all cost. And Weimar Germany teaches us how: it broke down because extremists thrive on economic collapse and international indifference. Not helping Ukraine, Russia, and the other states while pushing them to devastate their economies, polities, and societies can bring about the post-Weimar scenario. Only helping them reform themselves *gradually* can forestall catastrophe.

CHAPTER 1

Historical Perspectives on Ukraine's Independence

Conventional wisdom considers Ukraine a hotbed of nationalism and nationalism responsible for Ukrainian independence. Nothing could be further from the truth. Although nationalists and nationalism have made a difference in Ukrainian history, Ukraine's relationship with other states and power centers has largely determined the directions its society, polities, and economy have taken. Developments within the system of states to which Ukraine belonged deprived it of its medieval freedoms, and similar external developments also prepared it for and then thrust it toward statehood. Nationalists pushed the process along—and they certainly chronicled it—but without the decay of totalitarianism and the collapse of the Soviet empire their efforts could not have transformed Ukraine from a colonial territory into an independent polity.

In the twentieth century, Ukrainian nationalists have tried three times to build their own state: first in 1917–1921, when they failed; in 1941–1945, when they failed again; and in 1989–1991, when they finally succeeded. Success came the third time not because the nationalists tried harder or because they were stronger, but because the external conditions were right. Indeed, they were so right that sovereign Ukraine's leading nationalist proved to be the same person as Soviet Ukraine's leading antinationalist— Leonid Kravchuk. In a word, though Ukrainian nationalists, like all nationalists, would have us think otherwise, independence was

24   not so much won by, as bequeathed to, them. And because Ukraine has finally joined a receptive international community, over a hundred members of which have already recognized its statehood, in the absence of some world war, Ukraine is here to stay.

UKRAINE'S EARLY HISTORY

"*Ukraina*" means "borderland," and indeed Ukraine has been a borderland for much of this millennium. This contrasts with the early tenth through the mid-thirteenth century, when Ukraine comprised the heartland of one of medieval Europe's largest states, Kievan Rus'. Kiev, the capital, was a major center of trade, Orthodox Christianity, and old Slavic culture, and thus was a formidable political rival of Constantinople. The preeminent ruler of Kievan Rus', Yaroslav the Wise (1036–1054), codified its laws, established a stable administration, and thereby created the conditions for a golden age of culture. At a time when Moscow was an insignificant settlement and St. Petersburg did not yet exist, Yaroslav cemented his state's international ties by marrying his daughters to the kings of France, Hungary, and Norway.

Once Rus' collapsed under the impact of internecine warfare and the Mongol invasions in the mid-thirteenth century, however, Ukraine became a political *ukraina*, a frontier zone that for several centuries remained at the intersection of the continually shifting borders of the Grand Duchy of Lithuania, the Ottoman Empire, the Polish-Lithuanian Commonwealth, the Crimean Tatar Khanate, and Muscovy. The continued existence of Ukraine as a politically undefined territory, however, was incompatible with two interrelated world historical trends: the growth of the international system of states and the emergence of the modern state. The parcelization of the world into modern states, a process that began with the Peace of Westphalia in 1648, meant that borderlands such as Ukraine could not remain beyond the reach of some state or states. No less important, the transformation of the European state from a coercive, tax-gathering, and

war-fighting apparatus to a bureaucratic structure concerned with **25**
permanently administering and supervising a subject population—a development that coincided with the division of the world
into states and the development of new technologies and forms of
political organization in the seventeenth and eighteenth centuries—made Ukraine's integration into some state inescapable as
well. After 1648, in other words, not only was Ukraine's familiar
frontier status, especially in Europe, impossible, but incorporation
into a state necessarily entailed integration into the administrative, coercive, and financial systems supervised by some political
elite.

Ironically, although borderland status transformed Ukraine
into a political no-man's-land, it also contributed enormously to a
cultural, religious, and educational revival in the sixteenth and
seventeenth centuries, one that produced many of the elites that
eventually came to staff the Russian church and polity. To be sure,
a precarious existence at the intersection of several states had the
effect of assimilating local Ukrainian elites, who generally concluded that alignment with the culture and politics of Poland,
Lithuania, or Muscovy would enhance their interests. By the same
token, however, Ukraine's position also produced cross-cultural
fertilization and religious assertiveness—two processes that contributed greatly to the religio-cultural revival. The central event
was the Counter-Reformation, which militant Jesuits used to
convert the Ukrainian Orthodox population to Roman Catholicism. In 1596 their efforts bore fruit at the Union of Brest,
whereby several formerly Orthodox bishops pledged allegiance to
the Vatican on condition that their distinct Eastern Orthodox
liturgical rites be retained. In turn, the Catholic offensive provoked an Orthodox counteroffensive, led by Prince Konstantyn
Ostrozsky and the Kiev Metropolitan Petro Mohyla. Orthodox lay
brotherhoods dedicated to a religious revival sprouted throughout
the country; the clergy was mobilized in defense of the faith; and
the intellectual foundations of the movement were laid with the
establishment of the Ostrih Academy and the Kiev Mohyla Col-

26   legium, both institutions of higher learning dedicated to training Orthodox intellectuals.

By the mid-seventeenth century, therefore, Ukraine had become a center of cultural and religious activity—a fact also reflected in the painting and architecture of the period and in the unusually high rate of literacy among its population. One of the central fault lines in modern Ukrainian history also emerged at this time: the division between a European-oriented Catholic west and a Moscow-oriented Orthodox east. That division was mirrored in the political realities. Despite unstable and shifting borders, Poland controlled most of the Right-Bank Ukraine (i.e., the lands west of the Dnieper), while Muscovy controlled most of the Left-Bank Ukraine. As long as such a condition persisted, Ukrainian culture remained open to a variety of external influences and continued to be vibrant. By the late eighteenth century, however, Ukraine's ambiguous political status had come to an end. In a portent of things to come, authoritarian Muscovy defeated chaotically democratic Poland, with the result that Ukraine's window to the West was closed. The three partitions of Poland bequeathed most of the Right Bank to Russia, with only eastern Galicia going to Austria and remaining open to the Western world.

Incorporation and integration into Russia was in most respects a disaster for Ukraine. Culturally, the region became a barren province within several generations, as most of its elites moved north or adopted Russian language and culture. In a trend that contravened European developments, the literacy rate actually declined. Religiously, Ukraine was reduced to an appendage of the Moscow Patriarchate, and the intellectual debates that characterized the seventeenth century withered away. Economically, Ukraine became the Russian hinterland, serving almost exclusively as a source of agricultural products and raw materials. Socially, Ukraine lost its educated elites and became a country in which ethnicity and class overlapped and three distinguishable strata emerged: ignorant and impoverished Ukrainian peasants, wealthy Russian and Polish landlords, and, trapped between the first two, a stratum of socially precarious Jewish merchants. Politi-

cally, Ukraine lost the capacity for self-rule that it had had in the   **27**
seventeenth century and was transformed into a backwater of
Russia.

The Ukrainian Cossacks

The mid-seventeenth century represented post-Rus' Ukraine's
best chance of reestablishing an independent political existence.
Because of Ukraine's borderland status, something of a primitive
political elite had come into existence by the late sixteenth
century: the Cossacks. Cossackdom emerged as a haven for escap-
ing serfs, slaves, and peasants beyond the bounds of established
political authority in the vast Ukrainian steppes. Their lair was
the Sich, an island stronghold on the south Dnieper. From there
the Cossacks launched attacks on Turks and Tatars and defended
their autonomy from the encroachments of Poles and Russians.
Their exploits became the stuff of Ukrainian legend and, as argued
in chapter 3, the basis of Ukrainian national identity. In time,
some of these "social bandits" were co-opted by the Polish authorities, who "registered" them as frontier allies of the *Rzecz Pospolita*,
or Commonwealth. Even so, both registered and unregistered
Cossacks continually engaged in rebellions against the expansion
of Polish rule and obligations throughout most of the sixteenth and
seventeenth centuries.

The Cossack rebellions culminated in the great insurrection
led by their hetman Bohdan Khmelnytsky in 1648. Cossack defense of their prerogatives merged with popular dissatisfaction
with the harshness of Polish landlord rule and Orthodox opposition to the Counter-Reformation to produce a massive revolt that
encompassed all strata of Ukrainian society. As Khmelnytsky's
armies defeated the Poles in several battles, Orthodox battled
Catholics and peasants massacred Jews. In the end, Khmelnytsky
established an independent Cossack state. Independence was
short-lived, however, since in 1654, facing military threats on all
sides, Khmelnytsky signed a treaty of alliance with the tsar of
Muscovy at Pereyaslav. Several decades of incessant warfare then
followed, as Ukraine was transformed into a battleground among

28   Turks, Tatars, Poles, Russians, and Ukrainians. By the late seventeenth century, when the dust had settled, the Right Bank, utterly
devastated and largely depopulated, remained Polish, while the
Left Bank, which survived the period of the "Ruin" more or less
intact, remained home to the Hetmanate—but in a new incarna-
tion, as an autonomous political unit subordinated to the Russian
tsar. The Ukrainian hetmans defended their rights, but to no
avail. Hetman Ivan Mazepa actually attempted to secede from
Russia with the assistance of Charles XII of Sweden, but both went
down to defeat by Peter the Great at Poltava in 1709. Finally, by
the late eighteenth century, Catherine the Great, in her enthusiasm to establish a modern bureaucratic state, abolished the Hetmanate and destroyed the Sich as well.

Could the Cossacks have succeeded in maintaining an independent polity? An analysis of its international environment
suggests not. For reasons directly related to Ukraine's peculiar
status as an unincorporated territory situated at the intersection of
several realms, Ukrainian elites lacked the means to assert their
political will over the long run. Although the Cossacks were
formidable fighters, they were in the end no match for the well-
organized and better-supplied armies of the Turks, Russians,
Tatars, and Poles. Seen from this point of view, Khmelnytsky's
temporary success seems to have been due to the international
"correlation of forces" in general and in Eastern Europe in particular. Poland had been weakened by the Thirty Years' War, Muscovy had just emerged from the Time of Troubles, while the
Ottomans were pursuing empire in the Balkans and southeastern
Europe. With a power vacuum in Ukraine, the Cossacks were able
to assert themselves temporarily; once this window of opportunity
had closed, state-building became well-nigh impossible.

Three other factors also contributed to relative Ukrainian
weakness, all related to Ukraine's extended existence on the
margins of several political realms. For some four hundred to five
hundred years, Ukraine was the site of attempts at annexation,
plunder, and buffer-zone maintenance by Poles, Ottomans,
Tatars, and Muscovites. The constant incursions of all four into

the no-man's-land separating them destabilized Ukrainian society **29** and made indigeneous Ukrainian attempts at state-building exceedingly difficult. At the same time, such destabilizing conditions ensured that Ukraine would be the site of continual rebellions, uprisings, and revolts from the sixteenth through the eighteenth century, precisely the time of the most concerted Polish, Muscovite, Tatar, and Ottoman attempts to control the territory.

Furthermore, Ukraine's geographic features—flat steppe-lands amidst virtually no natural boundaries—have made it a natural invasion and migration route from East to West, for Sarmatians, Goths, Alans, Huns, Mongols, and many others, and, of course, from West to East for the armies of Poland, France, and Germany. Because there are few places that lend themselves to the sort of urban fortifications that were common in the Middle Ages in Western and Central Europe, the geography of Ukraine was conducive neither to easy defense nor to the development of settled stable societies in general and cities in particular. In turn, the relative lack of prosperous cities, a condition aggravated by the fall of Byzantium in 1453 and the concomitant elimination of the north-south trade routes that had contributed to Kiev's strength in the tenth and eleventh centuries, deprived the region of much needed capital and other resources. Not surprisingly, Ukraine would remain a political vacuum until modern states emerged and began dividing up the world.

The Nineteenth Century and After

Thanks to the modernization that radiated outward from the Moscow-Petersburg region, the nineteenth century witnessed the former Ukrainian borderland's progressive integration into the Russian polity and economy. Urbanization, industrialization, and transportation went hand in hand, as did education, communication, and social and ethnic differentiation. A Ukrainian working class began emerging in the late nineteenth century in the mining industries of the Donbas and in the oil industry of the Carpathian foothills of Galicia. A tiny Ukrainian bourgeoisie also came into

30   existence. Tensions with ethnic Jews grew as competition for jobs and housing in rapidly growing cities intensified. In all these respects, however, nineteenth-century developments in Ukraine differed little from developments in Russia as a whole, which is simply to say that the country was undergoing rapid change. A distinctly Ukrainian national intelligentsia was making itself heard, especially toward the end of the century, and its self-perceptions did differ somewhat from those of the Russian intelligentsia, if only because the tsarist regime assiduously pursued cultural Russification to the point of banning even Ukrainian-language publications. But, inasmuch as separatism was on virtually no one's agenda before 1917, Ukrainian and Russian intellectuals did not have fundamentally different political aspirations at the start of World War I. Liberals, socialist revolutionaries, social democrats, conservatives, and reactionaries were evident in Ukraine, as throughout the entire empire. Democracy, socialism, and autonomy may have been desired ends, but independence remained the goal of only a handful of ethnic Ukrainians.

Nevertheless, despite the Ukrainian elite's utter lack of interest in separation from Russia initially, in a preview of perestroika, several years of massive instability transformed Ukraine into something approximating a country. World War I debilitated the tsarist polity, economy, and society. The Bolshevik revolution of 1917 destroyed tsarism, while the Civil War that lasted until 1921 forced the non-Russian elites to fend for themselves and to choose sides. Ukrainians were forced to build a state and to respond to the military and political challenge of the Bolsheviks and the White Russians. Identical developments in state- and nation-building were also taking place in Finland, Poland, Belarus, the Baltic, Georgia, Armenia, Azerbaijan, and Turkestan. Clearly, the collapse of the Russian polity and economy, and not non-Russian nationalism per se, impelled Russia's constituent provinces and imperial possessions to opt for nationalism and pursue independence. Simply put, not only did independence begin to make sense to non-Russian elites, but by 1918 it was the only option that offered them refuge from imperial collapse and Bolshevik take-

over. So belated an appreciation of the benefits of independence **31**
meant that Ukrainian and other non-Russian elites were completely unprepared for the demands of statehood. They lacked
armies, bureaucracies, and citizenries willing to defend their borders. As a result, Ukrainian leaders generally improvised. They
reacted to events in Russia, they squabbled over utopian schemes,
they shifted positions and changed alliances, they fought on several fronts—and in the end they lost.

The Ukrainian Revolution

The first to lose were the democrats who had established the
Ukrainian People's Republic in 1917. Unable to stop the Bolshevik invasion of early 1918, they were forced to conclude a
separate peace with Germany and Austria-Hungary—a desperate
move that earned them the contempt of the West. In April, the
Central Powers replaced the democratic nationalists with General
Pavlo Skoropadsky, whose authoritarian policies proved so unpopular that the democrats were easily able to forge a broad-based
coalition that swept him from power in November. Once again,
however, the democrats failed to build a stable state. Chaos
reigned, as demobilized soldiers assisted land-hungry peasants in
expropriating landlords' property, warlords assumed control of
most of the country, and a myriad of parties, movements, and
armies vied for power. Ukraine became a borderland once again, as
Germans, Austrians, Poles, Bolsheviks, White Russians, and
Ukrainians of various political hues, from monarchist to anar-
chist, fought over the territory, a situation remarkably similar to
the Ruin of the 1670s. Unskilled, untrained, and unprepared
Ukrainian nationalist elites, lacking armies, industries, bureaucracies, and popular bases, were no match for such confusion.
Left-wing nationalists believed that social revolution alone could
save the cause; in time, they allied with the Bolsheviks. Right-
wing nationalists believed that a strong military and a strong state
were the only answer; they looked to Symon Petliura, a social
democrat turned general, for inspiration. Ironically, by
1918–1919, both sides had become irrelevant, as events in

32   Ukraine assumed a life of their own. The fact is that no one was in charge. What historian Arthur Adams called the "Great Peasant Jacquerie" devastated the country. Millions of Ukrainians and Russians died, falling victim to war or disease. Perhaps as many as 100,000 Jews were killed or wounded in pogroms initiated by peasants, warlords, and soldiers under Petliura's putative command, by Russian Whites, and by the Bolsheviks. By 1920, the nationalists, or what remained of them, had to flee.

Under conditions such as these it was virtually preordained that the Russian Bolsheviks would win control of Ukraine and most of the tsarist territorial holdings. Given Bolshevik organizational, military, and industrial superiority, none of the non-Russian provinces could escape Bolshevik reassertion of central control on its own. The Bolsheviks possessed a genuinely well-disciplined cadre party; they inherited the bulk of the former tsarist army; and their control of Russia's largest urban centers provided them with the industrial base without which victory in a major war would have been impossible. Not surprisingly, only where German or Allied intervention was strong enough and lasted long enough, as in Finland, Poland, and the Baltic states, did independent states actually manage to sustain themselves. In striking contrast, all of Austria-Hungary's successor states survived because what remained of Vienna was far too weak to reassert control over the former Hapsburg domains.

Within the Soviet Empire

Conquest presented the Bolsheviks with a dilemma. On the one hand, Leninist ideology, which had asserted that all nations have the right to self-determination up to and including separation and independence, forced the Bolsheviks to address the issue of ethnic inequality and separatism—the so-called nationality question that, they claimed, only they were equipped to resolve. On the other hand, the non-Russian political elites that emerged from the ruins of the Russian empire now possessed nationalist ambitions that could no longer be suppressed. The legitimacy of Bolshevik rule required paying some attention to ethnic concerns; the stabil-

ity of Bolshevik rule meant incorporating the emergent non-   **33**
Russian elites into the Soviet state, but on terms that had to be
different from those of the tsars.

The Bolshevik choice was empire masquerading as federation. In contrast to the tsars, who had openly trumpeted their
imperial ambitions, the Bolsheviks claimed that the Union of
Soviet Socialist Republics was actually a federation consisting
of sovereign and equal republics possessing their own symbols of
statehood and bound in a voluntary union. The reality was different. Effective political power was concentrated not in the republics, but in the Communist Party, which remained a thoroughly
centralized and Russian-dominated institution. By and large, republican Communists were little more than administrators completely subordinated to the dictates of the central Russian party
organs. The system built by Lenin and Stalin was thus unabashedly imperial since it was premised on the existence of a
distinct core elite—the Russian Communists in Moscow—and
distinct peripheral elites—the non-Russian Communists—with
the former possessing absolute political power and the latter serving only as an administrative class.

The USSR can be classified as an empire primarily because
political domination, not economic exploitation, was at its core.
Imperial holdings, or colonies, are usually exploited economically,
but this fact is not central to the definition. Economic inequality
and exploitation occur in all states, yet we would not say that the
Mezzogiorno is a colony of Milan or that nineteenth-century
Manchester with its atrocious slums was not at the very core of the
British empire. By the same token, there is no reason why colonies, even if exploited economically, have to be poor and underdeveloped. After all, some colonies live well: consider Hong Kong,
the American colonies, the Baltic German territories under the
tsar, and Greece in the Roman empire. We assume that colonies
are poor because our mental image derives from the British and
French experiences in Africa and Asia. This is not to say that
Soviet colonies did not suffer economic depredation. Some republics and Central European states were exploited more than others,

34   and all, including many parts of Russia, were exploited to some degree at some times. Ukraine in particular, while not resembling a "typical" Third World colony, actually transferred a far greater percentage of its material wealth to the center than most other republics.

The mature Soviet empire eventually came to consist of the non-Russian republics and all the satellite states of Central Europe. Russia—or, more precisely, the core Russian elite—ruled them all, while the Polish, Czech, Hungarian, Baltic, Ukrainian, Armenian, Central Asian, and other Communist elites acted as the colonial administrators of its imperial holdings. It is here that the crucial difference between the Russians and the non-Russians lies: while all experienced a totalitarian system, the Russians actually *ruled*, while the non-Russians did not. Life in the totalitarian Soviet empire was difficult for everyone, but Russian elites enjoyed the perquisites of imperial authority, and Russians in general had the satisfaction of being masters, even if decidedly impoverished ones, of an empire, in which their language, culture, symbols, and values reigned supreme. For Russians, the Soviet Union and much of Central Europe were home; for non-Russians, they were either a prison or a cheap hotel.

THE IMPACT OF IMPERIAL RULE

Although the imperial relationship between Soviet Russia and Soviet Ukraine closely resembled that between St. Petersburg and the Hetmanate in the eighteenth century, it represented a major step forward—from the point of view of Ukrainian elites—over that practiced by the tsars in the nineteenth century. Then, Ukraine had had virtually no distinct elite; by 1924, it could again boast of having the elite it had lost in the late eighteenth century.

But Soviet rule also decimated the very elites it created: first, during the 1930s, when the Ukrainian national Communists were purged and the budding Ukrainian intelligentsia was destroyed; then in 1939–1941, when the west Ukrainian elites were subjected to a terror that played a major role in inclining the population of Galicia to support Germany's attack on the USSR; in the **35** late 1940s, when "Ukrainian bourgeois nationalism" again became the target of Stalin's ire; and, finally, for most of the 1960s and 1970s, when the Ukrainian dissident movement was crushed in several waves of secret police repression.

More important than the fate of the elite, however, was that Soviet rule devastated Ukraine. Ukraine's population suffered enormous losses: millions died in the Great Famine of 1932–1933, and millions were shot, exiled, or incarcerated during the Stalinist terror of the 1930s and 1940s. As if Soviet rule were not enough, millions more perished during World War II as a result of Nazi Germany's genocidal policies toward Jews, who were slated for immediate destruction, and Ukrainians, who were to serve as *Untermenschen.*

In addition, Ukraine's culture and language were subjected both to the homogenizing influence of "Sovietization" and to the psychologically dislocating impact of "Russification." Ukraine not only became a cultural backwater with almost no ties to the rest of the world but also lost most of its historical memory. Ukraine's economy was subordinated to the dictates of planners in Moscow, who transformed it radically in the 1930s at an enormous cost in human lives and with the effect of destroying its agriculture, depleting its mineral deposits, poisoning its land, air, and water, creating inefficient monster industries, and producing a demoralized working class. Finally, Ukraine's society was atomized, its diverse organizational forms destroyed, and its population regimented in officially sponsored institutions.

In a word, Ukraine—its population, its elites, its many cultures, its economy, and its civil society—fell victim to a totalitarian state, whose central Russian elite exerted imperial control over its satraps in the republics. Nevertheless, the creation of an administratively bounded, symbolically sovereign territory called the Ukrainian Soviet Socialist Republic, forced industrialization and rapid urbanization, the development of a relatively modern educational, social, and communications system, and the emergence of a Ukrainian political class endowed with a certain bu-

36   reaucratic structure and some administrative skills effectively transformed what had been a backward province into a potentially viable Ukrainian state. Thanks to the Communists, and not to its own nationalists, Ukraine finally acquired all the prerequisites of statehood and could, as a result, become a state. Thanks to Soviet policies, Ukraine's administrative bureaucracies supervised its economic development, which in turn provided the territory with the urban resources and capital that state-building requires and that Ukraine had historically lacked. By the 1960s, Ukraine was actually in the position of being able, if external conditions permitted, of translating its symbolic sovereignty into genuine sovereignty.

Perestroika and Crisis

A closer look at 1914–1921 will be useful in isolating what such conditions had to be. At that time, a genuinely life-threatening crisis struck the Russian political system, which did not survive its impact. Just as World War I destroyed the Russian empire, so did it impel the provinces to turn nationalist and strike out on their own, while, at the same time, favoring the centrally located Bolsheviks in the resultant civil war. Had the Russian provinces of seventy years ago been endowed with the relatively experienced political elites and industrial and military resources of today's republics—or of the crownlands of Austria-Hungary in 1918—Bolshevik victory would have been far from certain.

Although the Soviet system was clearly beginning to run down in the 1970s, there was no reason to think that it could not survive, even if ineffectively, for a long time to come. Historically, empires—consider Roman, Byzantine, or Ottoman—have muddled through for centuries after decay has set in. Decay always sets in, however, because imperial rule rests on self-contradictory tendencies that, over time, reduce its effectiveness and thus make the system increasingly unviable. In a nutshell, imperial elites require of their vassals that they collect vast amounts of resources and funnel them to the center, whose absolute rule depends on the revenues and information vassals appropriate. But the self-interest of local administrators, the vassals, also demands of them that they **37** retain a portion of these resources as a means of safeguarding their own status against the claims of the imperial center. As vassals reduce the flow of revenues and information to the center and begin establishing their own bailiwicks, absolutism runs down and the efficiency and effectiveness of the imperial state decline. And what is true of the absolutist regimes of empires is doubly so for totalitarian states, whose appetite for resources, information, and control is wholly unrestrained.[1]

While both systems are doomed to long-term degeneration and decay, their rapid and comprehensive collapse can occur only if a crisis, on the order of a world war, so shakes the system, so incapacitates the center, and so emboldens the periphery as to lead to a complete breakdown in imperial relations. Such crises took place in both the Austro-Hungarian and tsarist empires, in the form of genuine war, and in the USSR, in the form of perestroika. The first peripheries to sever their ties with the imperial Soviet center were the countries of Central Europe, Poland, Hungary, and Czechoslovakia; the next were the republics of the Soviet Union, all of which declared sovereignty in the course of 1988–1990. Thereafter, the twin processes of "detotalization" (that is, undoing totalitarianism) and "deimperialization" were so advanced that there was no going back to the imperial relations that Gorbachev, in his version of the Union, wanted to resurrect.

Totalitarian Decay

In contrast to the traditional imperial state that extended its control over peripheral elites and some aspects of peripheral society, thus leaving a substantial space within which social forces could exercise autonomy, the totalitarian state controls all of society, both "vertically" and "horizontally." That is, the state attempts to penetrate all social institutions in depth and in breadth, with the result that none of the independent social and economic institutions characteristic of civil society and the market can exist. The cost of maintaining a totalitarian state is therefore extremely high, far higher than that required to maintain a run-of-

38   the-mill imperial state, while its tendency to suffer from the decay that afflicts all absolutisms is far greater as well. As a result, the totalitarian state is far more prone than other absolutist polities to lose effectiveness and finally to degenerate.[2]

A comparison with Austria-Hungary and tsarist Russia is instructive. In contrast to the Hapsburg and Romanov realms, which underwent rapid and dynamic economic growth in the last decades of their existence, the Soviet imperial lands all experienced steep, and apparently irreversible, economic decline. And the reasons for this critical difference are to be found, first and foremost, in the fact that the Soviet economy was completely subordinated to the imperial state and, as a result, came to suffer from all the pathologies of overcentralization typical of totalitarianism. In contrast, the Hapsburg and Russian economies were far less susceptible to the intrusions of the state, enjoyed a more or less autonomous existence, and could grow, even if unevenly.

Soviet imperial decay thus came to accelerate and be accelerated by totalitarian degeneration. The inefficiency of empire was compounded by the hypertrophy of totalitarianism, leading imperial decay to progress in tandem with totalitarianism degeneration. Perestroika was initially intended to stem both processes, to rejuvenate the totalitarian state, and to preserve the empire, at least within the formal USSR. Gorbachev's reforms, however, ended up, perhaps inevitably, accelerating totalitarian decay, indeed producing totalitarian collapse—the rapid and comprehensive dismantling of the totalitarian state. Once this happened, the imperial rule that was premised on the maintenance of totalitarian control of necessity had to dissolve. In a word, the collapse of totalitarianism led directly to the fall of the Soviet empire.

Explaining Totalitarian Collapse

Several factors deserve special attention in explaining how the collapse of Soviet totalitarianism came about. The starting point of the process was Gorbachev's decision to rein in the secret police, the KGB. Once repression of political dissent was withdrawn from the Soviet state's arsenal of social control mecha-

nisms, glasnost and the public expression of critical opinions **39**
became possible. Still, as long as glasnost remained within certain
bounds, any potential threat to the regime could always be contained. But everything changed when Gorbachev relentlessly encouraged the debunking of the past in order to discredit his
political opponents and to assert his own legitimacy.

Very quickly glasnost spun out of control. As a result, ram-
pant glasnost not only destroyed Soviet ideology and values—
however deserving they may have been of abandonment—but in
doing so it effectively transformed the Soviet Union into a criminal state. Close investigation of the many "blank spots" in Soviet
history led logically to repudiation of the entire Soviet experience.
As revelations of Stalinist and post-Stalinist crimes against humanity came to light (culminating in the discovery in Belarus,
Ukraine, and several other republics of mass graves containing the
mutilated remains of countless workers, peasants, and other
"bourgeois enemies of the people"), most Soviet citizens concluded that their regime was little different from what Hitler's had
been.

Worse still, Gorbachev's struggle against the Communist
Party bureaucracy, which was the major obstacle to reform and to
the consolidation of his power, weakened and ultimately undermined the linchpin of the totalitarian system. Ironically, Gorbachev's policies negated the possibility of real reform, since only
the party, which so completely defined and dominated the system,
was in a position to change it in a stable and predictable manner, as
for instance in Hungary under János Kádár or in China under
Deng Xiaoping. But Gorbachev's attempted pursuit of radical
economic reform also made it impossible for him to consolidate
control of the party without destroying its authority in the process.
In the end, reform could but fail, while the party, the country's
only effective political institution for nearly seventy years, could
but decay. Without the party, Gorbachev's own authority could
not extend beyond the Kremlin walls and the totalitarian system
lost its central institutional prop; without reform, new institutions

40   could not be created and Gorbachev's own legitimacy perforce went into steep decline.

Gorbachev's haphazard economic reforms and assault on the Communist Party also threw the economy into chaos. After all, the command economy functioned, albeit inefficiently, as long as the central bureaucracies determined inputs and outputs and the party possessed the authority to implement their decisions. Once the powers of central ministries were curtailed and the authority of the party was eroded, while little was done to introduce genuine market mechanisms, the Soviet economy was left with the worst of two competing economic approaches: neither capitalist nor socialist, it could only decay to the point of collapse. Under conditions like these, the hapless Gorbachev could do little more than lose his temper, fulminate about reform, and impose futile authoritarian measures, such as cracking down on so-called speculators and withdrawing large-denomination ruble bills from circulation.

Small wonder, then, that Gorbachev's attempt to create new political institutions under such conditions was certain to fail. There was no way for quasi-representative bodies, such as the Congress of People's Deputies, the revamped Supreme Soviet, or the Presidency, to assert their authority and to establish their legitimacy in circumstances of extreme ideological confusion, economic decline, and political decay. Indeed, Gorbachev's own transformation into an unpopular dictator was the inevitable consequence of his tinkering with totalitarian politics and economics. In contrast, Gorbachev's willingness to tolerate the emergence of political opposition under conditions of systemic collapse provided them with the very ideological, economic, and political ammunition they needed to promote themselves above the congenitally defective institutions he had created and those, such as the party, he had weakened. Particularly significant was that the loosening of the party's control over its republican branches left the non-Russian Communist elites defenseless against criticism from below, thus forcing them to be responsive to their ethnic constituencies, to adopt increasingly nationalist positions, and, finally, to forge informal coalitions with republican popular fronts against the **41** center.

Finally, Gorbachev's preordained failure to deliver on the many extravagant promises he made in the early years of his tenure, such as eliminating alcoholism and providing all citizens with adequate housing, led to frustration and contributed significantly to the popular perception of his rule as incompetent. Unlike other Soviet leaders who had also begun their administrations in this manner, Gorbachev made such promises while undermining both the economy's ability to deliver and his own ability to crack down should discontent arise.

These developments meant that Soviet totalitarianism was destroyed and that Gorbachev himself no longer had any stable, legitimate, and effective political institutions with which to pursue reform. The old Soviet institutions were either gone or ineffective; new ones were either bogus or as yet uncreated. Besides Raisa, Gorbachev's wife, there was nothing left at the imploding center but Mikhail Sergeievich himself, a president with formal powers far greater than those of most Russian tsars, and the forces of coercion, the army and secret police, two institutions of declining reliability. In contrast, the legitimate political institutions that did exist—popular fronts, national Communist parties, churches, and all the other groupings that constitute emergent civil societies—were in the republics.[3]

The End of Empire

All the republics began to abandon Moscow because perestroika produced chaos in the polity, economy, society, and culture. By unanimously declaring sovereignty in 1988–1990, the republics sought to break ties with the center, not because of uncontrolled nationalist passions or a desire for unbounded freedom, but because of a supremely rational, almost cold-blooded, calculation. They knew that survival meant relying first of all on themselves, not on an impotent central apparatus. The Russian Soviet Federated Socialist Republic's own declaration of sovereignty on June

42   12, 1990, was thus the logical culmination of the non-Russian rejection of imperial Russian dominance.

The impotence of the Leviathan state became manifestly clear on August 21, 1991, when the coup attempt led by Vice President Gennadi Yanayev, in a fashion reminiscent of perestroika's own fate, collapsed ignominiously. The days that followed witnessed the emergence of a populist Russian president, Boris Yeltsin, and of a Russia proud of its national heritage and reluctant to abandon its imperial past. No less important, the coup and its aftermath represented what Armenian President Levon Ter-Petrosyan aptly termed the "suicide" of the center. The total collapse of all central Soviet institutions and the relegation of the stubbornly pro-socialist Gorbachev to what Soviet propaganda used to call the "dustheap of history" meant that the republics, finally, were completely on their own. As soon as the center disappeared, the republics effectively became independent. In recognition of the new reality, all except Russia proceeded to declare independence as well. And if the world needed any more evidence of the seriousness of republican aspirations, it was provided by Ukraine's referendum of December 1, in which over 90 percent of the population supported a declaration of independence.

The creation by Russia, Ukraine, and Belarus, which were later joined by the Central Asians, Armenia, and Azerbaijan, of a Commonwealth of Independent States on December 8, 1991, delivered the coup de grâce to the Soviet state. Not only was their action as legal as anything that the Soviet authorities ever did—after all, legality is a fuzzy notion in a state that practiced mass murder for decades—but it also showed that the republican elites were rather more level-headed than their critics in Moscow and the West claimed they were. The republican willingness to create a transitional arrangement and to talk about their most pressing problems suggested that a future without the Kremlin need not be as bleak as Gorbachev pronounced.

Despite the good news, the Commonwealth was, by its very nature, doomed. The very inclusion of the non-Slavic republics ensured such a fate, since the greater the number of participants, **43** the more difficult it is for any body to make tough choices and to coordinate policy. More important, the vital interests even of the three Slavic republics were so different as to subvert any long-term cooperative venture. Compared with Russia, Ukraine and Belarus are small, homogeneous, evenly developed, and militarily weak. It was easy for the three to agree that the old Union was dead and that Gorbachev had to go. Rather more difficult was developing joint security and military policies in light of Moscow's insistence that the armed forces remain under its control and to agree on uniform economic and social policies that would affect their countries differently and cause their populations extreme hardship. Finally, and most important, if Russia was, as some Western economists believed, a genuine locomotive of economic development, then the incentive to cooperate with so large a country might be irresistible. If the more appropriate image of Russia was that of the *Titanic*, however, then the post-Soviet states were unlikely to stay on board. It was more probable that they would jump for the lifeboats, lest their own fortunes depreciate as rapidly as the ruble's value against the dollar.

Stirrings of Nationalism

Perestroika's destruction of the Soviet system provided the background for Ukraine's hesitant march toward independence. Few Ukrainians actually desired the creation of their own state, even as late as 1989. That most of the population then proceeded to vote for such a measure in late 1991 was, to be sure, the result partly of a bitter political struggle waged by Ukrainian nationalists against the Communist regime, but far more so, of Gorbachev's demolition of Soviet totalitarianism.

The leading nationalist organization, the Ukrainian Popular Front in Support of Perestroika (Rukh), emerged only in 1989. Until then, nationalist activity in Ukraine had been confined to the renewal of some of the dissident organizations crushed in the 1970s, such as the Helsinki Group, to the formation of several others, most prominent of which was the Ukrainian Culturologi-

44   cal [sic] Club, and to the agitation of Ukrainian writers—in particular, Ivan Drach and Dmytro Pavlychko, both of whom discovered a particular talent for mobilizational politics. Organizations such as the Helsinki Group focused on the defense of human rights, while those like the Culturological Club concentrated mostly on the "ecology"—that is, the existential status—of Ukrainian culture and language. Rukh itself was initially created to promote the goals of perestroika in opposition to the resistance of the conservative Ukrainian party authorities. Not surprisingly, writers were most vocal, both because they knew how to express themselves and because their professional concerns—language and culture—tended to coincide with those of nationalists.

Of great importance in making their audience receptive to the nationalist message was the nuclear accident at Chernobyl in May 1986. The catastrophe had not yet come to symbolize the Ukrainian experience in the Soviet Union, but its mishandling by the party authorities in Moscow and Kiev greatly contributed to a growing sense of unease and anger and to the erosion of party legitimacy. Chernobyl was a godsend for the nationalists because it conveniently combined several themes that were to become increasingly prominent in the years ahead: party incompetence, national suffering, and environmental destruction.

In contrast to the events rocking Central Europe in 1989, however, Ukraine still appeared—and largely was—quiet. Rukh's first major attempt at mobilizing mass public opinion took place on January 22, 1990 (the anniversary of the declaration of independence of the Ukrainian People's Republic in 1917), when the movement attempted to replicate the Baltic "human chain" of several months before. Incredibly, or so it seemed at the time, close to half a million Ukrainians turned out to join hands on the highways and roads between Kiev and Lviv. The action was a foretaste of things to come in 1990.

The Decisive Year

In March of that year, elections to the republics' supreme soviets took place. Although the democratic opposition in Ukraine had

only a month to campaign, and was not represented in all the **45**
electoral districts, it still managed to win nearly a third of the new
parliament's seats. Although the Communist majority, the
"Group of 239," controlled the legislature, for the first time in
Soviet Ukrainian history a vocal, talented, and vigorous opposition emerged and made itself heard. Most important perhaps,
although the democrats lacked numbers, they quickly showed that
they outclassed the Communists in political and oratorical skills—
a fact of no small consequence in the next year and a half.

No less important than the elections was the removal of
Volodymyr Shcherbytsky from the post of party first secretary in
late 1989. In power since 1972, when he initiated a vicious
crackdown on dissent, Shcherbytsky had embodied the ultraloyal
non-Russian official, committed to Communist rule and to the
preservation of Moscow's empire. His retirement, and eventual
death in early 1990, removed one of the major obstacles to the
development of a nationalist movement by permitting the hith-
erto monolithic party elite to divide into pro- and anti-perestroika
factions. The leader of the reformist wing became the unassuming
Leonid Makarovych Kravchuk, the former ideology chief who was
elected chairman of the supreme soviet in Ukraine in mid-1990.
The leader of the conservatives was Stanislav Hurenko, appointed
party chief in midyear and a man committed to Communist
hegemony, even if of a more humane kind. As Hurenko noted in
late 1990:

> It really is unfortunate that most of the new political parties that
> have emerged—we now have about twenty of them in the repub-
> lic—base their political programs above all on criticism of the
> Ukrainian Communist Party for both its past and its present activ-
> ities, and they direct their practical efforts towards the quickest
> possible elimination of the Communist Party from the political
> arena. From our standpoint, this does not promote a constructive
> solution of the problem, and, above all, it irritates people. We feel
> that this could—and I hope our opponents pardon me here—lead
> to undesirable changes both in politics and as regards the future of
> these parties.[4]

Not surprisingly, Kravchuk and Hurenko became involved in a
power struggle that pushed the former to ally himself with the

46   non-Communist opposition and to adopt increasingly nationalist positions.

Events in other republics also pushed Ukraine in a nationalist direction. Estonia, Latvia, and Lithuania declared sovereignty, by which they meant the primacy of their laws over Soviet laws, in 1988–1989. In March 1990, Lithuania went even further and proclaimed independence, an act that led Gorbachev to impose an economic blockade and Lithuania to suspend the declaration. Soon thereafter Russia and all the other republics followed in the Baltics' footsteps and also claimed to be sovereign.

SOVEREIGNTY AND AFTER

With Ukraine's own declaration of sovereignty on July 16, 1990, popular expectations of the parliament and government increased dramatically. Students demanding that the government actually behave in a sovereign manner staged hunger strikes in Kiev in the fall. Although some Communists called for repressing the demonstrators, the government itself wavered and finally made concessions to the newly assertive popular will. The prime minister, Vitaly Masol, was replaced by Vitold Fokin, who promised the immediate introduction of economic and political reforms. Large segments of the population finally realized that change, substantive change, was inevitable and that Ukraine really could control its own destiny.

That October, Rukh held its second congress, which together with the student strikes marked another turning point in the politics of Ukrainian nationalism. The movement condemned the Communist Party and expressly came out for Ukrainian independence. The Rubicon had been crossed. The nationalists dropped all pretense of supporting only perestroika. Ironically, their action put both the hard-line Communists and the national Communists in a bind: since both had supported sovereignty, they had to distance themselves from the maximalist demands of Rukh without appearing to contradict their pro-Ukrainian stance. Kravchuk especially had to maneuver between Rukh-style nationalism and what was probably his own preference, a looser Soviet Union with greater powers for Ukraine and the other republics.

Significantly, as of mid-to-late 1990, Rukh and only Rukh set the political agenda and determined the political discourse, at least in part because its language was palatable to Communists like Kravchuk. The language was nationalist, but not chauvinist, racist, or anti-Semitic; it had at its core the attainment of independence, of statehood, for the Ukrainian people, whom Rukh carefully defined in nonethnic terms that permitted Russians, Jews, Poles, and others to take part in and support its cause. Such a nationalism was at least potentially appealing to Communists because it promised them the opportunity of continuing to serve as an elite, if not the only elite, within a future Ukrainian state.

In the fall and winter of 1991, the forces of reaction, in alliance with Gorbachev, struck back throughout the entire Soviet Union. Eduard Shevardnadze's resignation as foreign minister and the crackdown in Lithuania and Latvia were important events. In Ukraine, conservatives attempted to subvert the nationalist movement by staging an obvious provocation against one of its more radical representatives, Stepan Khmara, in the hope of discrediting Rukh in general. No less strikingly, however, while the government remained inactive and the police were pursuing diversionary tactics against the nationalists, Kravchuk did not abandon the sovereignty line. Indeed, against expectations, he became one of the most forthright defenders of Ukrainian sovereignty—the only position, as he no doubt realized, that would permit him to retain power, to keep the conservatives and Gorbachev at bay, and to continue to court the nationalists.

Most of 1991 was occupied with the tug-of-war surrounding Gorbachev's many versions of a new Union treaty. The March 17 referendum on the desirability of the Union seemed to suggest that most Ukrainians wanted to have their cake and eat it, too: 70.2 percent came out in support of an unrealistically idealized union while 80.2 percent supported something called Ukrainian "sovereignty." Gorbachev lobbied for a more or less centralized federation, while the republics countered with confederative schemes.

48   Finally, in April, the Nine-Plus-One agreement seemed to herald
a compromise solution acceptable to all: Russia, Ukraine, Belarus,
the Central Asians, and Azerbaijan agreed with Gorbachev on the
general outlines of a new arrangement involving a radical devolu-
tion of authority from the center to the republics.

The August Coup

One day before the new treaty was to have been signed, however,
reactionaries in the party, military, and KGB staged their abortive
coup. The rest of the story is familiar. The coup leaders refrained
from using massive force, Kravchuk appeared to equivocate,
Yeltsin mobilized the opposition, and then the coup was suddenly
over. Within days virtually all the republics declared independence and suspended their Communist parties. Ukraine's own
proclamation was issued on August 24; its party took its richly
deserved place on the dustheap of history soon thereafter. Especially noteworthy was Kravchuk's apparent "flip-flop"—after neither endorsing nor condemning the coup, he suddenly painted
himself as the foremost defender of Ukrainian independence.
Although, as argued in chapter 6, there is more to Kravchuk than
meets the eye, his newly found nationalism was clearly the only
response that would have preserved his credibility under post-coup
conditions.

Would a Soviet-type Union have survived had there been no
coup? Obviously not. The forces that were driving the USSR to
destruction went much deeper than the day-to-day activities of
politicians and coup leaders. Once totalitarianism had been destroyed and the empire had collapsed, it was just a matter of time
before the republics' de facto independence, which they had
achieved well before the coup, attained de jure status. The coup
accelerated the process; to use Marx's phrase, it hastened the birth
pangs of history.

The real importance of the coup is not that it destroyed the
Soviet Union but that it destroyed Gorbachev, since it was he who
was ultimately responsible for placing the coup leaders in their
positions of influence in late 1990 and early 1991. Moreover,

Gorbachev's pathetic post-coup performance, his unwillingness   **49**
to acknowledge Yeltsin's heroism, and his embarrassing defense of
socialism sealed his fate. By late 1991 it was evident to all that
Gorbachev was completely out of touch with reality.

INDEPENDENCE AND ITS CONSEQUENCES

The final act in the drama of Ukraine's independence was the
December 1, 1991, referendum. Even the nationalists did not
expect such a resounding vote of support; indeed, many feared
that the population might actually vote *against* independence. But
their fears were unwarranted. Kravchuk and his former comrades,
all of whom were also fearful, but of being accused of insufficient
patriotism and, perhaps, even complicity in the coup, supported
independence and decided to use the old party machine to that
end. Several months of old-style "agitation and propaganda,"
incessant parliamentary debates that excluded other options as
unpatriotic, methodically staged rallies by Rukh and other nationalist organizations, the careful courting of key Russian and other
ethnic constituencies, and a media barrage concerning the historical inevitability of independence did the trick. Independence
became the only imaginable option. Even though many inhabitants of Ukraine were emotionally indifferent to the notion, an
overwhelming majority supported the government's initiative.
That continued membership in the Soviet Union meant having to
live with the widely despised Gorbachev, that the other republics
were also jumping ship, and, finally, that the administration of
United States president George Bush signaled its support of independence several days before the referendum only added to the
persuasive appeal of genuine statehood.

The referendum confirmed two facts. One was that nationalism was the only game in town, that the nationalist agenda was
completely victorious and set the terms of debate. The other was
that the former Communists under Kravchuk had managed to
retain influence by appropriating that agenda and, far more important, translating it into reality. The current political reality in
Ukraine is, as a result, especially complex. Independence was won

50   by people who for the most part had fought independence all their lives. The first of independent Ukraine's many Communist bene-factors was, of course, Gorbachev, whose destruction of total-itarianism forced all the republics to become free. The second such benefactors were the coup leaders, who hammered the last nail into the USSR's coffin. The third were Kravchuk and his cronies, who recognized that independence was the necessary condition of their survival under post-coup conditions. The bona fide national-ists did make a big difference: They mobilized the masses, spread the word, and developed the program that eventually became Kravchuk's. On their own, however, the nationalists could not have destroyed the system and rallied the entire population around the flag of independence. Only established elites, in Moscow and in Kiev, could and did do so by initiating and continuing a process, perestroika, that inevitably led to the destruction of totalitari-anism and, then, to the collapse of empire. Without perestroika, the USSR would not have collapsed in the way that it did, and Ukrainian independence would have remained a nationalist dream.

That Ukrainian independence came so abruptly and so unex-pectedly has enormous consequences for the future of the country. Virtually no one in or out of the government was prepared for independence or its aftermath. Inexperienced and untrained, Ukraine's postimperial elites must now cope with the herculean task of transforming a colony into an independent state and creating everything that totalitarianism had destroyed or stifled: a civil society, a market, the rule of law, democracy, the machinery of a state. In many respects, the challenges facing the post-Soviet republics are greater than those of most colonies, such as the new states that emerged from the French or British empires. However disadvantaged, these colonies had to overcome only the legacy of empire. By contrast, Ukraine and the other successor states must also overcome the legacy of totalitarianism. As the following chapters suggest, it is hard to imagine how post-Soviet elites can cope successfully with the huge problems bequeathed to them by several hundred years of Russian empire, seventy years of Soviet totalitarianism, and seven years of Gorbachev.

CHAPTER 2

Overcoming the Legacies of Empire and Totalitarianism

Two contradictory forces, one generated by the end of empire, the other by the end of totalitarianism, are now buffeting all of the Soviet Union's successor states. The collapse of empire encourages rapid and fundamental change. Thus the shock of collapse makes populations cognitively and emotionally more receptive to change. The socioeconomic disruption associated with collapse undermines existing power structures and creates dissatisfied popular groups. The attempts of newly emergent elites to appeal to and acquire the support of potential constituencies inclines them to adopt policies of radical change. And the emergence of new states intensifies the appeal of nationalism with its emphasis on assertiveness, regeneration, dynamism, and new beginnings. For all these reasons, the post-Soviet countries are in a seemingly excellent position to embark on rapid and full-scale transitions to new forms of political and socioeconomic organization.

The end of totalitarianism, however, thoroughly undermines the ability of post-Soviet elites to adopt radical policies and of post-Soviet populations to withstand them. After all, where the state is totalitarian and controls society in depth and in breadth, there can be no market, no democracy, no rule of law, and no civil society. As a result, post-totalitarian elites lack the political, social, and economic institutions and resources necessary for determined and consistent policymaking, while post-totalitarian

52   populations lack the social and economic bases that would permit them to survive radical transformations without undue hardship and disruption. Most important, perhaps, post-totalitarian societies are so atomized that the challenge before them is not the radical and rapid *transformation* of existing social, political, and economic institutions, but their wholesale *creation*. Consider, in contrast, postcolonial Mozambique and Angola. There, too, imperial collapse left the native populations lacking in many institutions and resources and facing staggering problems. But, unlike the Sovietized nations, the Mozambicans and Angolans did not face the task of creating market economies and civil societies from scratch. In this sense, their problems, however immense, were actually fewer and somewhat less complex.

The postimperial temptation of the successor states is to take advantage of imperial collapse and transform their societies relatively quickly. The post-totalitarian imperative, however, is for post-Soviet (*and* Western) elites to recognize that the successor states have virtually nothing to work with and that, while transforming what exists into something else may be possible, creating everything at once is not. Even God needed six days. Moreover, God's creation of the world was logical and sequential: first the heavens, then the earth, then plants and animals, and, only then, Adam.

Which legacy will win the day? Logic dictates that the post-totalitarian imperative sooner or later will assert itself and that the postimperial temptation, no matter how seductive, will eventually be resisted. Once elites see that constructive radical change is impossible, they should abandon the revolutionary agenda and adopt an evolutionary approach. While that may be the inevitable ultimate outcome, post-Soviet elites will probably succumb—indeed, some already have succumbed—to the blandishments of post-imperialism, which promises to satisfy their inflated ambitions *and* to meet with the approval of the West, and ignore the lessons of post-totalitarianism. The result is likely to be tragic: the elites will fail to transform their societies, but, in their attempt to do so, they will have destabilized their polities, angered their populations, destroyed their economies, and produced radical **53** backlashes of a dangerously post-Weimar type.

THE NATIONAL ADVANTAGE

Although the future of the successor states seems bleak, there are grounds for some optimism. In contrast to any version of the former Union—especially to such an anemic entity as the Commonwealth of Independent States—the successor states have one unique asset: They are the homelands of particular nations, which can serve as ready-made vehicles of consensus, civil society, and political stability. Since national identity is rooted in a sense of national community, it automatically provides for a certain amount of social cohesion. By the same token, national traditions—religious, political, or exclusively cultural—underpin the institutions of an emergent civil society. Finally, popular fronts, which enjoyed widespread legitimacy and support in all the republics, have endowed their political arenas with a modicum of stability as well as produced some of the requisite leaders and institutions.

But the nation and the institutions it generates can also be a double-edged sword. When distinctly national movements form the basis for the emergence of multiethnic civil societies, conflict and competition among ethnic majorities and minorities can easily result. Although the democratic popular fronts by and large managed to address the concerns of ethnic minorities before independence, some, such as the Estonian and Latvian movements, began to adopt more intemperate positions after independence. Neither the problems they now confront in building viable sovereign states nor the solutions they must develop to satisfy the legitimate demands of their own nations without alienating the Russian settler populations appear as obvious as they once did. And continued social, political, and economic disarray could easily increase interethnic strains and conflicts.

Ukraine's dilemmas are especially striking. Its Russian-speaking population is concentrated in the heavily industrialized

54   provinces of the Donbas. Market reforms will inevitably hit this region harder than the others, and it is possible that socio-economic grievances will then assume anti-Ukrainian overtones. By contrast, Ukraine's half-million ethnic Jews, among the best educated and most urban of the republic's population, are likely to benefit most from market reforms. If the rest of the population also does relatively well, anti-Jewish attitudes are unlikely to proliferate. But if, as seems more likely, ethnic Ukrainians and Russians suffer disproportionately, or see themselves as victims of a zero-sum game, class conflict might assume an anti-Semitic form, as has occurred all too frequently in the past.

Post-totalitarian Ruin

After three hundred years of Russian imperialism and seventy years of Soviet totalitarianism, Ukraine has joined the international community of states. Like the other non-Russian states, Ukraine is in ruins. Not quite literally, of course: while its buildings and factories and roads still stand, some in excellent condition; while its people in general are probably better educated than those of some states in the West—the United States comes to mind—the country lacks virtually everything required for a modern society. It has no democratic institutions and no rule of law; it has no civil society; and it lacks a market. Indeed, Ukraine even lacks a bona fide state, a set of political institutions, to use Max Weber's definition, that engage in effective taxation, administration, and policing of a certain territory. Ukraine is a land with people and things, but the organization of the people and things, the administration and arrangement of them, the relations between and among them, are still for the most part missing or undefined.

Like other post-Soviet states, Ukraine confronts a historically unique challenge. The problem facing its current leadership is to create more or less simultaneously a state, the rule of law, democracy, a civil society, and a market. In the West, not only did such processes take hundreds of years, but they also tended to develop sequentially, with states, rule of law, and markets emerging first, and democracies and full-fledged civil societies, as opposed to the exclusively religious institutions bound to the Catholic Church, emerging only later. For the new post-Soviet countries, however, such an option is not available. They cannot wait centuries because the legacy of totalitarianism, on the one hand, and Gorbachev's breathless destruction of it, on the other, mean that they have to save themselves now or perish. Moreover, due to both the contemporary human rights *Zeitgeist* and the democratic impulses generated by the struggle against communism, it is difficult, if not impossible, to neglect democracy, rule of law, and civil society, and concentrate only on state-building and markets. To make matters even more complicated, the West insists that the fledgling states of Eastern Europe respect human rights and maintain spotless democratic records, even as they embark on socioeconomic experiments that are likely to disrupt the lives of the vast majority of their populations.

Such difficulties may well be insurmountable. None of the USSR's successor states is likely to succeed at what appears to be an impossible task. Although something can be created on the basis of nothing, it is hard to imagine how nothing is supposed to be transformed, almost magically, into everything—without enormous tension, upheaval, and perhaps even bloodshed. Not only are the challenges great and the resources small, but the pursuit of some goals—say, markets—may undermine the achievement of others—say, democracy. In other words, some of the goals may, in the short run, be incompatible. Because some factors are necessary conditions of others and, as such, must precede them, sequential development appears necessary.

Post-totalitarian Capacities

In terms of these challenges, Ukraine is no different than the other successor states. In terms of ability, however, it is. Overcoming the legacies of empire and of totalitarianism is the central problem confronting all post-Soviet elites, from Estonia, to Ukraine, to Russia, to Kyrgyzstan, since all the republics were victims of totalitarianism and all formed parts of an empire. There are

56   degrees of totalitarian decay; likewise, the location of a successor state in the empire, in the former core or in the former periphery, makes a difference. Clearly, the greater the extent of totalitarian degeneration, the easier is a post-totalitarian transformation of the society and polity. Where some social, economic, or political institutions already exist, the radical change encouraged by imperial collapse becomes plausible, if not easy, because there is a starting place and there are already institutions that can be changed. Totalitarianism in Poland and Hungary had so lost the capacity to control life effectively that a fair amount of private enterprise could exist in both, and the Catholic Church and Solidarity were able to form the beginnings of a genuine civil society in Poland. No former Soviet republic, even Estonia, which had the greatest contacts with the West, can compare in this respect with Poland and Hungary.

Second, imperial cores have several disadvantages that imperial peripheries lack: burdened with the degenerate imperial state, with the lion's share of the imperial army, and with outworn imperial mentalities, former cores possess just those characteristics that are most likely to incline them away from reform and toward foreign policy adventurism (or what some Russians now call "enlightened imperialism")—a pattern that tends to recur historically. Consider in this light Weimar Germany's inability to come to terms with its perceived humiliation in World War I. If so, then Central Europe is most likely to change, the non-Russian republics are next, and the former imperial core, Russia, is least.

Several other factors influence the capacity of post-totalitarian states to embark on and attain radical change. One, already mentioned above, is degree of national homogeneity; the more homogeneous a population, the easier it is for a consensus to form and for the conflicts that change inevitably carries in its wake to be avoided or managed. Another is size: in general, smaller states and smaller societies, like smaller firms and plants, are easier to fix than larger ones because coordinating and synchronizing change is less daunting an organizational and managerial task. Three others are leadership, especially if it is charismatic, such as has been exercised by Walesa, Havel, and Yeltsin; economic potential; and extent of international support, that is, the willingness of other states, in particular powerful ones, to provide political, financial, or military assistance. A final factor is administrative uniformity: the greater the number of autonomous administrative units, the greater the challenge of coordinating semisovereign entities for the pursuit of some common good. In general, therefore, totalitarian ruin, imperial institutions, ethnocultural heterogeneity, large size, poor leadership, minimal economic potential, international isolation, and administrative complexity impede radical change, while their opposites encourage it.

Where do Ukraine and the other successor states stand with regard to these factors? Table 2.1 suggests a tentative answer. Countries could score 0 to 10 on any one factor, with lower scores indicating greater chances of reform. Given the roughness of my estimates, scores are intended only to be analytically suggestive, not statistically meaningful. The lowest possible, and thus the best, total score is of course 0; the highest possible total score is 90. In some cases, scores were assigned on the basis of statistical calculations; in others, on the basis of informed estimates. Thus the degree of totalitarianism was assumed highest (10) in most of the republics, somewhat less (6.6) in the Baltic states, the Czech Republic and Slovakia, and lowest in Poland and Hungary (3.3). The four Central European states were on the outer periphery (3.3) of the empire, the non-Russian republics on the inner periphery (6.6), and Russia at the core (10). The ethnic homogeneity index represents 10 percent of the relative size of a state's minority population. Thus Estonia's score, 3.9, is derived from 39 percent, the proportion of the total population that is non-Estonian. The population, area, and administrative uniformity scores for the non-Russian states are all pegged relative to those of Russia, which, with the largest population and area, and thirty-one ethnic administrative units, scores 10 on all three counts. Population size and geographic area are taken as indices of size. Russia and the Central Europeans, with the experience that im-

58

TABLE 2.1
FACTORS FACILITATING AND OBSTRUCTING REFORM
IN THE POST-COMMUNIST STATES

	A	B	C	D	E	F	G	H	I	Total
Hungary	3.3	3.3	0.8	0.7	0.1	0.0	0.0	1.0	0.0	9.2
Poland	3.3	3.3	0.2	2.5	0.2	0.0	0.0	1.0	0.0	10.5
Czech Republic	6.6	3.3	0.6	0.7	0.1	0.0	0.0	1.0	0.0	12.3
Slovakia	6.6	3.3	1.3	0.3	0.1	0.0	3.3	2.3	10.0	27.2
Lithuania	6.6	6.6	2.0	0.3	0.0	0.0	6.6	2.3	5.0	29.4
Estonia	6.6	6.6	3.9	0.1	0.0	0.0	6.6	2.3	5.0	31.1
Latvia	6.6	6.6	4.8	0.2	0.0	0.0	6.6	2.3	5.0	32.1
Ukraine	10.0	6.6	2.7	3.5	0.4	0.1	3.3	1.7	5.0	33.3
Belarus	10.0	6.6	2.2	0.7	0.1	0.0	3.3	4.5	10.0	37.4
Armenia	10.0	6.6	0.7	0.2	0.0	0.0	10.0	5.3	8.0	40.8
Georgia	10.0	6.6	3.1	0.4	0.0	0.3	10.0	3.9	10.0	44.3
Azerbaijan	10.0	6.6	1.7	0.4	0.1	0.2	10.0	5.3	10.0	44.3
Moldova	10.0	6.6	3.5	0.3	0.0	0.0	10.0	5.1	10.0	45.5
Turkmenistan	10.0	6.6	2.8	0.2	0.3	0.0	10.0	7.3	10.0	47.2
Tajikistan	10.0	6.6	3.8	0.3	0.1	0.0	10.0	8.2	10.0	49.0
Uzbekistan	10.0	6.6	3.9	1.4	0.3	0.1	10.0	6.8	10.0	49.1
Kyrgyzstan	10.0	6.6	4.8	0.3	0.1	0.0	10.0	7.6	10.0	49.4
Kazakhstan	10.0	6.6	6.0	1.1	1.6	0.0	10.0	4.5	10.0	49.8
Russia	10.0	10.0	1.8	10.0	10.0	10.0	0.0	2.8	0.0	54.6

Sources: *World Almanac, 1992; The Europa World Year Book,* vol. 1, 1992; *The Soviet Union at the Crossroads* (Frankfurt: Deutsche Bank, 1990); Roland Götz and Uwe Halbach, *Daten zu Geographie, Bevölkerung, Politik und Wirtschaft der Republiken der ehemaligen USSR* (Cologne: Bundesinstitut für ostwissenschaftliche und internationale Studien, 1992); *Malyi Atlas SSSR* (Moscow: Glavnoe upravlenie geodezii i kartografii, 1981).

Key: A: Degree of totalitarianism
B: Core/Periphery location
C: Homogeneity of population
D: Population size
E: Geographic area
F: Administrative uniformity
G: Elite capability
H: Economic potential
I: International support

perial and satellite status gave them, are assumed to have the best elites; Ukraine and Belarus, with their experience in the United Nations, and Slovakia, one notch below the Czech Republic, are next; the Baltics, more or less open to the West, are third; the remaining republics are last. Since the Deutsche Bank study did not rank the Central European states, Poland, Hungary, and the Czech Republic (to which conventional wisdom ascribes the highest potential) were assigned 1.0; Slovakia was ranked at the level of the Baltics. The Central Europeans and Russians have the most international support, the Baltics and Ukraine are next, Armenia enjoys some sympathy, and Slovakia, Belarus, Moldova, Azerbaijan, and the Central Asians are clearly of least concern to the richest and most powerful countries of the world.

The rankings are not for the most part surprising. As expected, the table indicates that Hungary, Poland, and the Czech Republic are in a class of their own and thus are most likely to reform successfully; that the Slovaks, Baltics, Ukrainians, and Belarusians lag behind the Central Europeans; that the Moldovans and Caucasians are further removed; and that the Central Asians are least likely to reform. In other words, even though Russia's ranking is unexpectedly lower than that of the Central Asians, there is no obvious reason to believe that the criteria are slanted or incomplete. That being the case, we can only conclude that the obstacles to a successful Russian transition are formidable indeed. Moreover, they would remain so even if Russia's scores were, arbitrarily, reduced across the board. The conventional wisdom claims otherwise, because Russia's two major assets—leadership and international support—are highly visible factors that appear to endow the country with an aura of invincibility. However important, Yeltsin and the West may not be enough to overcome the many objective and thus less visible obstacles to reform that Russia uniquely confronts. This is not to say that Russia is doomed, that, as Jeffrey Sachs put it, "The whole country is going over the cliff,"[1] but that its road to democracy and the market is most likely to be very long and very arduous. Five hundred days, which is the amount of time the so-called Shatalin Plan envisaged

60   as sufficient for the introduction of market reforms, are, to say the
least, not enough. Naturally, Russia's likely inability to achieve
effective economic and political reform cannot be encouraging for
Ukrainians or other non-Russians: if Russia collapses, then they
may, too. Lest such pessimism be exaggerated, chapter 4 will
discuss in greater detail whether Yeltsin's leadership or Russia's
economic resources may indeed save the day.

Post-totalitarian Challenges

Regardless of the assets individual countries possess, the tasks they
face—attaining civil society, democracy, a well-ordered state, rule
of law, and a market—cannot be achieved simultaneously, so it
becomes logically imperative to adopt some manner of sequencing. Deliberately or not, this is exactly what Ukraine's elite, with
its commitment to evolutionary change and continued state intervention in the economy, seems to be doing.

   If civil society is defined as the coherent set of autonomous
social institutions positioned between people as individuals and
the state and its own institutions, including religious associations,
political organizations, social movements, and clubs, then it is
obvious that nothing resembling a civil society can be said to have
existed in the Soviet Union before 1989–1990. There were, of
course, dissidents, but they never succeeded in creating institutions. There were some ostensibly nonstate institutions, such as
the Russian Orthodox Church, but in reality it was completely
subservient to and controlled by the political authorities. And
there were all sorts of unsanctioned individual behavior, such as
black marketeering, kitchen discussions, friendships, and the like,
but they, too, were neither institutionalized nor particularly public. In Ukraine, as in the USSR in general, there was nonsanc-
tioned *life*, but not civil society.

   An embryonic civil society began to emerge only during
perestroika, after the totalitarian state started crumbling under
the impact of Gorbachev's reforms and their unintended consequences. Once totalitarian controls were dismantled, individuals
could create their own organizations and associations. The many

thousands of informal groupings that sprouted in 1986–1988 were **61** the first manifestations of autonomous social activity. But it was only with the establishment of popular fronts and political parties, with the freeing of the churches and other forms of religious activity, and with the transformation of some informal groups into functioning organizations, that one can legitimately speak of something resembling civil society in the Soviet Union.

In Ukraine, as elsewhere, 1989 was the pivotal year: it witnessed the emergence of Rukh and the reemergence of the Greek Catholic Uniate Church from forty years of underground existence. Since then, a multitude of parties spanning the entire political spectrum from communism to fascism has arisen; the official trade unions have faded in importance and such organizations as the Ukrainian Organization of Worker Solidarity have taken their place; ethnic political and social organizations (for example, Jews for Jesus, the Russian Movement of the Crimea, the Hungarian Cultural Association of Subcarpathia, and the German Rebirth Society) have emerged; the Ukrainian Autocephalous Orthodox Church has been revived; Baptist preachers and missionaries have become ubiquitous; and independent journals, newspapers, and publishing ventures have mushroomed.

Yet, despite all this progress, it would be incorrect to say that Ukraine, or any other republic, already possesses a civil society. All these elements of autonomous social activity, while important as the basis of civil society, are not yet institutionalized. They have not yet become relatively stable, coherent, and adaptable patterns of social activity. In this sense, what Ukraine has experienced in the last six years is a quantum increase in the amount of nonstate social activity, but this quantity, to use a Marxist phrase, has not yet undergone a qualitative transformation into a genuine civil society. Ukraine's political parties—such as the moderate Democratic Party, the Green Party, the liberal Party of Democratic Rebirth, the progressive New Ukraine movement, the nationalist Republican party, the (formerly Communist) Socialist Party, the Peasants' Party, the Social-Democratic Party—are cases in point. Although there are scores of such self-styled political associations,

62   they are not yet "real" parties, but rather debating clubs of intellectuals. Typically, these parties group like-minded individuals
around some publication; they hold meetings, organize rallies,
distribute leaflets. By and large, they lack both a stable constituency and an organization concerned with maintaining relations
with that missing constituency. This is not to say that some, such
as Rukh, cannot mobilize people on certain occasions and on
certain issues. But even Rukh cannot really claim to have a solid
social base.

The striking degree of "diasporazation" of Ukrainian politics
provides additional evidence for this argument. Ukrainians from
the West are helping set the public policy agenda by virtue of their
resources, initiative, and organizational coherence. Some diaspora Ukrainians have come to occupy important advisory positions in the government; others have injected themselves into
public debates. In turn, some diaspora organizations are transferring all or part of their operations to Ukraine and, for the time
being at least, doing quite well. The liberal émigré journal *Suchas-
nist* [*Present Times*], for instance, has moved to Kiev, a welcome
development that can only raise the quality of Ukrainian debates.
But the Bandera wing of the Organization of Ukrainian Nationalists, a Munich-based group with what can generously be termed an
ambiguous relationship with democracy, is also making inroads; in
the spring of 1992 it even staged a huge congress in Kiev, at which
several respectable local intellectuals agreed to speak. Regardless
of how one evaluates these two cases, the important point is that
in both instances relatively marginal émigré groups—the *Suchas-
nist* liberals and the Munich extremists—have suddenly mounted
the political stage and have begun to play a role in the political
process. In and of itself, such a development is probably both
inevitable and to some degree desirable, since émigré Ukrainians,
like diaspora Jews, can make substantial contributions to their
putative "homelands." But, while the ability of a strong and large
Jewish diaspora to exert some influence on the political agenda of a
small country is not surprising, the diasporazation of Ukrainian
affairs is. After all, Ukrainian émigrés are neither particularly

numerous, nor particularly powerful, while Ukraine is a country **63** the size of France. But, of course, Ukraine also lacks the autonomous social institutions that generally set the public agenda, and compared with such a nascent civil society the Ukrainian diaspora not only looks strong but *is* strong.

DEMOCRACY, THE MARKET, AND THE STATE

An equally guarded conclusion should be drawn with respect to democracy in Ukraine. It has become common in the West to assume that democratically conducted elections are tantamount to democracy or that self-styled democrats constitute necessary and sufficient conditions for democracy. Alas, no. Although Ukraine has many political parties professing commitment to democratic ideals, a multitude of politicians who call themselves democrats, a parliament, and a president, and although it has held several democratically conducted elections, including those that brought Kravchuk to power in 1991, to say that the country has already become democratic would be premature.

Like civil society, democracy, as a set of procedures and rules by which the political game is played, must consist of regularized patterns of political behavior, or *institutions*. Elections are part of democracy, of course, but just as important are stable and accountable legislative, executive, and judicial branches of government, the regularized competition of genuinely representative parties, and the various procedures by which elites are brought into and removed from office. These things are not yet in place, through no fault of the Ukrainians, Russians, or anybody else: it is simply too soon. Institutions and procedures by their very nature take time to develop. Indeed, if the experiences of the West and of the Third World are instructive, then stable democracy may need centuries to take root, so the attempt to create it overnight may be doomed to failure. We should at least refrain from calling Ukraine and other successor states democratic until they have passed the political scientist Samuel P. Huntington's "two turnover test"—that is, that democracies cannot be considered stable until and unless

64   governmental authority has been turned over twice in regular elections.[2] Because of the four-to-five-year periods between elections, this cannot happen in less than a decade in most of the post-Soviet states.

Just as one can at best argue that only some elements of civil society and democracy are found in Ukraine, one can also make the case for at most an embryonic market. As in all the republics, black marketeering, moonlighting, and other such forms of private economic activity are widespread in Ukraine. Indeed, as visitors to the republics know, almost the only way one can procure scarce consumer goods or food is by means of under-the-counter transactions and bribes. Since 1990 a variety of private enterprises have emerged: stock markets, commodity exchanges, consulting firms, business schools, luxury shops and restaurants (Kiev even boasts a Lancôme boutique and a pseudo-Italian trattoria, while Vilnius now has its first Chinese restaurant), service stations, and others. But while private entrepreneurship has boomed, a market, as a complex institutional arrangement within which the free exchange of goods, labor, capital, and land can take place, is still absent. Private firms exist in a legal and economic limbo: the rules of economic activity remain unclear, regulations tend to be restrictive, vital information on the state of the economy is missing, and ties with other firms are generally informal and ad hoc. Western entrepreneurs interested in joint ventures in Ukraine can attest to the sense of being completely on one's own, of lacking all bearings in thoroughly uncharted waters. Far too much of the economy, over 90 percent, is still the property of the state, land still belongs to state or collective farms, and the scope of tolerated private activity is still narrow. Most important perhaps, it is hard to imagine a market without a meaningful currency—a name that cannot be applied to the fast-falling coupon, the karbovanets—acting as the means of exchange. Only after the hryvnia is introduced, an issue discussed at greater length in chapter 5, can there be talk of creating a real market in Ukraine, and even then, of course, the stability of the market will depend

greatly on the strength of the currency and the monetary and fiscal **65**
policies pursued by the government.

Especially distressing is that the emergence of widespread racketeering (Lviv enjoys the distinction of Ukraine's most corrupt city) on the ruins of the command economy is hindering the introduction of the market. Much entrepreneurship is generated by Mafia-like organizations, and their all too visible success at amassing fortunes, contributing to popular immiseration, and flouting the law is producing an antimarket backlash among a population that has come to associate the opening of the economy with the rise of organized crime, poverty, and other ills.[3] The situation has gotten so bad in some regions of the country that local officials are forging informal alliances with young nationalists in the hope of eventually using them as vigilantes against the criminals.

No less undeveloped than civil society, democracy, and the market is the state, here defined as the set of administrative, coercive, and extractive institutions with exclusive control over some territory. The Ukrainian bureaucratic apparatus is understaffed, inexperienced, and unstructured. As such, it is almost completely incapable of doing what states are supposed to do: effectively extract resources through taxation, administer laws, and maintain order. As a result, the rule of law—in contrast to the *passing* of laws—cannot yet be considered a reality in Ukraine. The rule of law presupposes a set of stable and coherent institutions that are capable of being ruled by law. The underdeveloped, and dreadfully corrupt, Ukrainian pseudostate requires laws to become a genuine administrative apparatus, but it is only then, after some semblance of regularity and stability has been achieved, that the legal procedures that rule of law embodies will be able to take root in the state apparatus.

The Army and Secret Police

Unlike Ukraine and the other republics, Russia does have an all-too-large state, because imperial Soviet institutions were located mostly in Russia and, to a large degree, are still intact. Understaffing is thus not as much of a problem in Russia; inefficiency, ineffectiveness, inexperience, and lack of structure are. Russia is

66   also exceptional with regard to another institution, the military, the coercive arm of the state. The former Soviet army, like the armed forces of the CIS, was not only overwhelmingly Russian, especially in terms of the composition of the officer corps, but its central command, located in Moscow, was inevitably Russian as well. However, inheriting the Soviet army is a mixed blessing for Russia. The army does provide Russia with clout both within the former USSR and abroad, but a bloated, frustrated, angry, humiliated, underpaid, and underfed military force, especially one that has substantial units posted in the non-Russian states, is unlikely to play a politically stabilizing or democratically supportive role. The lack of real armies in most of the non-Russian states may turn out to be one of their most important assets in effecting successful transitions to democracy.

By the same logic, Ukraine's decision to create its own army, one that may include as many as 400,000 soldiers, while understandable for security reasons, is less than encouraging. Like the Russian army, the Ukrainian armed forces are likely to demand, and get, substantial public resources for their needs. And like all armies under postcolonial conditions, the Ukrainian army will be sorely tempted to interfere in the political process. About the only positive statement that may be made about the Ukrainian and other non-Russian armies is that, at least initially, because they are the potentially patriotic servants of newly established states with no official links to the traditions of the humiliated Soviet armed forces, they are unlikely to share the Russian army's extreme sense of frustration and degradation and therefore may be less inclined to leave the barracks.

Further clouding the picture is that all the republics, including Ukraine, have retained the former secret police. Russia's inheritance is most problematic, as the former KGB directed its operations, in the USSR and throughout the world, from its headquarters in Moscow. Moreover, Boris Yeltsin, for reasons apparently having to do with opposition to his reforms, has decided to form something like an alliance with the Russian security service. No less worrisome is that many of the newly established national secret services are forging official ties with one another in **67** order to cooperate in the struggle against organized crime and, one hopes, nothing else.

The Ukrainian version of the former KGB, the National Security Service (SNBU), now claims to have become a regular intelligence agency cleansed of the KGB's maleficent behavior.[4] But the SNBU, like all its counterparts in the other successor states, has changed little of its personnel and operating procedures. We should not assume that its agents are admirers of democracy; nor should we assume that surveillance has ceased. The SNBU remains virtually the only state institution in Ukraine with any degree of coherence, competence, experience, and esprit de corps. KGB agents were, after all, among the best and the brightest of the former Soviet elite, and their institution was actually one of the most effective in the USSR. How will the SNBU interact with, and react to, the democratization of Ukrainian society? How will it protect its own interests? Will it interfere in politics? Will it resume its past practices? It is impossible to answer any of these questions with certainty. And therein lies the problem: with weak and unstable political, social, economic, and other institutions, an institutionally strong secret police represents an objective threat to democracy, and it will continue to do so as long as all the other institutions remain weak and undeveloped.

The Logical Necessity of Sequencing

The choice facing Ukraine, like that confronting all the other post-Soviet nations, is stark: to develop a state, the rule of law, a civil society, a market, and a democracy, more or less simultaneously *or* sequentially. Other than doing nothing, there is no third way. The citizenry insists on simultaneity, as does much of the elite and the West, while the legacy of imperial collapse suggests that all-or-nothing transformations are not only possible but also desirable. The legacy of totalitarianism, however, precludes simultaneity and warns against radical solutions to issues requiring patience and what Karl Popper calls "piecemeal social

68   engineering."[5] As suggested earlier, the legacy of totalitarianism must take precedence over the legacy of empire. As a result, sequencing is logically unavoidable and a Big Bang approach cannot work because some valued ends are preconditions of others and as such must be constructed first. According to Popper:

> The one thing people in the formerly Communist states must not do is to dismantle their industrial system abruptly. Change takes time, often a great deal of time. Factories have employees who need employment; they produce something that is needed, even though this something may not meet international standards. When demand disappears and unemployment can be taken care of by alternative employment and an extended social safety net, then, and only then, should the old type of "Socialist" enterprises be gradually phased out. . . . That is the way communism has to expire, not by suddenly dismantling what cannot be dismantled overnight. . . . We should say to them: "You should go on with your system until another has naturally replaced it." That is all that can be done, and it is irresponsible to suggest otherwise.[6]

Thus a state, indeed a strong, institutionally healthy state, is a necessary condition of democracy and rule of law; democracy being the set of procedures by which a state and its relations with society are run, and the rule of law, the coherence, regularity, and logic of those procedures. Clearly, the procedures—democracy—cannot precede what they are intended to regulate—the state. As Gorbachev realized, neither can they precede the rule of law, since without the latter the state's relations with society would be arbitrary and thus unregulatable in a democratic and open manner. A market also appears to be a precondition of democracy, insofar as the existence of private property necessarily curtails the reach of the state and thereby permits the establishment of rules governing its behavior within politically circumscribed bounds. Finally, democracy must also be preceded by civil society, which acts as a popular counterpoint to the state within the set of rules and regulations that democracy imposes on their relationship. In sum, no state, no democracy; no state, no rule of law; no rule of law, no democracy; no market, no democracy; no civil society, no democracy.

What, then, are the relationships between and among the state, rule of law, civil society, and the market?

Civil society appears to be a precondition of the market. As a **69** set of autonomous social institutions, civil society represents the sphere of social activity within which market transactions involving the exchange of goods, labor, and capital have to take place. Without such a sphere, without autonomous social institutions, it would be immeasurably more difficult, if not impossible, for market relations, and not just barter, actually to take root. At most, then, civil society is a necessary condition of the market; at the least, civil society strongly facilitates it. Thus, no civil society, very probably no market.

Clearly, states can exist without markets and primitive markets can exist without states. But modern markets, which are complex mechanisms regulated to a greater or lesser extent by the state, cannot exist without states to regulate them. States, in turn, cannot truly regulate things unless they themselves are ruled by law and thus possess the coordinated procedures by which they can do so. Thus, no rule-of-law state, no modern market.

As to states and civil societies, the former can obviously exist without the latter, if only in some feudal or totalitarian form. But can civil societies also exist without states? I am inclined to argue that the answer is "no." First, states define the territorial space within which a coherent and stable set of social institutions can emerge. Second, political authority is the point of reference of the autonomy of social institutions. In the absence of the state, therefore, social patterns of behavior obviously can and do exist, but in being territorially unbounded and defined exclusively in terms of the individuals comprising them, such behavior is more akin to the black-marketeering and kitchen debates found in totalitarian states and less akin to a genuine civil society. In sum, no state, most probably no civil society.

However, states in which rule-of-law prevails, as particular kinds of nontotalitarian or feudal states, must precede civil society. The autonomy of social institutions in nonprimitive settings must be recognized by the state for it to confer civil society status on those social institutions. And the state can recognize and coexist with such social autonomy only if it has coherent rules and

70   regulations itself that permit it to do so. In sum, no rule-of-law state, no modern civil society.

The above analysis, even if modified in some respects, necessarily leads to the conclusion that a radical, "all at once" approach to creating states, rule of law, democracies, civil societies, and markets cannot work because sequencing is necessary and because the correct sequencing is, most probably, the state first, rule of law second, civil society third, the market fourth, and democracy fifth. The dilemma confronting Ukraine and the other states, however, is that their populations demand democracy immediately, while the West demands markets immediately.

WHITHER UKRAINE?

What, then, is Ukraine likely to do? Virtually all political elites perceive state-building as the primary task—less so for the theoretical reasons outlined above than because they view a strong state as the sine qua non of Ukrainian independence and the guarantee of Ukraine's survival in a post-Soviet order dominated by a seemingly threatening Russia. State-building will also assume priority because a weak state—with, alas, a rudimentary army and a strong security service!—is in place, whereas only the foundations of democracy, civil society, rule of law, and the market can already be said to exist.

The construction of the rule of law and of a civil society should also proceed apace, because Ukrainian political elites appear sincerely committed to a legal process initiated by Gorbachev, because the amount of informal socioeconomic activity is already so vast, and because both the rule of law and civil society, unlike democracy, do not pose too much of a threat to the prerogatives and privileges of the state elite. Moreover, since civil society entails a huge expansion of permissible activities, it can function as an ersatz democracy, palatable to elites and attractive to society, at least for the time being.

In light of the imperatives of sequencing, Kiev's reluctance to address economic reform in a radical manner—a reluctance that is motivated as much by lack of purpose as by practical considerations—may actually redound to Ukraine's favor. A rapid, sudden, and total introduction of market relations before state, rule of law, and civil society are consolidated could ensure that all three would remain woefully undeveloped, that democracy would have to be put off indefinitely, and that the market would at best function haltingly. In short, economic shock therapy would probably wreak havoc on the polity and society, leading to either its own ineffectiveness or its own rapaciousness and thereby encouraging the weak state to call on the armed forces to reimpose "law and order."

Whatever the scenario, we should not expect Ukraine to become more than superficially democratic anytime soon. Considering the legacy it has to overcome and the past it has to reject, a quasidemocratic rule of law polity—say, one with an overly domineering president and a disorganized legislature—with a vigorous civil society and some elements of the market would not be all that unsatisfactory an outcome.

The course of events in 1992 appeared to validate this prognosis. The groups comprising the nascent Ukrainian civil society continued to multiply, perhaps even to excess; the legislature remained divided and ineffective, prompting calls for its dissolution and the holding of new elections; the president amassed ever more powers and evinced authoritarian inclinations. Most important perhaps, the draft of the new Ukrainian constitution unambiguously foresaw the creation of a strong presidential system. Nevertheless, Ukrainian society remained free, ethnic peace was maintained, and a sufficient degree of political and social consensus prevailed for genuine economic reform to be considered by the Kuchma government in early 1993. Things were far from ideal, but, in contrast to Russia, Ukraine appeared to be a relatively stable society poised to embark on serious change.

Ukrainian National Identity

Complicating the above developments will be the Ukrainian nation in general and Ukrainian nationalism in particular, the double-edged sword referred to above. National identity provides for consensus, for a shared set of values and world views, and these

72   in turn encourage the emergence of social institutions and demo-cratic (or for that matter any other kind of) rules of the game. National identity also provides some of the social solidarity, en-hances the willingness to sacrifice for the good of the cause, and inculcates the sense of mission necessary for weathering the shock introduced by marketization. Finally, national identity helps state-building by reducing the costs involved for the state in eliciting societal compliance with its administrative, extractive, and coercive measures. Nations will put up with more when running their own governments than when governed by others.

In each of these respects, Ukrainian identity can help Ukraine. Ukrainian groups and organizations with a distinctly Ukrainian agenda are contributing most to the formation of civil society. The sense of loyalty to and love of the *Vitchyzna*, the homeland that has finally become independent, also seems to be inspiring a willingness to accept economic hardship. And it is Ukrainian national identity that is permitting the Ukrainian state to assert its own international identity and to acquire legitimacy as well as establish its authority at home.

Nevertheless, while the commitment to Ukrainian state-hood aids state-building, as well as the construction of civil soci-ety, democracy, and the market, that same commitment can also undermine each of these processes if it unduly stresses the eth-nically Ukrainian identity of the state being built. After all, a distinctly ethnic Ukrainian national identity is exclusionary by definition, and that is the rub. In light of the fact that a very large proportion—anywhere from a third to half—of Ukraine's popula-tion is either ethnically Russian or Russified, Ukrainian national identity can only go so far in providing the basis for a vigorous civil society, market, democracy, and state. As argued in chapter 3, a new Ukrainian identity will have to be crafted on the basis of myths and symbols that also incorporate the millions of Russians and Russified Ukrainians.

Eastern Germany is a vivid example of both the opportunities and the limitations of national identity's interaction with radical reform: on the one hand, the sense of common nationhood has softened the blow of unification; on the other, excessive concern **73** for the future of the *Volk* has also contributed to neo-Nazi excesses against foreigners. The continued strength of the nonexclusionary variant of Ukrainian nationalism is thus necessary for the current experiment with independence to succeed. Because the nationalism propounded by Rukh, most political parties, and President Kravchuk has been of this variety, all ethnically non-Ukrainian minorities in Ukraine joined the proindependence coalition in the December 1, 1991, referendum. The Jewish community, for instance, supported Rukh consistently and independence overwhelmingly, with 93.6 percent of Kiev's Jews voting "yes."[7] Even most ethnic Russians support, or at worst are indifferent to, Ukrainian nationalism, with the sole exception being perhaps a sizable segment of the Russian population in the Crimea, although there, too, 53 percent of all voters, Ukrainian and Russian, endorsed Ukrainian independence.

Inclusionary Ukrainian Nationalism

Fortunately, the Rukh brand of inclusionary nationalism is not just a recent phenomenon. It has its historical roots in three sets of experiences. Most important is the dissident movement of the 1960s–1980s, which consistently promoted human and national rights, democracy, and ethnic tolerance. The explicitly ecumenical writings of Ivan Dzyuba, author of the seminal *Internationalism or Russification?*,[8] are typical in their assertion of distinctly Ukrainian rights within the context of rights and liberties for all. His appointment in late 1992 as minister of culture was thus an encouraging sign of Kiev's continued commitment to ethnic equality. Next in importance are the various strands of national communism that emerged in Ukraine in the 1960s under Party First Secretary Petro Shelest, in the 1920s under Commissar of Education Mykola Skrypnyk, and in the prerevolutionary activity of Ukrainian socialist parties. Ukrainian national communism, which also inspired such dissidents as General Petro Grigorenko and Leonid Plyushch, sought to reconcile the socially egalitarian and nationally liberating ideals of communism with the aspira-

74   tions to cultural authenticity and statehood of the Ukrainian people.[9]

Finally, inclusionary nationalism explicitly sees itself as a continuation of the historical precedent set by the Ukrainian People's Republic (UNR) during the 1917–1920 period of independence. Although armed units associated with the UNR engaged in over a thousand pogroms, thereby compromising the republic in the eyes of Jews and the West, the nationalist leaders themselves, who included the prominent historian Mykhailo Hrushevsky, the writer Volodymyr Vynnychenko, and even the man most associated with the UNR's unsavory side, the commander-in-chief of its armed forces, Symon Petliura, were among the most enlightened and philo-Semitic Ukrainian social democrats of the time. More important, the laws they passed, such as that on National-Personal Autonomy, were some of the most progressive in early twentieth-century Europe and, not surprisingly, initially won the UNR substantial goodwill among Jews. Enlightened thinking and good intentions were not, however, a barrier against Petliura's incompetence and indecisiveness, which, in combination with unruly soldier bands, anti-Semitic warlords, a rebellious peasantry, and sociopolitical chaos, produced a government that controlled only the territory that it physically occupied and could do little to save itself or others.

The challenge before Ukrainian policymakers today is no smaller than that which confronted the Ukrainian People's Republic. They must create an inclusionary Ukrainian national identity, one that permits all ethnic groups to consider themselves bona fide members of a Ukrainian nation, and reinforce the already existing variety of inclusionary Ukrainian nationalism, as an ideology that encourages all of Ukraine's peoples to participate in state-building. The first task is obviously of greater priority because it represents a precondition of the second: the people of Ukraine must first possess a Ukrainian identity before they can help build a distinctly Ukrainian state. Were this twofold challenge to be met, then social peace and political stability would be within Ukraine's reach. Neither part of this challenge can be met, **75** however, if Ukrainian elites succumb to the blandishments of their postimperial legacy and, throwing all caution to the wind, proceed to try to create a democracy, the market, the rule of law, and a civil society immediately and, in all likelihood, fail to attain any of their laudable goals.

CHAPTER 3

Forging a New National Identity

Paradoxically, the most visible presence in Ukraine is the *absence* of all traces of its Communist past. The experience, like the previous statement, can be jarring; Communist civilization has completely disappeared from a setting it dominated for three-quarters of a century. Such a thorough transformation is unusual. Very few civilizations—for example, those of the Maya and the Aztecs—have simply ceased to exist. Naturally, the residue of communism will long remain in people's minds, in the habits of their work, in the structures of society and state, but communism as an all-embracing and vital way of life is gone. Even the still ubiquitous statues of Lenin have become what Soviet propaganda used to call "relics of the past."

It is within this context that Ukrainian elites have to form a new, inclusive national identity capable of embracing all of Ukraine's many ethnic groups, in particular its Russian speakers. The disappearance of communism provides Ukrainian elites with the unprecedented opportunity to ground Ukrainian identity in those myths, symbols, and values that they alone choose to highlight, to combine, to redefine. To their disadvantage is the fact that the collapse of Communist culture has left conceptual chaos in its wake, within which words have lost their traditional meanings and communication has become exceedingly difficult. Here as well the legacies of empire and totalitarianism conflict: the former permits and encourages Ukrainians to craft an identity in

opposition to their experience with empire; the latter cautions **77**
them about assuming that identity-formation is easy under post-
totalitarian conditions of cultural ruin.

THE DEMISE OF SOVIET LANGUAGE

A brief discussion of the larger cultural context within which
Ukrainian identity must be created will be useful. The disappearance of communism as a civilization is less the result of the
death of the Communist Party than of the collapse of Communist
ideology—an event that preceded, and brought about, the party's
demise. And it was glasnost that killed the ideology. By suggesting
that virtually every leader, policy, and development in Soviet
history contributed to the deformation of socialism, glasnost ultimately left Soviet ideology with very little of its original content.

The consequences of Soviet ideology's deservedly igno-
minious extinction were numerous, but at least two merit special
attention. The end of ideology virtually necessitated that the
party abandon its formally leading role within the system. After
all, the party was Communist precisely because it possessed a
Communist ideology. An even more momentous development,
however, was the closing of the Soviet political discourse. Indeed,
the end of ideology led to a startling result—the expiration of
Soviet *language*.

Like ideology, Soviet language died. Obviously, people continued to speak Russian, Ukrainian, Armenian, and all the other
national languages. There was, however, no consensus on terminology and concepts. Under Brezhnev, when people talked about
certain things, they shared certain fundamentals. Terms, concepts, and referents were something upon which most people at
most times could agree. After glasnost, however, the terms and the
concepts were dissociated from the referents. The fate of the term
"democracy" illustrates the point. Until the late 1980s, the only
true democracy was "socialist democracy," while "bourgeois democracy" was only a form of "bourgeois dictatorship." Once so-

78   cialism lost the positive meaning it had, "socialist democracy" became unattractive and "democracy" pure and simple became the goal. But what was democracy? Rule of the people? Rule of law? Rule of parties? Rule of parliament? And which people, which law, which parties, which parliament? Although the term was retained, "democracy" came to have at least as many meanings as there were questions about its meaning.

This breakdown in terminology had several repercussions. One was that the resulting conceptual vacuum was filled by alternative languages, of which there were three. First, religious language, whether Orthodox, Catholic, Baptist, Muslim, or Jewish, and, second, ethnic terminology (the terms and concepts that are specific to a particular nation and its cultural tradition) were tailor-made for this role, since both had survived the Brezhnev years largely intact. Moreover, as the polar opposites of Soviet ideology, they were immediately attractive to those searching for radical alternatives to Soviet reality. And third, there was an attempt, mostly by the Soviet intelligentsia, to appropriate the language of the West. This involved using such words as "human rights," "democracy," "civil society," "rule of law," and "markets," very often in ways fundamentally different from their usage in the West. Especially interesting was the fact that a concept long banned from the western Sovietological lexicon, which was taboo in the Soviet context as well, began to enjoy a revival in the USSR: totalitarianism.[1]

In addition to the incapacity of Soviet society to agree on terminology, concepts, and language, the Soviet Union lacked an individual, group, or entity with the authority or ability to develop common definitions. The only institutions and individuals capable of reestablishing such a language were in the Soviet republics. Only they enjoyed popular legitimacy and wielded authority, and only they dealt with relatively homogeneous constituencies whose shared religious and ethnic symbols already inclined them to a certain degree of agreement over terminology.

NATION-BUILDING IN UKRAINE

Although the collapse of Soviet discourse led directly to a revival of ethnic values and concepts—a phenomenon welcomed by nationalists—it also confronted them with a dilemma. Narrowly ethnic values, most vividly expressed in songs, folklore, and traditions, do not yet constitute discourse; they are not yet a coherent *national* world view. Indeed, in the absence of such a consensus, republican elites will be hard-pressed to create real nations encompassing all the inhabitants of the state, and not just a certain ethnic segment, no matter how large.

Post-Soviet elites must therefore not only refashion neglected ethnic identities, but also forge thoroughly new *national* ones involving popular allegiance to myths and symbols that are neither narrowly ethnic nor conceptually vapid. Drawing on the folklore of only one ethnic group, no matter how rich and meaningful it may be, is not acceptable. Neither is creating thoroughly artificial symbols that lack meaning, resonance, or appeal to the population. An example from the American experience is illustrated. The Pilgrim heritage, however significant to some whites, may be too remote for Asian-Americans and Hispanic-Americans. The golden arches of McDonald's, however, are surely too insubstantial to bind together an American nation.

The creation of multiethnic nations is imperative, as argued in chapter 2, because the existence of such nations advances the construction and maintenance of effective states, civil societies, democracies, and markets. Ongoing ethnic revivals in Ukraine or elsewhere must therefore be incorporated into larger identities that offer them all a stake in the future of the inclusive new states. Exclusionary ethnic revivals are, as a result, wholly incompatible with new national identities. Latvians, for instance, must somehow integrate their country's Russian-speakers into a redefined "Latvian nation" if the Latvians are to survive. Equally problematic are ethnic traditions that are out of touch with the contempor-

80   ary world. Thus Russians cannot seriously expect Tatars, Bashkirs, and Russia's hundred-odd other ethnic groups to share their exalted views of tsarism and its imperialist adventures. And Ukrainians must craft an identity that would at a minimum encompass ethnic Ukrainians, who comprise 72 percent of the population, *and* Russians, 22 percent, *and* Russified Ukrainians, who probably constitute no less than a third.

Fortunately for Ukraine, most of its elites are at least aware of the challenge. In the words of the Lviv historian Yaroslav Hrytsak, Ukraine's goal must be "to create a new Ukrainian nation, which is based not on an exclusive ethnic, linguistic, religious, or cultural principle, but on the principle of the political, economic, and territorial unity of Ukraine."[2] But before Ukraine's liberal elites can even attempt to put these ideas into practice, they will have to overcome their major intellectual obstacle to such policies—*inclusionary* nationalism! Although inclusionary Ukrainian nationalism is certainly preferable to the exclusionary variety and is not necessarily inconsistent with a state-based national identity, it too views the ethnically Ukrainian nation as the cornerstone of state-building. In contrast, Hrytsak's proposal derives the nation in general and its multiethnic citizenry in particular from the state, thereby consciously emulating the thinking of Vyacheslav Lypynsky, twentieth-century Ukraine's leading political philosopher, a confirmed monarchist, and himself of noble Polish origins.[3] Unfortunately, if Lypynsky's reputation among Ukrainian nationalists is any indication of the likelihood that his ideas will soon take root, then people such as Hrytsak are in for a rough time. As a monarchist, Lypynsky was scorned by the socialist left. As a Polish Ukrainian, he was scorned by the right-wing nationalists. And as an opponent of inclusionary and exclusionary nationalism's fixation on Ukrainian ethnicity, he was ignored by liberal nationalists. At present, most Ukrainian elites in and out of elective office appear to share at least some of Lypynsky's views. Still, it would be premature to say that these views have triumphed and that ethnically based notions of the nation are mere "relics."

Nation-building Policies

Although their thinking may still be in need of clarification, Ukrainian elites have been exemplary in their deeds. The policies of Rukh have been largely symbolic, but even these have been extraordinarily important at a time of conceptual confusion and in light of Ukraine's historical record of interethnic strife. By going out of its way to address the concerns of ethnic Russians and Jews in its programs, to provide them with a meaningful voice and representation in the movement, to support their organizations both politically and materially, and to condemn Ukrainian chauvinism, Rukh succeeded in building a stable interethnic coalition and in ensuring that Ukraine's acquisition of independence would occur without bloodshed. Ironically, Rukh's record is least laudable with regard to its own constituency. Transcarpathian Ruthenians, like Russified east Ukrainians, appear suspect to many Rukh activists, who have greater difficulty dealing with individuals with dual or uncertain identities than with certified Russians, Jews, Magyars, or Slovaks—testimony, once again, to the tendency even among inclusionary nationalists to think in all too narrowly ethnic terms.

The Kravchuk government has also been unusually sensitive to Ukraine's "nationality question." According to official terminology, for example, the "people of Ukraine," and not the "Ukrainian people," are sovereign in the country. Russia and the "Muscovites" may be—and gleefully are—publicly criticized, but not the Russians of Ukraine. Ukrainian officials speak Ukrainian and Russian both privately and publicly. Language policies have also been eminently sensible. While attempting to enhance the woeful status of Ukrainian, which is the language of instruction in a minority of urban schools and universities, policymakers have prudently accepted the legitimacy and reality of Russian as the language spoken in most of Ukraine's cities, including Kiev, and used in much of Ukraine's media. Ukraine's Russian-speaking population is thus in no danger of being forcibly "Ukrainized," a specter inexplicably raised even by Anatoly Sobchak, the liberal

82   mayor of St. Petersburg. The Kiev government has been particularly concerned with reconciling ethnic Jews and ethnic Ukrainians. The commemoration in late 1991 of the Nazi massacre of
Jews at Babi Yar in 1941 and the construction of a stone menorah
on the original site of the tragedy have been symbolically most
important, while the establishment of diplomatic relations with
Israel and the adoption of policies permitting Jews to emigrate or
to return with impunity have been the most important practical
measures.

Obstacles to Nation-building

Thus far Ukrainian elites have done virtually everything right
with respect to their own national minorities. Creating a new
Ukrainian nation will require continuing along the same path for
some time to come. But there are three obstacles. The first
concerns Ukraine's Russian-speaking population. Although the
differences between most Russian speakers and most Ukrainian
speakers are so small as to warrant belief in the eventual rapprochement of the two groups, some in both groups would disagree
with this assessment. It is they who are the problem. Exclusionary
Russians in the Crimea, like exclusionary Ukrainians in Galicia,
will try to prevent a new non-exclusionary Ukrainian nation from
forming. It could be argued, however, that there will always be
extremists, and that ignoring them or not providing them with
ammunition for their cause may be the best policy. The former is
easy; unfortunately, the latter is not, especially if Kiev adopts a
policy of radical social and economic transformation that exacer-
bates existing tensions.

　　The second obstacle to a new national identity may be even
greater than the first. Ethnic Ukrainians, who must form the core
of the "people of Ukraine," are increasingly resisting Kiev's ethnically evenhanded policies and pronouncements. They see what
they believe to be *their* state as Ukrainian only in name; they resent
the continued widespread use of Russian, and they doubt the
loyalty of Russian speakers. The Lviv historian Yaroslav Dash-

kevych captured this *ressentiment* in his defense of the nationalist **83**
slogan, "Ukraine for Ukrainians": "Of course, Ukraine should
be for Ukrainians. After all, for hundreds of years it was for
everybody but Ukrainians!"[4] Dashkevych's argument is not un-
appealing, and if opposition to Kiev's nation-building program
comes to encompass substantial segments of the ethnic Ukrainian population in general and the elites in particular, the government, no matter how committed to incorporating Russian
speakers, will have difficulty ignoring its major constituency and
the source of its legitimacy.

The third problem concerns other states. Ethnic extremists
may receive support from outside forces. Kiev's hands-off policy
toward the heavily Ukrainian Trans-Dniestrian region in eastern
Moldova is emotionally painful but politically correct, since it
recognizes Moldovan sovereignty. In contrast, the Russian parliament's revocation of the 1954 treaty ceding the Crimea to
Ukraine, and the Congress of People's Deputies' decision to
review the status of the Crimean city of Sevastopol are emotionally
satisfying, but politically inappropriate. Russian policymakers'
concern for the 25 million Russians in the other successor states is
understandable, but, if taken too far, potentially dangerous because it could embroil Russia in ethnic conflicts throughout the
entire former empire. Wisely, Yeltsin so far has not followed the
Russian parliament's implicit suggestion that Russia emulate Serbia's attempts at ingathering Serbs in Croatia and Bosnia-Herzegovina. And yet, as the national passions surrounding the Kuril
Islands and the Russian army's repeated interventions in civil wars
in Moldova, Tajikistan, and Georgia suggest, there may be a limit
to how long Yeltsin can resist his own legislature, especially if
economic conditions in Russia worsen radically. And there may
also be a limit to how long Kiev will be willing to tolerate what it
considers Moscow's unwarranted interference in its nation-building project. If such a point is reached, all hope of Russo-Ukrainian
cooperation will end and a genuine "Cold War" between the two
states will be likely to break out.

MYTHS AND SYMBOLS

Ukrainian elites are drawing on several mythic elements from Ukraine's past in order to fashion a new Ukrainian nation. In general, they are propagating the image of Ukrainians as the European descendants of good peasant stock, of multiethnic pioneers, and of an ancient multiethnic state. The image reinforces Ukraine's aspirations to democracy and freedom, underlines its multiethnic character, and suggests that Ukraine is distinct from its neighbor to the north—Russia. It is unimportant whether or not such notions are historically accurate. All nations are, in the final analysis, mythic constructs with more or less imagined histories that purport to outline their emergence, development, and glory.

According to their own cultural assumptions, ethnic Ukrainians would be best characterized as a freedom-loving peasant nation. Not surprisingly, peasant motifs and libertarian themes abound in traditional folk music, poetry, and humor, as well as in contemporary film, art, literature, and even rock music. The embodiment of both qualities is supposed to be Taras Shevchenko, the nineteenth-century east Ukrainian national poet whose climb from serfdom to literary prominence is taken to symbolize the emergence of a Ukrainian nation and the qualities that it embodies. Shevchenko has been the focus of considerable scholarship, journalism, and literature, with some Ukrainians even arguing that a "cult of Shevchenko" serve as the basis for contemporary Ukrainian national solidarity. His closest competitor for such exalted status, Ivan Franko, is still a distant second, since he was both a west Ukrainian and, most damning, an intellectual.

That Ukrainians should, wittingly or not, see themselves as a nation of peasants is understandable considering that this is exactly what they were until several decades ago; even now, a very large proportion, up to a fifth, of all ethnic Ukrainians still live in villages. Like farmers all over the world, Ukrainians are supposed to have a special relationship with the land. It is the land—especially the rich, fertile, and abundant Ukrainian land—that

defines Ukrainians and provides them with everything they need. **85**
The Chernobyl disaster was, in this perspective, not just destructive of the country but also of the nation and its "soul." The
association with land presumably makes for stability, reliability,
dedication, indeed, for culture and civilization. Consequently,
only in the village are spirituality real, values honest, and people
hard-working—a view reminiscent of that encountered in the
small-town ideology espoused by many Americans. The village is
authentic; the city is not.

Although largely out of tune with the Ukraine of today—a
country that is relatively modern, about two-thirds urbanized, and
most of whose ethnically Ukrainian population, not to mention its
non-Ukrainian population, has assimilated urban values and has
no realistic hope or expectation of ever returning to its supposed
roots in the countryside—the peasant dimension is likely to remain, if perhaps relegated to a secondary role. "Peasantness" is a
convenient symbol of certain qualities related to one's origins that
dovetail well with the requirements of nation-building. Love of
land, this land, presumably translates into patriotism, and putative
peasant virtues, such as honesty and hard work, are just what a
new nation and a new state need. The fact that most urban
inhabitants have traditionally been non-Ukrainians need not
undermine the appeal of "peasantness," since ethnic Russians,
Poles, and Jews also have their own traditions of cultivating the
soil that can be merged with the Ukrainian perspective.

Again, the Cossacks

The second component of Ukrainian self-perception is the love of
freedom. According to the Ukrainian view, peasants know best
what genuine freedom is because only they have a direct relationship with nature and are unsullied by the corrupting influence of
the city. But Ukrainians are not just any kind of freedom-loving
peasants. They are the peasant descendants, historically and ethnically, of the Cossacks, the frontiersmen and social bandits par
excellence, who occupied the borderland that was Ukraine from
the fifteenth to the eighteenth century. Myth and reality overlap

86   in this view, since freedom from their masters was the main reason that Ukrainian, Belarusian, Russian, and Polish peasants would escape to the Ukrainian steppes. And it was this rag-tag collection of former serfs who eventually formed what has come to be known as the Cossack Host, which did indeed govern itself, at least initially, on the basis of a kind of raucous democratic order, one lauded even by Karl Marx.

To be sure, most ethnic Jews would dispute the association of the Ukrainian Cossacks with freedom. Because the Jewish population bore much of the brunt of the great rebellion led by Hetman Bohdan Khmelnytsky in 1648, Cossack freedom, for Jews, is tantamount to the loss of their freedom. And here, of course, the Jews are right. If differing perceptions were all there are to the issue, however, an irenic historical interpretation of the Cossacks would be within relatively easy reach. The problem is far more complex because the Cossack experience functions as a deeply rooted symbol crucial both to Jewish identity and to Ukrainian national identity. Cossacks are a source of negative identity for Jews and of positive identity for Ukrainians. In other words, this is a classic instance of the irreconcilable opposition of *two national myths* both offering oversimplified black-and-white interpretations of reality. The Jewish myth is straightforward: evil Ukrainian Cossacks killed innocent Jews. The Ukrainian myth is equally straightforward: innocent Ukrainian peasants and Cossacks rebelled against evil landlords, who were Poles, and their underlings, who were Jews. The adjectives "evil" and "innocent" are part of mythmaking; without them both myths would offer no emotionally appealing explanations for equally traumatic experiences for two peoples trapped in a conflictual relationship that neither ever chose to have. No matter how distasteful the Cossack symbol may be for Jews, therefore, Ukrainian mythmakers are unlikely to relinquish it. Like the cowboy in American lore, the Cossack will remain an important part of the Ukrainian myth, despite the disrepute with which both images are held by significant minority populations, be they Jews or Native Americans.

Exemplifying both the mythic character of the Cossacks and its continued tenacity is the satirical poem, "Eneida," written in

the late eighteenth century by Ivan Kotlarevsky, a Ukrainian **87**
aristocrat from the Poltava region. Based on Virgil's classic poem
the *Aeneid*, Kotlarevsky's version depicts the survivors of Troy and
the founders of Rome as Cossacks. The implications are obvious:
although the Cossack stronghold, the Sich, had been destroyed in
1775, Kotlarevsky was suggesting that a still brighter future lay in
store for the Ukrainians. Kotlarevsky's message aside, his choice of
the *Aeneid* as the model for his own work clearly placed the
Cossacks in the realm of myth, which is where they have remained
ever since. To bring the story up to the present, it is, as the
Communists used to say, "not accidental" that, in 1991, the year
of Ukraine's independence, a Kiev-based film studio released an
animated version of "Eneida." Troy is lost, but the Ukrainian
Cossacks outsmart their enemies, enjoy the favor of the gods, and
eat and drink their way toward founding Rome.

But there is more to the Cossacks than their centrality in
Ukrainian mythology. The freedom-loving—or is it freeboot-
ing?—element of Cossackdom can be especially appealing to
modern nations nurtured in the language of human rights. Cossackdom exemplifies individualism, freedom, and perhaps even
licentiousness in its rejection of social constraints and disregard for
societal norms. Moreover, the Cossacks represent just what the
contemporary Ukraine presumably wants and needs to create: a
community of individuals ostensibly committed to freedom and
the well-being of the multiethnic entity they represent. The moral
of the myth is clear: just as anyone could presumably have become
a Cossack, so can virtually anyone become a modern Ukrainian.
The only requirements are love of freedom and commitment to the
collectivity. An elderly gentleman captured the point nicely at a
public gathering on Kiev's Independence Square by asking—in
Russian—"Where is our Cossack soul? Where is our Ukrainian
spirit?"

The Myth of Kievan Rus'

If multicultural myths are most likely to become the constituent
elements of a new national identity, then two more symbols can be
expected to occupy pride of place alongside the Cossacks. The first

88   such symbol is Kievan Rus', the princely state that dominated Eastern Europe from the tenth through the thirteenth century. The state itself appears to have been established by Vikings and its population consisted of East Slavic tribes. But Ukrainian nationalists have traditionally taken their cue from West European historiography by insisting that the centrality of Kiev, in yesterday's Rus' and today's Ukraine, is analogous to the centrality of Rome in the Roman Empire and modern Italy and that, as a result, Rus' is as much an integral part of Ukraine's history as Rome is of Italy's. Although their insistence on such an interpretation was largely a response to Russians' appropriation of Rus' for their own history and thus a means of asserting national authenticity in colonial circumstances, the Kievan period is certain to become even more prominent after independence than it was before. Claiming lineage from a large and powerful medieval state enhances national pride and prestige even today. Far more important, however, the Kievan state, though perhaps logically a part of Ukrainian history, was not ethnically Ukrainian in any meaningful sense of the word—a point that all but the most fanatical Ukrainians would recognize. By the same token neither was Rus' Russian. Rather, the Slavs who inhabited the Kievan state were, at best, pre-Ukrainians, pre-Russians, and pre-Belarusians. The Kievan state therefore can easily be interpreted as the historical ancestor of the future Ukraine, the home of ethnic Ukrainians, Russians, and Belarusians.

Ironically, Ukrainian elites are likely to take the standard Soviet version of Rus' and stand it on its head. According to Moscow's former line, Rus' was home to "three fraternal peoples, Russians, Belarusians, and Ukrainians," who were tragically separated in the aftermath of the state's disintegration, fortunately reunited by Khmelnytsky's treaty with the tsar in 1654, and happily united, forever and ever, in the Soviet Union. The Soviet version assigned a historical purpose to Rus', claiming that it culminated in the USSR. Ukrainians, likewise, argue that all the peoples of contemporary Ukraine, as descendants of a common history, are fated to remain together, not in the Soviet Union, and

not as the "Soviet people," but in the direct descendant of Kievan   **89**
Rus', Ukraine, and as the "people of Ukraine."

THE FUTURE AS EUROPE

While backward-looking myths are crucial for galvanizing a nation, most valuable of all are those that promise a glimpse of the
future. These, too, Ukrainians expect to have. Ukraine as a great
power and Ukraine as a carrier of peace are two such images. The
first is clearly an exaggeration, but the second, rooted in Kiev's
willingness to part with nuclear weapons, perhaps somewhat less
so. Most attractive, however, is a word that captures everything
Ukrainians aspire to become and everything some Ukrainians
claim always to have been: Europe. For them this is a nearly
magical concept, with unclear content but with virtually limitless
connotations of all the many good things that the future holds in
store. From the Ukrainian point of view, while Ukrainians supposedly represent Europe, Russians allegedly incarnate Asia. The
myth is especially convenient because it coincides with the Cossack and Kievan origins of the contemporary Ukrainian nation:
after all, the Cossacks, like ancient Kiev, occupied a geopolitical
position straddling East and West. In this sense, although Ukrainians cannot quite claim to be full-fledged members of the West—
as can, for instance, Poles—they can nevertheless define themselves as the frontier of two worlds. They thereby create a unique
role for themselves: as intermediaries, as bridges, between two
ostensibly "alien" worlds, those of European "civilization" and of
"nomadic" Russian "barbarism." Such a self-perception has the
good fortune not only of differentiating Ukraine from Russia but
also of providing Ukraine with an indispensable role in reconciling
East and West.

What then will the new Ukrainians be like? Surely they will
speak Ukrainian, if not as a first language then as a lingua franca.
And, just as surely, they will search for the roots of identity in the
history and future of the land they inhabit. One example of such
an individual may be the remarkable Petro Prystupov, an ethnic

90   Russian who lives in Kiev, speaks perfect Ukrainian, and com-
poses music to the poetry of the eighteenth-century Ukrainian
philosopher Hryhory Skovoroda. Prystupov discovered the intro-
spective philosophy of Skovoroda in the 1970s, when there was
little opportunity for creative public expression. At present, he
dreams of establishing a World Association of the Singers of
Skovoroda, considers himself a true follower of Skovoroda's ascetic
philosophy, and also remains committed to his Russian roots. Is
Prystupov Ukrainian or Russian? Ethnically, he is the latter.
Nationally, however, he has clearly committed himself to being
the former. Another example may be Konstantyn Morozov, ethnically a half-Russian, half-Ukrainian general appointed
Ukraine's minister of defense in 1991 and a staunch defender—
impressing even Ukrainian nationalists—of Ukraine's sovereign
right to its own armed forces. Yet another is Vilen (as in *V.I.
Lenin*) Martyrossian, an ethnic Armenian who headed Ukraine's
Union of Officers. Or perhaps the talented ethnic Ukrainian
historian Serhii Plokhy, who was raised in the heavily Russified
Donbas, speaks perfect Russian and Ukrainian, and studies the
church politics of seventeenth-century Ukraine. Or Hryhory Lifa-
nov, the chief engineer at Kiev's Obolon Brewery, a man who
spent most of his life in the Donbas, speaks little Ukrainian, yet
considers himself Ukrainian. Or, finally, Yaroslav Asman, whose
German roots, Ukrainian-speaking Russian wife, English-speak-
ing Ukrainian son, and job in the Ministry of Foreign Affairs make
him and his family the classic kind of political Ukrainians the
Polish-Ukrainian Vyacheslav Lypynsky envisioned in his political
writings. While such individuals still may not represent the norm,
they are hardly exceptional and they do point to the direction in
which Ukrainian nation-building will have to go if Ukraine's
experiment with democracy is to succeed.

EXPLAINING UKRAINIAN TOLERANCE

How are we to explain the fact that Ukrainians, with a reputation
in the West for unrefined emotionalism, now seem to have be-

come so tolerant? Several answers come to mind. First of all, the **91**
reputation is not wholly deserved. Ukraine's record of interethnic
discord is arguably no worse, but no better, than that of most other
countries—consider, for example, America's treatment of its Native American population. Second, ethnic conflict in Ukraine
can be explained without reference to some perverted Ukrainian
"soul." In Ukraine as elsewhere such conflict generally broke out
during periods of particular social stress, when values and structures were challenged by outside forces—the armies of the tsar, the
Ottoman Sublime Porte, the Kaiser, or the Führer. This is not to
absolve Ukrainians of racism, anti-Semitism, and the like, but
only to suggest that Ukrainian history cannot be reduced to one
long pogrom.

Another factor is that the Soviet Union's assiduous promotion of Ukrainian assimilation to Russian culture did have one
unquestionably positive consequence: ethnic Ukrainians and ethnic Russians living in Ukraine really do know each other extremely well. They speak and/or understand each other's
language: the distance between Ukrainian and Russian is virtually
nil compared to that between Russian and, say, Estonian. They
know each other's cultures; to a certain degree, they share a half-
Ukrainian/half-Russian culture. Not surprisingly, street discussions, television talk shows, and radio interviews are usually conducted, simultaneously, in Russian, Ukrainian, and some hybrid
of the two. Such familiarity—or what Soviet propagandists used
to call "friendship of peoples"—makes it easy for Ukrainians to
treat Russians with respect and encourages the Russian willingness
to respond in kind. It also means that just as it was always
relatively easy for Ukrainians to adapt to Russian culture and
language, it should not be difficult for Russians to adapt to Ukrainian culture and language, especially if these are redefined in a
nonethnic way.

Finally, many of the contemporary elites, in Ukraine and
elsewhere, are former dissidents. Like Natan Sharansky, who has
fond memories of Ukrainian political prisoners whom he regards
highly for their integrity and bravery, many Ukrainian prisoners of

92   conscience established excellent relations with Baltic, Caucasian, Jewish, Russian, and other dissidents in the time they spent in prison or in concentration camps. This was an opportunity to meet, to get to know one another, to discuss one another's agenda, to become friends. An outstanding example is the longstanding relationship between Yevhen Sverstiuk and Semyon Gluzman, a Jewish dissident; while incarcerated, the two began an honest discussion of Ukrainian-Jewish relations in the 1970s, and they have continued their dialogue into the 1990s.[5] And it is these friends who are to a significant degree setting the tone for inter-ethnic relations in Ukraine as well as in many of the other republics.

Nation-building Assets

The nation-building agenda outlined above may be logical, but Ukraine's elites will have no small task in implementing it. Fortunately for them, they have two assets. One is Russia itself, which may be unwittingly pushing the inhabitants of Ukraine toward acceptance of a Ukrainian identity defined in anti-Muscovite terms. Russia's hegemonic behavior or, what for present purposes amounts to the same thing, the widespread perception in Ukraine of Russia as a bully—a perception that the Ukrainian media, still beholden to their old habits of kowtowing to the government, do their utmost to cultivate—may have the opposite effect of that apparently intended. Most inhabitants of Ukraine, whether Ukrainian- or Russian-speaking, do seem to identify with their homeland. They appear to have no intention of moving, and by and large they do not appear to aspire to become another province within the vast Russian state. Despite the pro-independence activities of the Russian Movement of the Crimea, the Crimean population itself is far from committed to annexation to Russia. According to a poll taken in January 1992, only 15 percent desired to join Russia, as opposed to 42 percent who preferred to stay in Ukraine[6]—a fact that may have played a role in the Crimean parliament's September 25, 1992, decision to acknowledge that the Republic of the Crimea is a part of Ukraine.

The second asset is that the "people of Ukraine" may have **93** already begun to think in nonethnic terms. The overwhelming vote favoring independence in the December 1991 referendum cannot be insignificant, even if patriotism was not the primary motive. If nothing else, those who voted helped create a national icon: they took part in the ritual of nation-building that all other nations have undergone. In this sense, the referendum was less important as a barometer of public opinion than as a catalyst of national feelings and emotions, which should help create a new national identity. Growing popular acceptance of the post-Soviet, formerly nationalist Ukrainian, symbols of state, the trident and the blue and yellow flag, also reflects this emerging sense of identity.

Liabilities

Despite these positive indicators, however, the obstacles to the emergence of a new identity are formidable. Economic crisis, chauvinist government policies, the spread of extremist national-ism, and undue pressure by Russia could all serve to derail Ukraine's hopeful experiment in nation-building.

The importance of economic crisis is obvious. At a time of fragile social cohesiveness and ethnic solidarity, the shock of extreme economic disarray and misery could block the rapproche-ment of Ukraine's ethnic groups. More than that, the competition for scarce resources—jobs, housing, or consumer goods—will inevitably accentuate ethnic tensions in Ukraine, as it does every-where else. In this sense, Ukraine, like all the other post-Commu-nist entities, faces a wrenching choice: the lack of economic reform will in the long run produce economic catastrophe and make the peaceful coexistence of different nations difficult, if not impossible. Rapid reform, however, even if salutary in the very long run, may be so disruptive as to be fatal in the short run.

No less problematic would be Kiev's adoption of exclusionary policies that could alienate those non-Ukrainians and Russified Ukrainians who have doubts about a strictly ethnic Ukrainian identity. The possibility of such a course change is not merely

94   hypothetical since the Ukrainian government's main source of
legitimacy is, and must be, the ethnic Ukrainians in Ukraine.
And because their symbols, myths, language, culture, and heroes
will probably form the core of the emergent national identity,
there is always the chance that non-ethnic Ukrainians will feel
uncomfortable with an identity they could all too easily interpret
as a smokescreen for narrowly defined Ukrainian values. Especially in times of economic stringency or outside threat—as, say,
from Russia—appeals to Ukrainian patriotism could override the
commonalities that the "people of Ukraine" share. There already
exists a tendency in Ukraine to interpret all things in terms of their
contribution to state-building—negative, positive, or indifferent—and to categorize politically marginal views as "harmful"
rather than simply as different. Although these attitudes appear to
be the products of the old Soviet way of thinking, they can be
easily reinforced by the existing socioeconomic disarray and, as a
result, are unlikely to fade away any time soon.

The situation is all the more complex because Ukraine also
has a tradition of exclusionary nationalism with roots in the
interwar experience of Galicia, the west Ukrainian province that
emerged from Hapsburg tutelage in 1918 only to be swallowed up
by Poland after a moderately successful experiment in democratic
self-rule. In the 1920s and 1930s Galicia was the home of the
Ukrainian Military Organization (UVO) and the Organization of
Ukrainian Nationalists (OUN). Both groups employed what
would today be called terrorism in their struggle against Polish
authority. In contrast to the more apolitical UVO, the OUN
developed a political program with strong authoritarian, if not
quite fascist, overtones; it was most inspired by the extremist
writings of Dmytro Donstov, a fiery publicist who fancied himself
the savior of the nation and who admired the experience of Italy
under Mussolini and Germany under Hitler.[7] The OUN also
espoused the slogan of "Ukraine for Ukrainians," hoping to
achieve its goals through a military alliance with Nazi Germany.
Berlin had other plans for the Ukrainians, however, and in the
summer of 1941, after the OUN proclaimed Ukrainian indepen-

dence in Lviv, the Nazis smashed the organization, drove it underground, and incarcerated its leader, Stepan Bandera, in the Sachsenhausen concentration camp. Paradoxically, repression proved to be the best thing that could have happened to the OUN, saving it from the collaborationist fate of the Croatian Ustasha or the Slovak People's Party. Once underground, the OUN initiated an anti-Nazi armed struggle, while its new and more realistic leaders eventually abandoned the authoritarian platform associated with Bandera's name and officially adopted a hybrid nationalist–social democratic program by 1943. And it was on the basis of this surprisingly progressive program that the nationalists established the Ukrainian Insurgent Army, extended their appeals to all the peoples of Ukraine, and waged a bloody guerrilla struggle until 1953.

The history of west Ukrainian nationalism deserves particular attention because it is currently enjoying a revival, both in Galicia and in other parts of Ukraine, such as Kiev, Kharkiv, Dnipropetrovsk, and Sumy. Fortunately, some adherents of the OUN look to its post-1943 history for inspiration. Many, if not most, however, admire the authoritarian tenets and fanatical commitment to state-building evident in Dontsov's writings, Bandera's postwar pronouncements, and the pre-1943 period. One such grouping, for instance, called "State Independence of Ukraine," has even appropriated—unwittingly, one hopes—the slogan "Ukraine above everything." Not to be outdone perhaps, the Ukrainian Nationalist League proposes "Everything immediately!" as its motto. The Social-Nationalist [sic] Party aspires to promote its four "basic principles"—patriotism, religion, sports, and aesthetics—while the Ukrainian National Party believes that Ukraine's boundaries should be extended to include all so-called Ukrainian ethnographic territories—from eastern Poland, down through the Kuban, where the Zaporozhian Cossacks were relocated after the Sich was destroyed in the late eighteenth century, and all the way to Gorbachev's hometown of Stavropol!

So much for the bad news. The good news is that this kind of exclusionary nationalism is virtually absent among the genuinely

96   influential political and cultural elites, especially where it matters most, in Kiev. Its popularity is more or less confined to Galicia. Indeed, it is hard to imagine its catching on in the Russified eastern and southern provinces. Equally encouraging is that the current infatuation with authoritarian nationalism may be as much the product of ignorance about the checkered history of the OUN as anything else. Once balanced treatments of Ukrainian nationalism begin to appear, as they already have, once would-be nationalists stop glorifying everyone Soviet propaganda condemned—especially such mediocre personalities as Bandera—inclusionary nationalism will probably carry the day and the exclusionary kind will likely remain confined to even smaller groups of marginalized individuals. But this is far from certain. Extremism, whether that of David Duke, French National Front leader Jean-Marie Le Pen, Austria's Freedom Party chairman Jörg Haider, Russian fascist Vladimir Zhirinovksy, or Dmytro Dontsov, thrives in hard and uncertain times, and the immediate future of Ukraine promises to be just that.

In particular, 1992 witnessed two potentially disturbing trends: the polarization of the Ukrainian political spectrum and the growing sense of popular frustration with the status quo. Former Communists won sympathizers, as did radical nationalists, with each side viewing the other as the source of all evil—in marked contrast to Russia, where a "red-brown" coalition was forming. Moreover, Ukrainians and Russians in Ukraine became increasingly disillusioned with the meager benefits that independence had brought them. Ethnic Ukrainians began to realize that declarations of independence do not immediately translate into national states or great power status, while Russians blamed independence for the decline in their living standards. The pool of potential extremists grew as the militancy of existing extremists intensified. Complacency is not in order, all the more so since some relatively well-endowed émigré groups—such as the Munich-based Bandera wing of the OUN, the peripatetic Anti-Bolshevik Bloc of Nations, and others—are actively funding their extremist compatriots in Ukraine.

THE PROBLEM OF RUSSIA

The possibility of exaggerated Ukrainian patriotism is closely
related to the problem that Russia poses for an independent
Ukraine. While Russia's pressure on Ukraine may be reinforcing
the Ukrainian elite's efforts at creating a new national identity,
such pressure could undercut solidarity if, on the one hand,
internal conditions in Ukraine deteriorate so much as to make
Russia begin to appear as an alternative, and more attractive,
source of loyalty, and, on the other hand, if the Kremlin, not just
extremists within the government, officially begins to pursue a
distinctly anti-Ukrainian policy. The second possibility should
not be discounted, if only because the forces pushing Ukrainian
leaders toward chauvinist positions will be no weaker, and probably far stronger, in Russia.

Moreover, unlike the Ukrainians and other non-Russians,
the Russians have to contend with an imperial mentality that
reinforces overbearing attitudes toward other peoples. Ukraine has
traditionally occupied an especially important place in the Russian mentality—a point discussed in greater detail in chapter 4—
and the loss of it is surely a major blow to Russian self-esteem.
Although the amount and the way Russian political culture affects
Russian policy are difficult to ascertain, an imperial mentality
certainly limits possibilities, by suggesting what is and what is not
attainable and desirable. That Ukraine's separation is not desirable from an imperial Russian point of view goes without saying;
whether its independence should therefore be crushed is another
matter.

The Crimean situation illustrates the problem. As indicated
in the introduction, there is no plausible argument proving that
the peninsula is historically Russian (or, for that matter, Ukrainian). From the thirteenth century until 1944, the Crimea was
the homeland of the Crimean Tatars. Still, Russia's absorption of
the territory in the late eighteenth century is a fact. Thus to
contend that the Crimea should belong to Russia or Ukraine for
geopolitical reasons or for international legal reasons may be

98   perfectly valid, but that is not the argument made by most Russians. Rather, they speak of emotional bonds to the peninsula, as if their feelings were of greater priority than those of the Tatars, who were driven from their homeland by the tsars and later by Stalin. The emotional content of the Russian position reveals that not logic, but a certain mind-set is at work. It is the hegemonic mentality that one encounters in every imperial nation's feelings about past glory.

As the next chapter suggests, Russia itself is unlikely to be a role model, or a haven, for Russians and others living in Ukraine. Despite the optimism generated by the Yeltsin government, Russia faces huge, perhaps insuperable, obstacles to democracy, a market economy, political stability, and economic prosperity. If Russia, like the USSR that it resembles far too closely for its own good, descends into political instability, economic chaos, and social warfare, Russians in Ukraine and other republics will not aspire to return to a decaying homeland.

As with all scenarios, this one can be invalidated by a change in surrounding conditions. Yet barring some unusual catastrophe in Ukraine alone, we should not expect the attractiveness of Russia to grow. Quite the contrary, since all the former republics are currently experiencing the same problems and developing in more or less the same manner, we should expect the relative, if not absolute, appeal of Ukraine and other regions to increase by default: they are unlikely to degenerate as far and as fast as Russia. A deteriorating Russia, however, will pose an even greater *security* risk than a stable Russia, and an economically prostrate Russia will in all likelihood abort economic reform in Ukraine. Either way, Ukrainian nationalists have no grounds for *Schadenfreude* because Ukraine will face some unpleasant alternatives. Indeed, it may even be in a no-win situation.

CHAPTER 4

Engaging a Post-totalitarian Russia

U krainians have an overwhelming preoccupation—Russia. It is their foremost foreign policy concern, and their primary source of negative identity. Indeed, for most Ukrainians, it is their major, if not only, problem. So powerful an obsession has deep historical roots. For several hundred years Ukraine has been the colony and Russia, the empire; Ukraine, the province, and Russia, the metropolis; Ukraine, the countryside, and Russia, the city; Ukraine, the borderland, and Russia, the center. Ukraine has traditionally defined itself with reference to, and against, Russia: Ukraine is that which Russia is not.

Not surprisingly, centuries of subordination have left a scar on the Ukrainian psyche, creating both a profound sense of inferiority and an even greater mistrust of all things Russian. Like most postcolonial peoples, Ukrainians should eventually transcend their paranoia, but not before a genuine sense of national self-worth, involving the creation of a new identity and the assertion of a historical memory, emerges.

But the legacies of empire and totalitarianism clash once again, with the result that Ukrainians cannot afford to be too paranoid about Russia, even if many of their fears are warranted. Centuries of close relations cannot be sundered without excessive harm to both sides. The intertwining of Ukrainian and Russian lives, cultures, languages, and histories—not to mention the

99

100   necessity of creating a new Ukrainian identity—makes reconciliation between Ukrainians and Russians in Ukraine and between Ukraine and Russia imperative. And yet, reconciliation,
however urgent, may be easier said than done in postimperial and
post-totalitarian circumstances. The postimperial legacy is one of
profound resentment and mistrust, which all former imperial
centers and colonies feel for each other. Empires resent colonies for
depriving them of their glorious heritage, of what they perceive as
rightfully theirs. Colonies mistrust the motives of former empires,
which they accuse of desiring to reestablish the hegemony they
once enjoyed. In marked contrast, the post-totalitarian legacy
argues for cooperation between two kindred peoples confronted
with the same ruin, the same devastation, and the same despair.
Reconciliation is possible, but only if both Ukraine and Russia,
and Ukrainians and Russians, accept the reality of imperial collapse and structure their relations on the basis of equality and
respect.

Although resentment and mistrust characterize both sides,
the sentiments of the colonizers and the colonized do not have
equal moral value. Typically we identify with, or at least publicly
support, slaves, peasants, and the downtrodden; just as typically,
we condemn slaveowners, lords, and exploiters. My point is not
that Ukrainians are innocents, but that Ukrainian attitudes toward Russians are secondary reflections of Russian attitudes toward non-Russians in general and Ukrainians in particular. Both
sides have their own phobias and complexes, but it is hard to see
how Ukrainians—or Balts, or Central Asians, or Bashkirs—can
rid themselves of theirs if Russians do not come to grips with their
imperial past and their postimperial present.

It would obviously be incorrect to assign moral responsibility
to *all* Russians and moral exculpation to *all* non-Russians. Nevertheless, Russians, like all imperial peoples, do bear a special
burden, a point that progressive Russian intellectuals, such as
Andrei Sakharov, have always understood. Even Lenin recognized that "Great Russian chauvinism" was a greater evil than
"non-Russian nationalism," because the first preceded, if not

provoked, the second. The non-Russians in general, and the **101**
Ukrainians in particular, would therefore do well to come to terms
with the Russians as soon as possible; but Russians will have to
learn to come to terms with them first and, in light of the difficulty
that imperial nations have of abandoning colonial stereotypes,
that may take a long time.

HISTORICAL DISPUTES

Different national mythologies have resulted in radically different
interpretations of common historical experiences. Ukrainians and
Russians have constructed virtually incompatible accounts of
their past. The Russian version generally relegates the Ukrainians
to the status of ungrateful cousins or younger brothers, the Little
Russians. The Ukrainian version sees Russians—better known as
moskali, the Muscovites—as usurpers of Ukrainian freedom and
destroyers of Ukrainian culture. Ethnic stereotypes correspond to
these interpretations: for Russians, Ukrainians are sly and lazy; for
Ukrainians, Russians are cold and vulgar.

As might be expected, Ukrainian and Russian constructions
of history begin to diverge with the period of the Kievan Rus' state.
Both Ukrainians and Russians consider it to be part of their
heritage. From the Ukrainian point of view, their Kiev brought
religion and culture to the Russians in the north, who repaid the
debt by sacking Kiev in 1147. From the Russian point of view, Kiev
is the "mother of all Russian cities." Who is right and who is wrong
in this conflict of symbols and icons is less important than the fact
that Ukrainians consider Russian claims to Kievan Rus' an assault
on their sense of national authenticity, while Russians believe
Ukrainian claims to the Kievan heritage are tantamount to a
violation of their very soul.

The next stage in the historical dispute dates to the Cossack
period. Above and beyond the fact that Russians can also claim
Cossacks as their own—for instance, those in the Don, Kuban,
Terek, and other regions of Russia—the key issues concern two
Cossack Hetmans: Bohdan Khmelnytsky, who signed a treaty

102   with Tsar Alexei in Pereyaslav in 1654, and Ivan Mazepa, who joined Charles XII of Sweden against Peter the Great and went down to defeat at Poltava in 1709. For Ukrainians, Khmelnytsky's treaty is little more than a personal union of two heads of state. For Russians, the treaty represents a union of two states. From the Ukrainian vantage point, the heroic Mazepa joined Charles to oppose Russian encroachments on Ukrainian autonomy, as allegedly guaranteed by the Pereyaslav accord, while Catherine the Great's dissolution of the Hetmanate was a crass violation of the agreement. Russians see things differently: despite Lord Byron's sympathetic portrait of "Mazeppa," the Ukrainian hetman was a usurper and a traitor, while Catherine's action was merely the logical, and perhaps long overdue, culmination of the treaty.

Nationally conscious Ukrainians and Russians diverge completely in their understanding of the remainder of their shared history. Ukrainians see the nineteenth century as a time of serfdom and colonialism, during which their nation was exploited and its culture and language officially persecuted. Russians, however, view these as years of the gradual merging of the Little Russian group into the Great Russian nation. Consequently, the "national liberation struggle" of the 1917–1921 period is perceived by Ukrainians as a glorious period in their "awakening," while it is condemned by Russians—as, for instance, by the writer Mikhail Bulgakov, then resident in Kiev—as another instance of "German intrigue." Modern Ukrainian nationalism, that is, the desire of Ukrainians for their own state, is therefore a dangerous and unnatural aberration for most Russians and a benevolent and necessary aspiration for most Ukrainians. In contrast, the tsarist state is a brutal empire for Ukrainians and a civilizing force for Russians. The disagreement could hardly be more thoroughgoing.

The Soviet period did nothing to bridge the chasm between Russian and Ukrainian understandings of their relations. Not only did the largely Russian leadership in Moscow always keep Kiev on a very short leash, not only were Ukrainian party members and intellectuals always required to speak and think the "language of the great Lenin," not only was linguistic and cultural Russification

a policy goal of Moscow, but opposition in Ukraine to the political   **103**
leadership of Russian apparatchiks or to the hegemony of the
Russian language and culture invariably resulted in execution,
incarceration, or deportation. Ukrainians thus see the physical
destruction of Ukrainian national Communists and intellectuals
in the 1930s and the crushing of Ukrainian dissent in the 1970s as
inevitable by-products of Ukraine's belonging to the Soviet
Union. To be sure, Ukrainians admit that Russians also suffered,
but unlike Ukrainian and other non-Russian nations, Russians,
they claim, suffered not for being Russian, but for being anti-
Communist or anti-Soviet. The following evaluation by a Ukrainian historian is typical of Ukrainian sentiments: "While the
Russians built Great Russia (even if partly on their own bones),
the Uzbeks, Armenians, Ukrainians, and Lithuanians served as
the construction material."[1] The Great Famine of 1932–1933,
which cost some four to six million lives, symbolizes for Ukrainians their experience within the Soviet Union.

The result is that contemporary Ukrainians are completely,
almost congenitally mistrustful of Russians. There is, in this
regard, virtually nothing that Russia can do that would put Ukrainians at ease. If a rapprochement takes place, and it should, then
it will do so only after more or less normal relations persist for a
decade or two and Ukrainians acquire sufficient self-confidence
not to interpret every Russian action as a threat to their identity
and independence. By the same token, however, it is imperative
that no real, as compared with imagined, Russian threats actually
occur.

Russo-Ukrainian Misunderstandings

As the previous section suggested, Russians have no less a Ukrainian problem than Ukrainians have a Russian problem. If Ukrainians suffer from a sense of inferiority, Russians suffer from a sense
of superiority. If Ukrainians resent Russians for dominating them,
Russians resent Ukrainians for rejecting them. Not surprisingly,
misunderstandings, tensions, and conflicts have increased expo-
nentially with the collapse of the empire and the emergence of two

104   states, Ukraine and Russia, both suffering from severe anxiety
about their own identities. Compounding the difficulty of sorting
out accurate from inaccurate perceptions is the fact that the
collapse of Soviet ideology, which provided Russians and Ukrainians with a set of common terms and understandings, has generated two distinct, and almost untranslatable, discourses—one
nationally Russian, the other nationally Ukrainian. Different
discourses, different myths, different historical interpretations,
and different national interests have produced a virtual breakdown
in communication precisely when the postcolonial and post-totalitarian legacies have to be dealt with. The objective difficulty of
disentangling a post-totalitarian colony from the empire has become all the greater because of the inability of both Ukrainians
and Russians to interpret each other's actions and motives from a
position outside the tangled web of misperceptions in which both
are caught.

The manner in which the ongoing Russo-Ukrainian war of
words has escalated illustrates the problem. Until Ukraine declared independence on August 24, 1991, everything was fine.
Boris Yeltsin and Leonid Kravchuk had signed an exemplary
interstate treaty the year before, in which both sides pledged
themselves to noninterference, mutual respect, and recognition of
sovereignty and existing borders. The reality of Ukrainian independence, however, spurred Yeltsin to make imprudent remarks
about Ukrainian borders in late August.[2] Ukrainians reacted with
alarm, but the resulting tensions were defused with the signing of a
joint communiqué, which repeated the points of the 1991 accord.
Soon thereafter, however, the unsettled Ukrainians began talking
seriously about creating their own army, as a means of enhancing
security. This time, their neighbors reacted with alarm, while
Anatoly Sobchak, the mayor of St. Petersburg, went so far as to say
that a Ukrainian army would pose "a huge threat to mankind as
a whole."[3]

The December 1 referendum was the next stage in the evolving conflict. Concerned with maintaining his Union at all costs,
Gorbachev inflamed the situation by arguing, "We shall not view

a decision by the citizens of Ukraine in favor of independence as a **105**
break with the Union. To push matters in that direction would
mean heading toward disaster: for the Union, for Ukraine itself,
for Russia, for Europe, and for the world."[4] Ukraine did choose
independence, and several days later the presidents of Ukraine,
Russia, and Belarus met to declare the end of the Soviet Union
and to found the Commonwealth of Independent States (CIS).
From the outset, however, Ukraine and Russia disagreed on what
the Commonwealth entailed. Ukrainians insisted that it was
exactly what its name said it was: a loose association of fully
independent states. It naturally followed that no one state could
claim the property or obligations of the former USSR, that no one
state should set the pace of reform on its own, and that a single
army under Moscow's command was unacceptable. By contrast,
many Russian policymakers—with the important exception of,
perhaps, Yeltsin—seem to have viewed the CIS as a federation
within which significant elements of sovereignty, especially as
pertaining to military and economic policy, would remain in the
hands of the center. In light of such profound differences, the
Commonwealth was still-born.

The War of Words

Post-Soviet conditions created further complications. Despite the
existence of the CIS, the reality of independent successor states
meant that, as of late 1991, Russia, Ukraine, and the other former
republics had to pursue their own interests. And it is at this point
that they initiated policies that fed into their mutual resentments
and thus accelerated the spiral of misunderstanding. It is impossible to determine who "started it." Clearly, both Russian and
Ukrainian policymakers engaged in unnecessarily provocative
actions.

RUSSIA'S MISTAKES

First on the list of Russian mistakes is the Crimea. The irredentist
statements of a number of Russian policymakers, in particular Vice

106   President Aleksandr Rutskoi and his supporters in the Russian parliament, are cause for alarm. However much some Russians in the Crimea may want to join the Russian motherland, Ukrainian policymakers were right to insist that the internationally sanctioned practice of generally *not* adjusting borders in line with ethnic boundaries and thereby actively pursuing the dismemberment of existing states—as opposed to unviable empires, such as the USSR had become under Gorbachev—be applied to the post-Soviet states. Although the nationalist argument regarding the imperative of complete self-determination does have moral merit, it has little practical value—other than producing the kind of ethnic violence that plagues Nagorno-Karabakh, Moldova, and Bosnia-Herzegovina. The international community's imperfect solution to the problem is to insist that national minorities be granted complete civic and human rights, a stance also adopted by Yeltsin, who appears to realize that pressing the Crimean case to the point of pursuing its annexation by Russia would set a legal precedent for border revisions and, as a result, greatly accelerate the separatist movements of the Chechen, the Ingush, the Tatars, the Bashkirs, and many other non-Russians *within* Russia.

In any case, despite Russia's interference in the Crimea, the issue appeared to be defused in mid-1992, after the Crimean parliament's declaration of independence on May 5, 1992, provoked a vigorous response from the Ukrainian legislature and president, which in turn induced Crimean policymakers to back down from a confrontation with Kiev and to comply with its demand that the Crimea's constitution and laws be brought into line with Ukraine's. Subsequent negotiations, which focused on the attainment of maximal autonomy for the Crimea within the Ukrainian state, suggested that both governments could reach a mutually satisfactory solution to their dispute if left alone by Moscow to deal directly with each other and with their own extremists. Logic argued that the Crimea should remain within Ukraine. As a semisovereign autonomous republic and the home of the Black Sea Fleet, it would enjoy exalted status vis-à-vis Kiev;

as one of more than 1,800 Russian administrative units, the **107** Crimea would unavoidably exert far less leverage on Moscow.

Russia's second mistake was in displaying insensitivity to the republics' claim to be equal entities in the international arena. Whereas the 1991 Minsk and Alma-Ata accords concerning the CIS recognized Russia as the successor state of the USSR in the United Nations Security Council *only*, Russia proceeded to declare itself—with the West's approval—the Soviet Union's successor state in all respects. Moscow claimed priority in such questions as debt repayment and disarmament, and, worst of all, immediately seized all *Soviet* property at home and abroad, along with all hard currency and gold reserves and all of the former USSR's embassies and consulates. Russia's rationale appeared to hinge on a technicality: since the non-Russians left the Union, while Russia never declared independence, everything that belonged to the Union perforce belongs to Russia. In effect, Russia's unilateral move bankrupted the other states, effectively denied them any chance of being represented abroad—none of them had the hard currency to buy or rent buildings of their own—and made a mockery of the successor states' aspirations to sovereignty. Ukraine, for instance, was forced to stoop to negotiating with Ukrainian diaspora organizations over use of their buildings in New York, Washington, Chicago, London, Ottawa, and other Western cities.

The third mistake was Yeltsin's unilateral decision to liberalize prices in early January 1992. In so doing, Moscow signaled to the other states that Russia alone would determine the course of economic reform. That Kiev was utterly unprepared was of course its own fault, but the Ukrainian request that Russia delay its reform by more than two weeks fell on deaf ears, even though waiting would not have made much economic difference. Thereafter the Russian government's further plans for economic shock therapy largely ignored the impact of developments in Russia on the other states, thus appearing as instances of great power *diktat* and of beggar-thy-neighbor policies.

108

UKRAINE'S MISTAKES

Ukraine also made three miscalculations. As already noted, first on the list was the question of a Ukrainian army. Although it is hard to dispute a sovereign state's right to its own military, Kiev's approach was poorly conceived and, because it was unilateral, unnecessarily alarming. To be sure, with some 700,000 soldiers stationed on its territory, and with Moscow sending mixed signals about the inviolability of Ukrainian territory and sovereignty and clear ones about its own appropriation of Soviet property, the Ukrainian government came face to face with a genuine dilemma. On the one hand, the continued presence of so many soldiers under Moscow's effective command appeared to pose a clear threat to Ukrainian independence—as it did to Polish, Czechoslovak, Estonian, Latvian, Lithuanian, and Moldovan independence. On the other hand, to demand that the troops be withdrawn immediately not only would have been impractical but would also have negated Ukraine's own claims to Soviet property. Kiev thus decided on three parallel courses of action. First, Ukraine resolved to build its own army, one smaller than the Soviet forces in Ukraine, thereby claiming its share of the armed forces and compelling the rest to be demobilized or withdrawn. Ukrainians believed this would reduce the military threat to Western Europe, not, as Sobchak suggested, somehow increase it. Second, by deciding to surrender the strategic and tactical nuclear weapons stationed on its territory (for reasons also related to popular fears of another Chernobyl), Kiev hoped to force Russia to eliminate its atomic presence in Ukraine as well. And third, by claiming neutrality as its ultimate goal, Ukraine expected to be able to distance itself from Russia for good.

The logic behind what Kiev somewhat too grandly calls its "military doctrine" may have been sound, but Ukrainian policymakers made several errors in implementation. By not informing their neighbors of their thinking beforehand, they needlessly alarmed the West by suggesting that the rationale for the army was

offensive, rather than defensive. By originally suggesting that the **109**
army would be half a million strong and by taking decisive steps
toward building their own armed forces *after* signing the Commonwealth accords, which referred to single "military-strategic" spaces
and joint commands, not separate military forces, the Ukrainians
created the impression that they were hot-headed spoilers of
interrepublic amity and cooperation. Worst of all, Ukrainian
behavior struck Russians as a repudiation of the CIS and as a
needlessly rash attempt to impose a fait accompli on the question
of the former Soviet army, which, as thoughtful Russians and
Ukrainians realized, simply could not be demobilized or reformed
overnight.

The Ukrainian decision to require that soldiers stationed in
Ukraine take an oath of loyalty to the republic seemed to typify
Kiev's inability to proceed slowly and with caution. Forcing the
issue did lay the groundwork for a Ukrainian army, but it also
provoked ethnic tensions within the ranks and encouraged
Ukraine's own Russians to take sides in the Russo-Ukrainian
dispute. Benign neutrality vis-à-vis Ukrainian independence became increasingly more difficult for them, which accentuated
Russo-Ukrainian differences at home and abroad.

Also unnecessary was Ukraine's second mistake: the decision
to claim *all* of the Black Sea Fleet. Whatever the rationale, Kiev's
move missed the mark on three counts. First, it was absurd to
think that the entire fleet would ever be Ukraine's, if only because
a certain proportion could be classified as strategic and thus
subordinate to joint CIS command. Second, it was foolish to
expect a nationally resurgent Russia not to react passionately to
the loss of so large a portion of the former Soviet armed forces. And
third, Kiev's timing was terrible: claiming the fleet while soldiers
were being asked to swear loyalty and the Republic Movement of
the Crimea was talking of separation played into the hands of
Yeltsin's archconservative opponents, who linked all three issues,
ascribed intensely emotional overtones to them, and, as a result,
both reduced Yeltsin's political maneuverability and confronted

110   Ukrainian policymakers with the possibility that their claims on
the fleet could generate official Russian claims on the Crimea. In
time, Kiev reduced its claims to 30 percent, but the damage to
Russo-Ukrainian relations had already been done. Russians would
not forget Ukrainian unilateralism, while Ukrainians could not
forget Yeltsin's remark that the fleet "has been, still is, and will
remain Russian"[5]—a statement reminiscent of Russian Interior
Minister Pyotr Valuev's notorious claim in 1863 that there "has
not been, is not, and will not be" a Ukrainian language.[6]

Kiev's third mistake concerned nuclear weapons. After promising in 1991 to transfer all tactical and strategic weapons to
Russia, Ukraine appeared to backtrack from its decision several
times in the course of 1992. After appropriate pressure by and
concessions from the United States and Russia, Ukraine gave up
its tactical warheads and joined them, along with Belarus and
Kazakhstan, in signing the Strategic Arms Reduction Treaty
(START) in May 1992. Kiev got what it wanted, international
recognition, but it paid a heavy price by appearing irresponsible
and willing to jeopardize international peace and security for the
sake of debating points with Russia.

Kiev's image suffered again in late 1992 when policymakers
and parliamentarians insisted that Ukraine's ratification of
START I be made contingent on further concessions from the
West. Angry at Washington for seeming to take Ukraine for
granted, Kiev linked its dismantling of the 176 missile launchers
and silos on its territory to security guarantees, financial compen-
sation, and assistance in dealing with the environmental hazards
posed by nuclear fuel. Linking disarmament to these conditions
may have been a sound bargaining strategy, but it came at a most
inauspicious time—just as Presidents Bush and Yeltsin signed
START II and universally held hopes for a new, nonnuclear age
were particularly high. Because START II could not come into
effect without ratification of START I by Ukraine, Belarus, and
Kazakhstan, Kiev appeared to be engaging in a form of nuclear
blackmail that threatened to alienate both Russia and the West.
Worse still, Ukrainian policymakers gave the impression that they

were irrational enough to believe that their land-based nuclear **111**
arsenal could actually serve as an effective deterrent against a
potentially hostile Russia capable of delivering both a devastating
first and an equally crushing second strike.

RUSSO-UKRAINIAN COMPROMISE

The mistakes made by Russia and Ukraine reflected the mind-sets
discussed earlier: the Russian sense of superiority vis-à-vis Ukraine
and the Ukrainian sense of inferiority vis-à-vis Russia. Willfully or
not, Russia seemed like a bully with respect to the Crimea, Soviet
property, and economic reform, while Ukraine appeared irrational
with regard to the army, the fleet, and nuclear weapons. The
impression arose that neither Russia nor Ukraine could be trusted—
the former because it wanted to impose its preferences by force, the
latter because it wanted to impose its preferences by stealth.

Yet, though the Russo-Ukrainian conflict over the army and
the fleet alarmed observers in the West, it was never quite as
serious as it seemed. Despite some faux pas by both, Kravchuk and
Yeltsin actively sought reconciliation, and once the military command conceded to former republics the right to field their own
armies on December 31, 1991, in Minsk, the ultimate resolution
of the problem could only involve some variant of the Ukrainian
position. That is to say, part of the army, like part of the fleet,
would become Ukrainian, while the rest would in time have to be
withdrawn or divided among Russia and other republics. Yeltsin's
eventual decision to create a Russian Ministry of Defense and a
Russian army followed logically. Pushing both sides to accept this
solution was perhaps the strongest argument of all: the desirability,
or permissibility, of a Ukrainian army was becoming moot, as ever
growing numbers of soldiers—some 500,000 between January and
March, 1992—swore allegiance to Ukraine, no doubt as much out
of a preference for its pleasant climate as out of patriotism. No less
important was that over half the officer corps of the Black Sea Fleet
had also taken the oath of loyalty to Ukraine by late 1992.

112   Kravchuk and Yeltsin succeeded in resolving or, at least, temporarily shelving their differences at two meetings, in the south Russian town of Dagomys on June 23 and in Yalta on August 3. The accords they signed achieved breakthroughs on all the points of contention and, significantly, represented Russian concessions to all of Ukraine's demands. First, by explicitly not addressing the Crimea in either agreement, Russia in effect admitted that the issue was of domestic political importance for Ukraine. Second, by agreeing to transfer 16.37 percent of all Soviet property overseas to Ukraine, Russia conceded that it was not the only successor state to the USSR, while Ukraine, naturally, got the buildings it sought. And third, by agreeing to place the Black Sea Fleet under joint Russo-Ukrainian command for three years, during which the question of ownership was to be resolved, Russia acknowledged the validity, in principle, of Ukrainian claims.

Ukraine also made concessions, the most important of which was that, domestic nationalist opposition notwithstanding, the Russo-Ukrainian border was to remain open. On balance, the accords represented a victory for Kravchuk and a testament to his persistence, diplomacy, and craftiness. Some Ukrainian extremists viewed the agreements as sellouts—"Kravchuk gave away our fleet!" was one such sentiment voiced frequently in public—but, premised as they were on the absurd notion that Ukraine already had what Kravchuk allegedly gave away, these views appealed only to politically unsophisticated fringe elements in the radical nationalist camp.

The accords of Dagomys and Yalta did not spell the end of the Russo-Ukrainian war of words. Continued discord over nuclear weapons and Yeltsin's 1993 decree declaring Russia the USSR's sole heir testified to that. Nor did the agreements exclude the possibility of intensified conflict, even real war, in the future, especially if socioeconomic conditions worsen in both countries and extremists come to exert greater influence on government policy. But the accords did signify that Ukraine was not as unreasonable as some Western policymakers and the media suggested.[7]

Throughout 1992 Ukraine was merely asking to be treated as the **113** sovereign nation it presumably became after independence. Once Russia acknowledged the reality of Ukraine's independence, as it seemed to do with the two accords, the major points of contention receded, even if only temporarily. The moral of the story is simple: that continued Russian appreciation of the end of empire is the best means of dispelling Ukrainian paranoia about Russia and of ensuring amicable relations in the future.

EVALUATING YELTSIN

It is clearly imperative for Ukraine and Russia to maintain a modus vivendi that avoids a continually escalating semantic war. From Ukraine's point of view, a successful Russian transition to democracy and the market would be most desirable, because it would signal Yeltsin's victory and the triumph of nonideological moderates inclined to resolve issues peacefully and to mutual advantage. Naturally, a successful Ukrainian transition would be no less desirable for Russia.

Will Russia succeed? Can it succeed? As suggested in chapter 2, of all the post-Soviet states Russia may face the greatest obstacles to success. Not only is Russia the inheritor of the imperial center and the victim of full-blown totalitarianism, but it is too big, too complex—with thirty-one ethnic administrative territories comprising 53 percent of its territory—and too unevenly developed for reform to proceed smoothly, if at all. But Russia has two advantages: a relatively skilled elite, in particular a forceful president, and the enormous mineral wealth undergirding its economic potential. Table 2.1 suggested that these assets would not suffice to overcome its disadvantages. The following discussion will explore these questions in greater detail by focusing on Yeltsin's chances of surviving as a democrat and Russia's chances of developing a democracy, a market, and a civil society.

Although there is no reason to doubt that Boris Nikolaievich Yeltsin believes in democracy, certainly no less, and perhaps even more, than Gorbachev, Kravchuk, Shevardnadze, or any other

114 former apparatchik, the degree of his personal commitment is almost irrelevant to assessing the likelihood that his government will remain, however vaguely, democratic. Even if we assume that Yeltsin will never depart from Jeffersonian ideals in his thinking, we should not conclude that he, like Alberto Fujimori in Peru, would not do so in practice to remain in power. Indeed, Yeltsin's unsavory wrangling with Gorbachev and the latter's unwillingness to recognize the authority of Russian courts suggest a meanness of spirit that fits neither man's exalted image in the West.

Consider the enormity of the task facing Yeltsin. Like all the other republics, Russia has to cope with the collapse of the Soviet system. The Russian polity, economy, society, and culture are in complete disarray and even the most optimistic reform scenario— rapid and effective macroeconomic stabilization, liberalization, and restructuring—would ensure deindustrialization and a massive contraction in Gross National Product. If the experience of eastern Germany is any indication of what awaits Russia, then widespread unemployment, a resurgent radical right, and interethnic conflict appear all but inevitable.

For the sake of argument, however, let us assume that Yeltsin succeeds in bringing about maximal change within the next year or two, an assumption that may be unrealistic in light of Yegor Gaidar's replacement as prime minister by Viktor Chernomyrdin in late 1992. If so, Yeltsin will certainly confront even greater political opposition than that which toppled Gaidar at the Congress of People's Deputies. Yeltsin may also face a social upheaval of revolutionary proportions. No democratic leader in the West could survive such dire straits—witness George Bush's preelection difficulties in 1992 with the declining American economy and John Major's backtracking on his own decision to close most British coal mines because of widespread protests—and if Yeltsin remains genuinely democratic, he will have to step down, especially since he foolishly staked his political survival on an improvement in Russian living standards by the fall of 1992. If, however, Yeltsin chooses to remain in power, despite such massive political

and social unrest, he will have to become a dictator, de facto if not **115**
de jure.

Although the December 1992 session of the Congress of
People's Deputies forced Yeltsin to sacrifice radical reform on the
altar of popular discontent, for most of that year circumstances
pushed him in an authoritarian direction. His manner of seizing
power from Gorbachev, however justified in view of the latter's
pathetic self-identification with the Soviet state, was not an
exercise in democracy. Yeltsin's rule by decree and appropriation
of the premiership, while also understandable in light of the
previous government's inability to embark on reform, represented
a potentially dangerous accumulation of powers. And Yeltsin's
decision to subordinate local government to prefects directly an-
swerable to him—again, a perfectly sensible move considering
local resistance to reform—was not precisely in the democratic
spirit that many in the West believe him to embody.

Evidently, Yeltsin understands that radical economic reform
and political democracy may be at loggerheads in today's Russia.
His willingness to dismiss Gaidar at the behest of conservatives
grouped about Arkady Volsky's Civic Union testified to Yeltsin's
unwillingness to abandon democracy in late 1992. Of course
Yeltsin's priorities may change—he had already threatened to
impose presidential rule before the meeting of the Congress—
especially if the post-Gaidar government adopts antimarket measures and the West insists that capitalism be favored over democracy in Russia.

OBSTACLES TO RUSSIAN REFORM

What, then, are Russia's chances of attaining democracy, the
market, and civil society? Russia's post-totalitarian condition is
even less enviable than that of the other republics. Like them, it
has no civil society, market, or democracy, if defined as sets of
coherent institutions. Unlike them, however, Russia has inherited
two large disadvantages, the imperial state and the imperial armed
forces. Although the foreign policy elite is competent, as it should

116 be after decades of negotiating with the United States, nothing else about the Russian state is: Russian apparatchiks are no less unskilled, corrupt, and inept than their non-Russian colleagues— but with one important difference. Russian bureaucracy is over- staffed to such an extent that much of the Russian state already is the parasitical, semi-autonomous entity that the non-Russian states may become.

Worse still, the Russian state has already forged an alliance, as a legacy of the Soviet period, with a huge army and an equally huge military-industrial complex. Indeed, to say that the military- industrial complex *is* the Russian state would not be much of an exaggeration. The non-Russians will soon face the prospect of having large, hungry armies to deal with; Russia already has this problem, and, despite talk of reducing the size of the army and converting military industry to civilian use, it is more likely that the army will remain large—the politically intrusive officer corps will see to that—and that military-to-civilian conversion, as in the West, will be minimal, especially at a time of economic constraints and hard currency shortages. Compared with the powerful institutions of a bloated state and a potentially hostile military, the Yeltsin "team" really was just a group of well-meaning individuals.

Inevitably, Russia's state and army will be among the greatest obstacles to democratic change. To be sure, elections will probably continue to be held and the legislature will meet, but democracy, as a set of procedures and institutions, will be subverted by a state and a military with no interest in maintaining them except as fig leaves. We may expect the apparatchiks to sabotage reforms and the generals to claim that the army is indispensable—a claim that will seem increasingly plausible if and when Russians living in non-Russian states come under attack or are forced to adjust to the requirements of life in new national states. And both will be increasingly tempted to intervene in politics to defend their own interests and to control the chaos that successful reform is sure to unleash. Can Yeltsin overcome the resistance of such powerful

institutions without becoming dictatorial? Can he overcome it **117**
at all?

There are additional obstacles to Russian democracy. The lack of a democratic political culture may be, as many observers note, a fatal flaw, since overcoming hundreds of years of authoritarian thinking cannot be easy. Furthermore, the Slavophile rejection of Western liberalism—a longstanding Russian tradition currently enjoying a resurgence—is functioning as the ideological glue binding Russian nationalists and Russian Communists in an anti-Western alliance. Slavophilism also gives meaning to the many ordinary Russians distraught by the loss of empire and superpower status.

Moreover, it is uncertain just how many supporters Yeltsin and democracy really have. Democracy ostensibly triumphed in August 1991, but most of Moscow, indeed most of Russia, took the putsch in stride and remained indifferent to the dramatic struggle between Yeltsin and the putschists—as did most non-Russian republics. The forces of democracy are unlikely to be strengthened by the probable influx of embittered and impoverished Russian *pieds noirs* abandoning Central Asia and other republics under pressure of local accusations of imperialism and colonialism. Finally, there is the problem of geographic size, a brutal fact that will hinder the even "spread" of democratic institutions and procedures. Even if they do catch on in some parts of the country, such as Moscow and St. Petersburg, most of Russia will lag behind, and because Russia is so huge, it will take much longer for Russia to become democratic than it would for a country only a fraction of its size, such as Estonia or, for that matter, even Ukraine.

Market and Civil Society

Size will also undermine Russia's attempt to marketize. The difficulty of reforming the Russian economy is far greater than that of doing so in any other post-Communist state. Big, complex, geographically dispersed economies make for bigger and more difficult challenges, which greatly increases the time required for success and the chances of failure. Moreover, Russia's economy is so

118   regionally segmented and development is so uneven—consider
the vast differences among the Non–Black Earth Zone, the Urals,
and Siberia—that reform, even if consistently applied, would
have a differential impact. As a result, the problem of coordinating and synchronizing economic development will be far greater in
Russia than in any other republic. The state and the military will
also complicate the economic challenges facing would-be reformers. Marketization is not in the interest of either institution,
and it would be unrealistic to think that venal apparatchiks and
power-hungry generals will not resist schemes that promise to
undermine their status and position.

Finally, a bona fide civil society is unlikely to take root soon
in Russia, despite the proliferation of parties, groups, clubs, newspapers, and the like. It is here that Russia's own "nationality
question" will play the decisive role. Russia currently has thirty-
one ethnic administrative units, ranging from Tatarstan southeast
of Moscow to Sakha-Yakutia east of the Urals to Chukotka in the
Far East. For reasons discussed in chapter 3, the collapse of Soviet
discourse has resulted in the emergence of a plethora of national
languages that made the creation of a consensually based *Soviet*
civil society impossible. The same argument holds for Russia, with
the added complication that, while the USSR was ostensibly
supranational, Russia, despite the Russian-language distinction
between ethnic Russians (*russki*) and a supposedly supraethnic
Russia (*Rossiya*), is generally viewed as the land of the *russki*.
Rather than transfer their allegiance to Russia, Tatars, Yakuts,
Chukchi, and others are more likely to establish their own civil
societies and not participate in some pan-Russian one. Eventually,
Russia may come to have many civil societies, a development that,
while a boon for cultural pluralism and artistic creativity, will not
result in what civil society is supposed to do: curb the state and
protect the citizenry from its encroachments. In particular, a
Babel of civil societies will not be able to act as a solid buffer
against the acutely Russian problem of a parasitical state and a
politically meddlesome military.

The emergence of non-Russian civil societies within Russia, **119** especially under conditions of continued economic and political hardship, may accelerate non-Russian drives toward independence, in very much the way the republics behaved during the Gorbachev period. Checheno-Ingushetia declared independence on March 12, 1992; Tatarstan's March 1992 referendum purported to endow it with sovereignty in its relations with Russia; and another twenty-nine such actions may be waiting in the wings, despite the fact that a Russian federal treaty was signed on March 31, 1992.

Indicative of future trends may be the August 13, 1992, joint statement of the presidents of Tatarstan, Sakha-Yakutia, and Bashkortostan in which they condemned Moscow for infringing on the sovereignty of their states. Bashkir President Murtaza Rakhimov's sentiments, so similar to those that glasnost unleashed in 1987–1988, appear to reflect the feelings of many non-Russians in Russia: "The republics have to be treated with respect; it's necessary to sit down and figure out who owes how much to whom. For 75 years they pumped the blood out of us and left us impoverished and face-to-face with environmental problems, and now they want us to go back to living the old way? That won't play anymore!"[8] Even if economic reform works, therefore, Russia could very well have its hands full with secessionist movements— a development that will both complicate reform and strengthen the position of the military as the only institution willing and able to prevent the further disintegration of the country.

The prospects for Russia are bleak. Will its vast mineral resources make the difference? It is difficult to see how, even if Russian oil production, which contracted by 14 percent in 1992,[9] miraculously revives and begins providing the country with massive sums of hard currency. As Western policymakers reluctant to provide financial aid to the former republics realize, lack of money is only a part, perhaps the smallest part, of the problem. The real difficulty involves the successor states' lack of appropriate institutions to absorb the aid and channel it in appropriate directions. Even if Russia generates its own hard currency, there is little

120   likelihood that large sums of money will more than marginally
assist reform unless Russia also succeeds in reforming and reducing
its state apparatus, curbing its military, and creating democratic
institutions, a civil society, and a market. Contrary to most
expectations in the West, none of these goals is likely to be
achieved soon.

The experience of Third World oil-producing states is also
instructive. Hard currency earnings, even in fabulous sums, can
spur development, as in Indonesia, and they can raise living
standards, as in the United Arab Emirates. But they can also
sustain dictators, as in Libya, leave outmoded political structures
unaffected, as in Saudi Arabia, and, if misused, encourage revolution, as in Iran.

Prospects for Interstate Tensions

Because of Russia's dominant geopolitical position in Eurasia, a
Russian failure to achieve democracy, civil society, and a market
will have a profoundly negative effect on Ukraine's own efforts. No
less important, Russia's failure may mean that its relations with
the former republics and Ukraine in particular will become, or
remain, exceedingly strained. The outlook is depressing, no matter how one looks at the issue.

It might, for instance, be argued that Russia's remaining a
regional giant will be stabilizing. Because its military strength will
be undermined by its political, social, and economic weakness,
however, Russia will be unable to play the role of a genuine
"hegemon" and impose order on Eastern Europe, the Caucasus,
and Central Asia. But unsuccessful attempts to do so are likely to
enhance non-Russian insecurity and, as a result, to provoke unnecessary conflicts. That the Russian military may have lost some
of its élan will only contribute to Russia's inability to play the
hegemonic role that advocates of an assertive foreign policy recommend.

Peaceful norms can reduce interstate tensions, but such
norms not only do not yet exist, but are also unlikely to be
established soon. Non-Russians will probably interpret any at-

tempts by Moscow to create such mechanisms as smokescreens for **121** Russian hegemony. And no outside force—that is, Europe— could impose a ready-made normative framework by integrating a country the size, and with the problems, of Russia and expect its own institutions to remain intact. Consider Germany's difficulties with its newly incorporated eastern provinces. Peaceful standards may be inherent in democracies, and it may be true that democracies never fight one another, but the fact that Russia will almost certainly not be democratic, while few of the post-Communist states are likely to become so soon, is obviously cause for concern.

Worse still, a variety of currently popular myths and ideologies might propel Russian and non-Russian leaders to adopt aggressive policies. Russia and the post-Soviet republics are self-consciously national states with an assumed responsibility for their ethnic brethren in neighboring countries: the fate of the millions of Russians living in the non-Russian states has already spurred some Russian generals and policymakers to favor military intervention in potential trouble spots. Border disputes have also emerged—for instance, Russia's claims on the Crimea—and they are likely to remain on the agenda so long as most of the successor states employ national identity to legitimize themselves.

The most hopeful news about relations among the successor states is that most of them lack developed armies, military-industrial establishments, and civil societies. As a result, there are at present few groups with a direct interest in fanning aggression and conflict. Naturally, as these countries become "normal," such forces will begin to emerge and may then come to exert a nefarious influence on foreign policy. As noted above, however, the two countries with already existing powerful pressure groups are Russia, which has inherited most of the Soviet army and military-industrial complex, and Ukraine, which is establishing an army and possesses a sizable chunk of the military-industrial complex as well.

Russia's armed forces, however, are alone in having the dubious distinction of being stationed in all the non-Russian suc-

122   cessor states. Their presence in the periphery, a typical legacy of all empires, will remain a source of instability until they are withdrawn. That time is unlikely to come soon, both because they have no place to go in Russia and because Moscow's concerns for Russian settler populations in the former republics will enhance the appeal of keeping troops stationed abroad. Even Yeltsin, on October 7, 1992, linked Russian troop withdrawal from Estonia and Latvia with greater "minority rights" for Russians in both states.[10] Inevitably, then, the Russian military's involvement in non-Russian conflicts will not remain confined to Moldova, Tajikistan, Abkhazia, and South Ossetia, while non-Russian resentment of "imperial intervention"—on the order of that voiced by Georgian President Eduard Shevardnadze—is sure to grow.

Ongoing debates in Russia lend weight to these theoretical reflections. Whereas earlier proponents of a strong and interventionist Russian foreign policy tended to be extremists, such as Zhirinovsky and Vice President Rutskoi, or members of the military establishment, such as Marshal Yevgeni Shaposhnikov, current supporters of "enlightened imperialism" include such figures as Sergei Stankevich, a widely respected politician and adviser to President Yeltsin, and Andranik Migranian, one of Russia's most original political theorists. Stankevich, for instance, has gone on record with the following sentiments:

> The attitude toward the Russian population and the Russian heritage [!] is the most important criterion for Russia in determining whether a given state is friendly. In turn, a whole complex of our bilateral relations—from the question of the fate of troops to economics and finance—cannot help but depend on this. All the accusations of an imperial syndrome notwithstanding, such a policy has nothing in common with imperialism.[11]

In light of his overly protective concern for something as ambiguous as the "Russian heritage," Stankevich's last assertion is not, alas, persuasive. Migranian's recommendations are even more alarming:

> Russia should declare to the world community that the entire geopolitical space of the former USSR is a sphere of its vital interests. This does not at all presuppose a threat to solve problems

by force; Russia is opposed to any conflicts in this space and is prepared to play there the role of intermediary and guarantor of stability. . . . Russia should say openly that it is opposed to the formation of any closed military-political alliances whatsoever by the former Union republics, either with one another or with third countries that have an anti-Russian orientation. And that it will regard any steps in this direction as unfriendly.[12]

The problem facing Yeltsin or an equally enlightened successor is obvious. If an assertive foreign policy becomes part of Russian mainstream thinking, then he may have no choice but to bow to popular pressure. On February 28, 1993, even Yeltsin asked that Russia be granted "special powers as a guarantor of peace and stability in the region of the former union."[13] Russian "revanchism"—whether motivated by sinister or noble intentions—would probably mean the end of the CIS and of all hope for a non-Russian rapprochement with the former empire.

UKRAINE MOVES WESTWARD

Despite the best intentions of leaders like Yeltsin, Russia's neighbors, and especially Ukraine, will long have a major security problem on their hands. They have already expressed their concerns about this. Poland, Moldova, Estonia, Latvia, and Lithuania are pressing Moscow to withdraw its troops as soon as possible; Belarus, Azerbaijan, Kyrgyzstan, and several other republics have already begun building their own armies; Kazakhstan, whose population is half Slavic, may retain some nuclear weapons as a bargaining chip with Russia.

Seen from this perspective, the evolution of Ukraine's foreign policy after independence makes perfect sense. Despite conflicting signals regarding atomic weapons, Kiev has gone out of its way to court American favor and recognition, in the hope—unceremoniously dashed by Secretary of State James Baker III[14]— that the United States might be willing to provide security guarantees in exchange for Ukraine's disavowal of nuclear status. Ukrainian policymakers have been even more energetic about establishing a high profile at the United Nations, lobbying at the International Monetary Fund and the World Bank, and inserting

124   themselves into European institutions, such as the Conference on
Security and Cooperation in Europe, the North Atlantic Cooperation Council, and the Council of Europe. The official explana-
tion for Ukraine's interest in Europe is, as Foreign Minister
Anatoly Zlenko put it, that "Ukraine is a European nation. More
than that, Ukraine is a great European nation which can enrich
the all-European process. Everything European is characteristic of
us."[15] The real reason is, of course, fear of Russia. Whatever their
motivation, however, Ukrainian hopes are likely to be frustrated.
Although the European Bank for Reconstruction and Development has developed a program supporting privatization in
Ukraine, European countries have not reciprocated Ukraine's
enthusiasm for rapid inclusion in the institutions that matter
most, such as the European Community.

More likely is the third component of Ukraine's move west-
ward—growing cooperation with Warsaw, Budapest, Prague, and
Bratislava, with which Kiev has already signed a variety of cooperative treaties. Ukraine's goal is rapid integration into the "Vise-
grad Quadrangle" composed of Poland, Hungary, the Czech
Republic, and Slovakia. In particular, President Kravchuk has
publicly stated that Poland, not Russia, will become Ukraine's
major partner in the future: on February 3, 1993, both countries
signed a "defense cooperation agreement." More important
than these policy moves, however, are several deeper forces that
make Ukraine's eventual integration into Central Europe a
virtual certainty. A common cultural legacy stemming from the
Polish-Lithuanian Commonwealth and the Hapsburg Empire, the
economic interdependence fostered by CMEA, fear of Russia's
enlightened imperialist inclinations, and the unwillingness of
Western Europe to accept any of them into the EC in the near
future should in time impel Poland, the Czech Republic, Slovakia,
Hungary, Ukraine, and perhaps Belarus and the Baltics to create
an East-Central European commonwealth. Such an association
would have far greater chances of survival than the post-Soviet
version, the CIS, whose current members share two burdensome

legacies of the past and few, if any, promising prospects for mutu-   **125**
ally beneficial relations in the future.

Although Ukraine's prospects for joining Western Europe
may be good in the very long run, the legacies of empire and
totalitarianism demand immediate solutions to its pressing problems. From this point of view, even the "Russian problem" takes a
back seat to the necessity of political, social, and especially economic reform. At a minimum, the course of reform in Ukraine will
be no less important to Ukraine's future than developments in
Russia. If Ukraine turns viciously nondemocratic, if ethnic conflict explodes, if the military attempts to "save" the country, it will
matter little what happens in Russia. Most important, if Ukraine's
economy collapses, with all the attendant political, social, cultural, and ethnic consequences, Russia's own slim chance of
successful reform will dwindle completely away.

CHAPTER 5

Transforming a Dependent Economy

O f all the problems bequeathed to Ukraine and other successor states by the collapse of empire and totalitarianism, that of creating a viable economy has attracted the most attention in the West. Yet, although the long-term prospects of all these states directly depend on their economic vitality, Western observers have tended to treat the problem of economic reform in isolation from the many other challenges confronting Ukraine and other states. Creating a market economy is hard enough. As this chapter argues, creating one under post-totalitarian conditions is especially difficult because it compels policymakers to consider a range of issues that are not exclusively economic and to choose between equally pressing and equally valid social ends. Once again, Ukrainian, Russian, and other policymakers face an unpleasant choice: either rapid economic reform and the likelihood of massive social and political unrest or greater attention to social and political stability and the possibility of continued economic decline. In the aftermath of independence, Russia opted for the first approach; Ukraine for the second.

COLONIAL TIES

For almost three hundred years, Ukraine's economy has been an integral part of Russia's. Dependent status meant primarily that economic development in Ukraine was subordinated politically to

126

the economic priorities set by the imperial authorities, first the **127** tsarist ministers in St. Petersburg and then the State Planning Committee (Gosplan) in Moscow. Dependency meant that Ukraine's economic relations—trade, capital, and labor flows, as well as communications and transport—have been overwhelmingly with Russia. Western Ukraine was an exception to this rule until its integration into the USSR after 1945; the backward Galician economy was directed toward Austria until 1918 and toward Poland in the interwar period. Eastern Ukraine itself might have been poised to overcome its complete dependence on Russia in the late nineteenth and early twentieth centuries, when substantial French and Belgian investment flowed into the region. But that connection ended with the establishment of the USSR, whereupon capital flows and trade became confined to Russia and the other republics.

Suddenly, that dependent relationship, in terms of both priority setting and developmental flows, has been rent asunder not by Ukrainian nationalists scheming at autarky, but by Mikhail Gorbachev dreaming of perestroika. Gorbachev's economic policies pushed the economy to the brink of collapse, producing massive inflation, disrupting production, and lowering living standards in the process. Not surprisingly, in 1991 Soviet gross national product declined 17 percent, while the consumer price index and wholesale industrial prices rose 96 percent and 240 percent respectively. Ukraine, meanwhile, suffered a 9.6 percent decline in net material product in 1991 and a 137 percent rise in the retail price index. The figures were even worse for 1992: the gross national product contracted 18 percent, wholesale prices increased 22.5 times, and the budget deficit equaled 44 percent of GNP.[1]

As production and trade relations between and among republics broke down, as the planning mechanism ceased to function, all the republics were forced to defend themselves against the vagaries of a chaotic postcolonial economy. Cooperation should have been the order of the day, but it is hard to cooperate when production shortfalls in all the republics reduce the overall supply

128   of needed inputs and force individual states to practice beggar-thy-neighbor policies. This was especially the case because energy suppliers, such as Russia, Kazakhstan, and Turkmenistan, expected to demand world prices from cash-strapped successor states. Like the other republics, Ukraine had no choice but to take control of its own economy and formulate its own policies in an environment of economic disarray. Its policymakers never expected to be confronted with so many challenges so quickly. And least of all did they ever imagine that they would be required to preside over a transition to, of all things, a market.

THE UKRAINIAN ECONOMY

Under tsarism, Ukraine served largely as an agricultural producer and source of raw materials and metals. The much heralded "breadbasket" of Europe accounted for 98 percent of Russia's wheat exports in the early twentieth century. In turn, the Donbas-Kryvy Rih industrial area produced 70 percent of the empire's coal, 87 percent of its iron ore, 67 percent of its pig iron, 58 percent of its steel, and almost 100 percent of its machines. Overall, the Ukrainian economy accounted for 24.3 percent of Russia's total gross industrial output in 1913.[2] Although many Ukrainians were workers, some 90 percent of the ethnic Ukrainian population still lived in the countryside, while the cities, the largest of which were Kiev, Kharkiv, Katerynoslav, and Odessa, were the preserve of ethnic Russians and Jews. Austrian Galicia was even more underdeveloped economically—indeed, it appears to have experienced actual "de-industrialization"—producing mostly dairy products and petroleum, while its urban population was overwhelmingly Polish and Jewish.

World War I and the revolution and civil war that followed devastated Ukraine, which served as a central theater of military operations from 1914 until 1921. Human losses may have been as high as three to four million, out of a total population of about twenty-six million. In addition, much of Ukraine's political, cultural, and economic elites were either killed during the civil war or

emigrated to the West to escape the Bolshevik takeover. At least   **129**
50,000 Jews perished in pogroms, and many more fled, leaving
behind a devastated system of trade.

The interwar period provided little respite for Ukraine. The
Ukrainian territories in Poland, eastern Galicia and Volhynia,
were hit hard by the Depression. Soviet Ukraine was hit even
harder by the forced collectivization of peasants, the famine of
1932–1933, the destruction of agriculture, and rapid industrialization and urbanization. In striking contrast to Galicia and Volhynia, where Ukrainians remained ensconced in villages and the
Ukrainian working class was minuscule, Soviet Ukraine's social
structure underwent a profound transformation, as large numbers
of impoverished and hungry peasants were forced to move to cities
and become workers. The structure of the Soviet Ukrainian economy also experienced major changes: production of agricultural
products and natural resources remained central, but the machine-
building, metal-working, and producer goods industries expanded
severalfold. Ukraine's share of total Soviet investment, however,
declined from 20.5 percent during the First Five-Year Plan
(1927–1932) to 14.9 percent in the Third (1938–1941),[3] probably due to Moscow's perceived military needs, which appeared to
require locating heavy industry far from the reach of potential
Western attackers, that is, beyond the Urals and not in Ukraine.

World War II again devastated Ukraine, inflicting enormous
damage on the cities, factories, farms, and, of course, the population. Ukraine's economic losses represented about 45 percent of
the Soviet total, amounting to approximately 285 billion rubles.[4]
Some 6 million people died in Ukraine during the war, of whom
about 1 million were Jews. About 2 million Ukrainians were also
drafted for forced labor in Germany; several hundred thousand fled
West with the return of Soviet forces.

Reconstruction proceeded rapidly in the late 1940s and
1950s, when Ukraine registered exceptional annual growth rates,
in the 13 percent range.[5] Despite some experiments with decen-
tralization under Khrushchev and Brezhnev, however, economic
development remained wholly subordinated to the planners in

130   Moscow. More funds flowed out of than into Ukraine; an unusually large proportion—a third—of its population remained occupied in agriculture; and some 90 percent of all industry was under the jurisdiction of Union ministries in Moscow. Most important perhaps, the Ukrainian economy became a virtual appendage of the USSR's military-industrial complex. Dnipropetrovsk, one of Ukraine's largest industrial cities, was transformed into the center of the Soviet aerospace industry, while Kharkiv became a leading producer of military goods. At present, the defense industry accounts for some 28 percent of total industrial production in Ukraine and employs about 18 percent of its industrial workforce.[6] Like Slovakia's tank production facilities, Ukraine's arms industry produces goods capable of attracting foreign buyers (such as India, which agreed in October 1992 to exchange medicine and cloth for Ukrainian weapons)[7] and, despite assurances to the contrary, we should not expect it to be converted to civilian use in the near future, especially if the perceived Russian threat persists.

Throughout the Soviet period, Ukraine's economy remained highly dependent on that of the USSR in general and Russia in particular. Sixteen percent of Ukraine's production consisted of exports to the other republics, while 18 percent of its consumption was dependent on imports.[8] At present, Ukraine produces between 20 and 50 percent of the former USSR's coal, steel, rolled ferrous metal, steel pipes, iron ore, bricks, rail cargo cars, chemical industrial equipment, agricultural machinery, and many other goods, while relying on Russia proper for trucks, tractors, and much of its oil and natural gas.[9] As a result of such interdependence, the decline in Russia's energy industry and the virtual collapse of the former Soviet economy together have produced the equivalent of an economic blockade of Ukraine. For their part, Ukrainians are all too ready to interpret Russia's inability to manage its own economy as deliberately hostile behavior. The paper shortage, for instance, has affected all the successor states, contributing to even *Pravda*'s temporary closing in early 1992; for many Ukrainians it appeared to be a Russian plot to destroy Ukraine's democratic press.[10]

Economic Dilemmas

The legacy of Soviet economic development is not all bad. Ukraine's population is highly educated, many of its scientists are world-class, urban transport is more than adequate, agriculture is potentially very productive, and the industrial base is quite large. But the system of higher education is recognized as being in need of an overhaul; Ukraine's agriculture is woefully inefficient since alarming amounts of produce are lost en route to markets; consumer goods are shoddy; worst of all perhaps, the vast majority of its plants and factories are incapable of producing things of value by world standards. Indeed, much of Ukraine is a large and heavily polluted rustbelt, like Polish Silesia, northwestern Bohemia, and parts of eastern Germany.

The decaying Donbas, with its thoroughly inefficient coal mines, is especially worrisome. In the short term, the region might play a positive role by supplying Ukrainian industry with some of the raw materials it cannot buy abroad because of either hard currency shortfalls or disrupted trade links with Russia and Kazakhstan. If and when interrepublic trade relations improve, however, and comparative economic advantage begins to assert itself as a policy principle, Donbas coal may become an economic burden and environmental blight that Ukraine cannot afford. Cleaning up and modernizing the area, however, will be socially disruptive because of inevitable job cutbacks and retooling, politically destabilizing (recall the clout of miners in Poland, Russia, Romania, and South Africa), and financially prohibitive. Moreover, because the work force is largely Russian or Russified, ethnic considerations will combine with economics to prevent Kiev from pursuing market-oriented solutions to the Donbas's woes single-mindedly.

The dilemmas facing Kiev appear even more acute in light of Ukraine's energy needs; 22 percent of those needs are currently met by ten nuclear power stations,[11] most of which, fortunately, are not of the alarmingly unreliable type found in Chernobyl. Closing down some stations may be environmentally impera-

132   tive—all of them are unsafe by Western standards—and politically attractive, but this is economically impossible, as Ukraine has few other untapped energy resources. Even Chernobyl is slated to remain in operation for the foreseeable future: a walk down Kiev's darkened streets at night suggests why. The breakdown in oil production in Russia and Moscow's desire that petroleum eventually be paid for in hard currency and at world prices have further intensified the economic woes of Ukraine and the other republics. Ukraine produces only 58 percent of its primary fuel, so Kiev is actively seeking external solutions to what is in fact an energy crisis. Ukrainian metal, petrochemicals, and perhaps arms are being exchanged for fifty million tons of Iranian oil; plans are also afoot for a pipeline to be built from Iran.[12]

Ukraine's economic problems, even without consideration of the massive challenges that marketization represents, are formidable. What, then, should Ukraine do? The short and easy answer is a sweeping, rapid transformation, but how exactly is this miracle to be brought about? Although no one, not even Western economists, really knows, one fact does appear certain: if a successful transition to the market is to occur—even if we define success as entailing massive unemployment and other severe hardships—it can do so only *within* Ukraine, perhaps by cooperating with the other successor states in a customs or payments union, but not within a resuscitated economic union.

AN ECONOMIC UNION?

Although the argument for resurrecting an economic union among the post-Soviet states is attractive, it is unrealistic and could even subvert the very reforms it is meant to bring about. The reality of post-Soviet economic life is marked by two facts. First, interrepublican economic relations are either in disarray or, as with the Commonwealth of Independent States, nonexistent. And second, fledgling postcolonial republican institutions have remained intact, while assertive republican elites have emerged.

These constraints must be taken into account in any serious **133** discussion of economic reform.

The central implication is that economic associations and economic reforms cannot work on the basis of the Commonwealth as a whole. Because the economy is in shambles, to insist on the greater economic rationality of larger, common economic spaces—insofar as they enhance coordination, reduce transaction costs, and permit economies of scale, among other things—is to impose economic categories, which may make great sense in a functioning economic setting, such as that of Western Europe, but make no sense when grafted onto the economic equivalent of a Hobbesian state of nature. Larger economic spaces are optimal only after a certain level of development has been reached. But the former republics have yet to reach that level, and it is uncertain whether the post-totalitarian legacy will permit them to do so soon.

Ongoing debates over broadening or deepening the European Community are instructive. Notwithstanding the political rationale for bringing in the Central Europeans, it is unquestionably true that the vast differences between the economies of, say, Poland and France immeasurably complicate the task of economic integration. By the same token, the West Europeans agreed at their conference on European integration in Maastricht, the Netherlands, in late 1991 that the economic policies and performance even of individual EC members must first be brought into line before monetary unification could occur later in the decade, lest the irresponsibility of one country harm the economies of the others. If even the far more developed West is concerned about the possible repercussions of premature unification—and the currency crisis that befell Western Europe in the fall of 1992 indicates that such concern is fully warranted—then the case for a Soviet economic space appears baseless.

The reform experience of Poland and Hungary offers another important lesson. Had they remained bound to some coordinating economic mechanism in Moscow, they almost certainly would *not* have embarked on genuine economic reform. Their own thinking

134 was ahead of that of the Kremlin, which would have held them back. More important, successful coordination could have ensued only if Russia were endowed with the authority to coerce Poland and Hungary to submit to painful policies. But, under post-Soviet conditions, a centrally coordinated economic mechanism, as opposed to a voluntary association such as a free-trade zone, would, in order to be genuinely effective, have to be the sole repository of sovereignty as well—a requirement that is not only impossible to fulfill but also unacceptable to the sovereign successor states.

The Absence of Resources

Even if we assume that the case for economic integration is strong, under post-totalitarian conditions, integration would actually guarantee the failure of radical economic reform. First, the economic and political overhaul Western economists recommend can succeed only if there are vast resources—whether coercive, material, or normative—available to induce or compel individuals to go along with the transformation and not attempt to resist or abort it. Second, the closer the relations between and among formerly Soviet republican economic institutions and actors, the greater their incentive to continue with business as usual and to avoid change.

With regard to resources, coercion is not an option, both because of the West's insistence that human rights be respected and, as the failed coup proved, because it could not be applied effectively anyway. Material resources are minimal, perhaps even nonexistent, in a collapsing economic environment, and there seems little chance that the vast sums required by reform—perhaps several times as much per year as Bonn is investing annually in eastern Germany—will be forthcoming from the West. Certainly the inability of Poland, the former Czechoslovakia, and Hungary to break through to Western markets and acquire more than token assistance augurs poorly for the former Soviet Union.

All that leaves, then, is what might be called normative resources: appeals to legitimacy, patriotism, and the like. These do exist in Poland, the Czech Republic, and Hungary, because each of these countries can claim to be pursuing a national revival, an **135** anti-imperial cause, and an anti-Communist struggle. Although their economies are only marginally less decrepit than those of most of the republics, these three states can countenance and even embark on radical reform because their governments possess reserves of legitimacy that permit them to encourage citizens to submit to economic ordeals voluntarily. As Poland's difficulties with pushing through radical reform suggest, however, even legitimacy may not be enough. But if there is any legitimacy in the former Soviet Union, it is to be found only within the successor states. Like Estonia, Latvia, and Lithuania, S. Ukraine, Belarus, Russia, and other republics represent promising experiments with national independence, cultural revival, and democratic transitions. Nothing of the sort can be said of the CIS, which cannot command significant loyalty, or of a forcibly reconstituted Russian empire.

REPUBLICAN ELITES

The collapse of interrepublic economic relations, while devastating for popular well-being, also represents an irreversible breakdown of the Soviet command economy and is probably the best incentive for republican elites to consider serious reform. Were the economy to be reintegrated and coordinated in the manner that some economists suggest, the incentives for the untrained, unskilled, and formerly Communist elites of the successor states to continue with past practices would be irresistible. The collapse of the imperial economy not only forces them to apply their own ingenuity and initiative to immediate economic needs, but also permits them to follow the politically expedient path of blaming their troubles on a vanished empire, which can reduce popular pressure at a time of hardship. There is, then, a potent economic rationale for reducing relations between and among republics until they pursue reform. Once they begin creating market economies, self-interest will push them to reestablish economic ties with one

136   another, but on the basis of economic rationality, not political expedience.

One more point concerning republican elites deserves to be made. It is not in their personal political interest to surrender their newly acquired powers, and the fledgling democracies over which many now preside will prevent them from doing so. Because their own still shaky legitimacy is so deeply rooted in national revival, and because their authority depends on their ability to prevent the disintegration of republican economies, they will not give up their prerogatives to some nebulous and illegitimate center. The consolidation of democracy in the successor states would actually prevent them from embarking on such a step, even if they desired to do so. Democratic politics are popular politics, and if "the people" reject economic subordination to a center they perceive as imperial and/or Russian, there is little that democratic politicians—especially weak ones in weak democracies—can do. Ukraine in particular is so supportive of sovereignty and so mistrustful of a junior partnership with an "elder brother" inclined to be a Big Brother that any association involving the creation of authoritative central institutions with the power to override Ukrainian ones would simply be impossible. No genuinely democratic, or career-minded, Ukrainian leader can take the risk of alienating most political elites and the public.

Mistrust of Russia does not preclude trade and cooperation, however, as long as they take place on equal and fair terms. Former Russian Prime Minister Yegor Gaidar's suggestion in May 1992 that Ukraine pay world prices in hard currency for Russian energy if it left the ruble zone was thus exactly the kind of Russian leadership Ukrainians and other non-Russians resent and reject.[13] Gaidar's warning assumed the priority of Russian economic interests, put Ukraine in a no-win situation, and dismissed alternative solutions, such as a payments union, even from consideration. Most disturbing from the Ukrainian point of view was that explicitly linking the manner of payment to Ukraine's disavowal of its own national currency appeared to be an intended affront to Ukrainian dignity precisely because a payments union would have

permitted both Russia to stop subsidizing Ukraine with cheap **137**
energy and Ukraine to retain its symbols of sovereignty.

ECONOMIC REFORM IN UKRAINE

But even if reform can take place only within the successor states,
are they, especially Ukraine, capable of the kind of change that
the times demand? In light of the Ukrainian elite's lack of expertise—the former Communists still tend to think in "command-
administrative" terms, while the present democrats have only a
vague understanding of what the market actually involves—the
answer appears to be "no." The number of Ukrainian economists with any understanding at all of real economics may be less
than ten.

Not only do Ukrainian elites lack economic expertise, but
Ukraine lacks the economic institutions and procedures needed
even to run, let alone reform, its economy. The Ministry of
Finance is merely a collection of clerks used to taking orders from
Moscow and little else; the National Bank was established only in
March 1991 and, despite its pretentions to being the country's
central bank, has insignificant currency reserves; the budget process is undefined, and the budget itself is largely an ad hoc shopping
list; there is no coherent and effective system of taxation; customs
and duties are virtually nonexistent; economic data are either
inaccurate or incomplete; and, last but not least, no real currency
is in place. In sum, Ukraine, like most postcolonial states, lacks all
the resources, mechanisms, and means required for economic
policymaking, or even policymaking in general.

Not surprisingly, the Ukrainian government did little on
economic reform in 1992. Until the August 1991 coup, most
political elites probably did not think of independence as a serious
option; their primary concern was winning greater authority from
the reluctant Gorbachev. Thereafter, the main task was to push
through the referendum on independence. It is, thus, only since
December 1991 that the Ukrainian government could have been
expected to develop an economic reform program. Even so, it is

138   still striking how little genuine economic thinking, even of a wild-eyed variety, was to be found within the corridors of power in Kiev in the months following independence. Communist clerks-turned-nationalist policymakers were still unduly troubled by private entrepreneurship, or what they called "speculation," ruinous taxes were still being imposed on private businesses, the relationship among prices, supply, and demand was still uncertainly grasped, and the intricacies of banking remained almost a complete mystery.

In general, the Ukrainians formulated their economic policies in response to those implemented in Moscow, which, having toyed with reform since 1987, had a five-year headstart on Kiev. Despite their ultimate ineffectiveness, the many economic reform programs developed under Gorbachev at least addressed certain key issues: private enterprise and private property, the excess rubles in circulation, economic overcentralization, state subsidies to inefficient enterprises, and banking. Russian economists, such as Grigorii Yavlinsky, Stanislav Shatalin, and Gaidar, have been dealing with questions that Ukrainians and most other non-Russians, with the exception of the Estonians, have only just discovered. Small wonder that the Yeltsin administration was able to formulate a reform package in 1991, while most of the other successor states were still groping in the dark.

Coupons and Currencies

The case of the coupons, introduced in mid-January 1992, is an excellent example of Ukraine's reactive economic policymaking. The Yeltsin government had already announced in the fall of 1991 that it would adopt a radical economic reform involving the liberalization of prices. Preoccupied with its own political concerns, Kiev barely responded. After the December 8, 1991, signing of the Commonwealth agreement in Minsk, Russia restated its intention to proceed with economic reform. At this point Ukraine, Belarus, and other states panicked and begged Moscow to delay the reform. Yeltsin agreed to wait—but only for two weeks. Thus, the price rise of early January 1992 found the

Ukrainians completely unprepared. Russia did not help matters by **139** failing to supply Ukraine with the requisite amount of rubles needed to absorb some of the shock of huge price increases. Still, in response to the liberalization of prices in Russia, Ukraine felt obliged to raise its own prices while introducing coupons to alleviate the cash shortage and to protect the Ukrainian market, in which prices of agricultural and other products were generally lower than in Russia, from Russian consumers.

In time, the coupon developed into a second currency, squeezing out the ruble, which Ukrainians, in turn, began dumping on the Russian and Moldovan markets, thereby contributing to inflation in those two republics. But since the Soviet currency continued to exist alongside the coupon—after all, the ruble remained the unit of accounting between firms, while the coupon was supposed to function only as a cash supplement—Ukraine quickly came to possess not just two currencies but, if one includes the dollar, three. There ensued uncertainty, speculation, a further reduction in the already deteriorating relations of Ukraine's factories with their suppliers and buyers in the other republics, and a contraction in trade that further lowered living standards. Worse still, as the government printed coupons to cover debts, the coupon quickly lost its value against the ruble, with the result that its protective function broke down as well and hyperinflation became a reality.[14]

Even if a Ukrainian currency had not been desirable before the introduction of the coupons, it became so thereafter. Only a single monetary unit can reduce uncertainty, restore consumer confidence, return some order to accounting, and provide for financial stability, assuming that prices are genuinely freed. But a currency is no panacea. Whether or not the hryvnia, as the Ukrainian currency is called, will actually have such beneficial effects depends on the monetary and fiscal policies of the government. Uncontrolled printing of hryvnias, together with easy credit, deficit spending, and unbalanced budgets, would only repeat Russia's mistakes and bring about a hyperinflation that would destroy the economy and discredit the currency. Kiev,

140   fortunately, appreciated this danger. In late 1992, when Ukraine officially left the ruble zone, the government refrained from introducing the hryvnia prematurely and instead chose to retain the coupon, rechristened the karbovanets, as a temporary currency.

Agriculture and Industry

Although many Ukrainian nationalists see only the symbolic importance of a national currency, most policymakers do at least appreciate that many other reforms must accompany the creation of the hryvnia. Of these, decollectivizing farms, privatizing small enterprises, shops, and restaurants, and encouraging entrepreneurship in the service and trade sectors are the easiest to introduce and would bring immediate benefits to hard-pressed Ukrainian consumers. Despite the lack of significant progress in 1992, privatization at least appeared to be on the agenda of Leonid Kuchma, who was appointed prime minister in October of that year.

Land reform is especially critical at a time of food shortages, but how far it can go in Ukraine is uncertain since the village population is elderly and understandably risk-averse; capital, fuel, seed, and machinery are still mostly allocated by state-run distribution systems that favor collective and state farms over private ones; and collective farm chairmen have powerful incentives to sabotage wholesale decollectivization. Even so, merely increasing the size of private plots, which already produce large proportions of vegetables, eggs, and other foodstuffs, would have a great impact on food production. And growing urban unemployment may incline some younger workers to return to their villages.

Russia's difficulties with privatizing agriculture and Armenia's relative successes are both important for assessing Ukraine's chances. By mid-1992, Russia had some 100,000 private peasant farms, while Armenia, which is 0.17 percent Russia's size, had some 1.5 times as many.[15] The size and complexity of the Russian economy and the persistence of Armenian peasant entrepreneurship may account for Armenia's lead over Russia. If so, then the outlook for Ukraine is mixed. The agriculturally more important eastern Ukraine, whose peasantry was crushed in the **141** 1930s, will probably lag behind western Ukraine, whose peasants have retained some of the productive habits they acquired under Austrian and Polish rule.

As tiny Hungary's and giant China's successful transitions to private agriculture show, however, the problems Ukraine and the other successor states face go beyond size, complexity, and initiative. Budapest and Beijing embarked on agricultural reform while their economies were still intact. Overall production had not broken down, supplies of vital goods could be assured, and the economic system continued to function. None of these conditions exists in the former Soviet Union, where demoralized peasants are being encouraged to risk their livelihood and take a leap of faith under economic conditions that are anything but stable, predictable, and normal. To be sure, some especially enterprising peasants will take the plunge, but the vast majority will probably prefer the certainty of a tolerable, if hardly comfortable, existence in a collective farm to the possibility of catastrophe on their own.

Private entrepreneurship in the cities will not be able to flourish unless industry is demonopolized and the stranglehold on the economy of organized criminal gangs, often intimately connected to former Communist functionaries, is broken. Freeing prices makes little sense under such a scenario because monopolist firms will respond—and have responded—by raising prices and reducing supply. The largest challenge facing all post-Soviet states—including the former German Democratic Republic, which experienced major labor unrest in 1992, especially in the ship-building industry in Mecklenburg-Vorpommern—is thus heavy industry, which employs a high percentage of the urban population. Closing down unproductive plants may be economically rational, but it is sure to be so disruptive socially as to be almost unimaginable politically. Selling off industry is hard, as even the Treuhandanstalt, the German agency responsible for privatizing the east German economy, has learned. The economic difficulties involved in investing in Ukraine are still too great to attract more than a few foreign firms, those large enough to take

142   risks and focus on the long term, such as Johnson & Johnson, R. J. Reynolds, Siemens, and A T & T. Modernizing industry without foreign participation is unlikely in the face of a lack of capital and know-how. Privatizing industry by placing it in the hands of "work collectives"—as the (formerly Communist) Socialist Party of Ukraine recommends—might be the worst possible solution, because it could result in only nominal privatization and, indeed, might guarantee that the new owners, the workers themselves, would do everything possible to prevent reforms that threaten their jobs.

If eastern Germany is a portent of Ukraine's future, a large proportion of Ukrainian industry will have to shut down during the transition to market relations, resulting in up to 40 percent real unemployment. Public works projects, the likely growth of the private sector, emigration to the West, and reemigration to the countryside will soften the blow, but popular dissatisfaction and suffering will remain dangerously high. And besides, public works projects will have to be limited during a period of supposed fiscal restraint; the private sector may be hampered by the absence of reliable nonstate suppliers of agricultural products (in striking contrast to Poland, whose private farmers were immediately able to sell their goods once prices were decontrolled); the West may not be willing to absorb many immigrants; and the countryside will have limited appeal to urban dwellers. Neither Russian nor Ukrainian miners in the Donbas will accept immiseration passively.

Emergent Entrepreneurship

There may be some good news. Entrepreneurship is appearing at the level of firms, individuals, and provinces. Increasingly, in a development known as "nomenklatura privatization," plant managers in all the former republics are effectively expropriating their factories and reestablishing ties with suppliers and sellers and modernizing their equipment and production processes. Their behavior may be of dubious legality, and it is not inconceivable that they may one day be punished; yet it is also having the

beneficial effect of promoting a kind of grass-roots economic **143**
reform. Of course, a major drawback of such privatization from
below is that it looks like, and arguably is, a form of racketeering.
Plant managers and their formerly Communist cronies in crucial
sectors of the economy and government are grabbing the wealth by
virtue of their having supervised it for so many years. Whether or
not they are so fabulously wealthy as people believe is less important than the facts that most Communists-turned-capitalists are
probably poor entrepreneurs, inclined to compensate for their
incompetence with their rapaciousness, and that popular anger
may one day translate into an understandable desire for retribu-
tion, a desire that could undo the practical good brought about by
such spontaneous expropriations.

Equally significant is the average person's response to economic breakdown: black-marketeering. West Ukrainians have
taken to trading with Poland with a passion; all Ukrainians are no
less assiduously engaging in private exchanges, shady deals, and
moonlighting in order to make ends meet. Ends do meet for most
people—except perhaps for the very poor and the very old—and
despite constant talk of famine, people do have enough to eat.
Informal trade relations with peasants, who appear to be doing
relatively well, play an especially important role in providing for
some continuity in food supplies. While such black market activities may not lay the foundations of a genuine market, they are
alleviating shortages as well as encouraging self-reliance and en-
terpreneurship, which are crucial to the establishment of market
relations.

Bona fide entrepreneurs are also seizing the initiative and,
despite heavy taxes, are providing many of the services that the
Ukrainian economy so sorely needs. Restaurants and cafés, auto-
mobile service stations, commodity exchanges and stock markets,
and advertising firms have already taken root in much of the
country. Some firms, such as Kiev's Biznex, offer consulting advice
to Western companies and Ukrainian policymakers. Others, such
as Lviv's Halimport, traffic in used cars. There are still others,
such as Viktoria-2 in Donetsk, which is planning to construct a

144   supermarket, produce beer, and bottle mineral water.[16] The talent exists, and, despite a less than enthusiastic reception from government bureaucrats, Ukrainian entrepreneurs are poised to assume an even greater role in the transition to market relations.

Finally, the inability of the central government in Kiev to adopt effective economic policies has forced provincial and district authorities to develop strategies for economic survival. The Lviv provincial government is a case in point. Although there are clear limits to how much they can do, the Lviv authorities have managed to keep their oblast above water by developing ad hoc responses to particular economic needs. In 1991, for example, some revenue was raised by imposing customs duties on the flow of products from Poland into Ukraine. An impending food shortage was averted by exchanging, on a barter basis, construction materials for Polish meat. In light of Kiev's paralysis, Lviv's economists have also begun developing elaborate privatization schemes, while the province's peasants lead Ukraine in creating private farms. Other oblasts are responding in a similar manner, with Odessa and the Donbas hoping to become free trade zones and Transcarpathia developing closer relations with Hungary and Slovakia.

The weakness of the Ukrainian state is thus something of a boon for the country. Incapable of extending their authority, the incompetent state bureaucracies at the center are in effect compelling local officials to cope on their own, even when, as is so often the case with former Communist apparatchiks, the locals might prefer business as usual, that is, doing nothing. The resulting economic regionalism may not work to every province's advantage, but, for the foreseeable future, it will surely play a crucial role in enabling Ukraine to weather the economic crisis.

ALTERNATIVE APPROACHES

How, then, should the Ukrainian economy be reformed? In the final analysis, Ukrainian policymakers must choose between embarking on macroeconomic stabilization, economic liberalization, and structural reform rapidly and more or less simultaneously, or cautiously and sequentially. Most Western economists agree that **145** the command administrative system must be felled in one blow— in true neo-Bolshevik fashion!—and that only then can a market be created. The costs of such a Big Bang, or even Little Bang, would be enormous: a massive contraction of productive capacities; huge price rises on all products and services with, one hopes, eventual stabilization; massive unemployment; and a radical, if temporary, drop in living standards. Political scientists might add that conditions of such extensive stagflation would also be likely to breed strikes, social tensions, ethnic conflict, political instability, dictatorial ambitions, military interventions, and so on—not immediately, as the cases of Poland and Russia might suggest, but in due time, as tensions accumulate, compound one another, and eventually lead to an explosion.

The alternative approach involves introducing the above measures slowly, sequentially, haltingly, and deliberately, with one eye to economic reform and the other to social peace and political stability. Many economists decry this approach as unworkable; a command administrative economy, they say, is so tightly intermeshed that partial and/or sequential reforms would be absorbed and reduced to ineffectiveness, with the result that economies will continue to contract and social and political instability will erupt anyway.[17] To this, other economists respond that some elements of economic reform, like some elements of political and social reform, are preconditions of other elements and so must be introduced first.[18] In other words, sequencing is logically inevitable and practically imperative with regard both to reform in general, a point made in chapter 2, and to the economy alone. Just as transitions to the market may occur only if certain political and social preconditions are present, so certain elements of market reform must precede others even when those political and social preconditions already are at hand.

Perhaps the neo-Bolshevik economists are right and their neo-Menshevik opponents are wrong: from an exclusively economic point of view, it may indeed by desirable to do everything immediately rather than some things sequentially. The legacy of

146   totalitarian ruin suggests otherwise, however. Because the economies, polities, and societies of the successor states are in shambles, it is incorrect to think that piecemeal economic reforms will be absorbed by "the" system, as they were in the past when undertaken by Communist reformers. The totalitarian system no longer exists, and the task facing reformers cannot be to transform it, but to escape its legacy of ruin altogether by creating things—markets, civil societies, democracies, and states—that do not yet exist. Moreover, it is highly unlikely that democratic governments will commit political suicide, and thereby usher in military takeovers or civilian dictatorships, by ruthlessly pursuing revolutionary reform. Poland's difficulties with radical economic reform are surely instructive. No less instructive is eastern Germany, which cannot resist Bonn's radically transformative policies to a large degree because most of its former elites have been purged for past association with the secret police, the Stasi.

The countries of Eastern Europe, and in particular the Soviet successor states, face a genuine dilemma. If they impose excruciating pain on their populations and do not waver in their commitment to such impositions, they cannot remain responsive to their populations and therefore be democratic in any meaningful sense of the word. Alternatively, if they remain responsive, they will have difficulty imposing such pain. It seems, then, that the post-Soviet states may have to choose between rapid economic reform with all its putative benefits and political dictatorship, and sequential economic reform with all its putative drawbacks and political democracy. So far, Poland, Hungary, the Czech Republic, and Russia appear to be muddling through on both counts, but soon they will have to go in one of the two directions.

A THIRD WAY?

The case for only some economic reform and only some democracy, at least with respect to Ukraine, is not unpersuasive. Dictatorial republics are likely to be aggressively chauvinist states, a development that would herald a revival of Russian imperialism

and a reversion in Eastern Europe to the policies of the interwar **147**
period. A dictatorial Ukraine, meanwhile, would probably mean
an end to the interethnic rapprochement negotiated by Rukh and
continued by the Kravchuk government. It could spell the end of
ethnic peace between ethnic Russians and Ukrainians and between both and ethnic Jews. Finally, a dictatorial Ukraine, like a
dictatorial Russia, would be most unlikely to inspire the kind of
economic entrepreneurship discussed above, and, as Third World
military dictatorships suggest, to accomplish the transition to
market conditions. Quite the contrary: a Ukrainian or Russian or
Slovak dictator would be hard-pressed not to embark on an alliance with the military-industrial complex. As Soviet citizens
under Brezhnev demonstrated, risk-taking, creativity, and effective policies do not happen by decree. If the political climate is not
conducive to free thinking, then neither is it likely to be conducive to the creation of free markets. That being the case, while
markets may be preconditions for democracy, political freedom
may be no less of a precondition for the economic entrepreneurship without which even incipient markets cannot survive.

As Kravchuk and Yeltsin appear to understand, all good
things do not go together, especially in light of the totalitarian
legacy. For policymakers to pretend otherwise is to invite disaster
in the forms of frustrated expectations and an antidemocratic and
antimarket backlash. If promoting democracy and human rights is
also important, then there simply must be an alternative to the
extraordinary dislocations that a Big or even a Little Bang promises. And that alternative must recognize the importance of freedom—of speech and of association—not only as a value in and of
itself, but also as an ingredient of the very market Ukrainian,
Russian, and other policymakers dream of creating in their countries. If, however, there really is no such alternative, if the economic tailspin in the former Soviet Union can be halted only
through the massive disruption of human existence, then the West
will have no choice but to prepare itself for the inevitable break-
downs in democracy, violations of human rights, and, perhaps,
emergence of Communist-fascist alliances that aspire to impose a
post-Weimar stabilization on Russia, Ukraine, and other states.

148   Needless to say, such a scenario would also spell the end of reform and would usher in a period of enormous political instability and international insecurity.

Is there such an alternative? The eminent British economist Alec Nove argues that the most sensible "third way" between immediately introducing laissez-faire market relations and doing nothing is a policy of government intervention in key sectors of the economy—in other words, an industrial policy.[19] Like the countries of Western Europe after World War II, the Soviet successor states have experienced the equivalent of war with all its attendant economic consequences. And like the West Europeans, Russia, Ukraine, and the others have no alternative to rebuilding their economies deliberately and with continued government guidance. If, instead, the successor states adopt the all-or-nothing policies recommended by most Western economists, Russia and Ukraine are doomed to experience continued deindustrialization because of insufficient investment capital, further declines in living standards, and the extreme likelihood of economic collapse, political instability, and social conflict. According to Nove:

> Russia is in a situation very different from that of the Czech republic, especially without Slovakia. But in these countries the transition to a market economy is accompanied by a steep decline in output, in living standards, and in the provision of social services. In all of them the decline in state-financed investments is not and cannot be replaced by private-sector investment. Yet there is a reluctance even to consider an investment *strategy* or industrial *policy*, as if a real capital market already exists.
>
> It is perhaps understandable that from the extreme of total state monopoly and state-party domination the pendulum swings far in the opposite direction. Yet in several countries, Russia in particular, it is hard to see how one can rely on a market mechanism that has yet to be created, while decline accelerates and a new Time of Troubles looms ahead. To create the preconditions for a market economy surely requires action, "interventionism," under conditions of dire emergency analogous to a wartime economy, with the real supply side in such disarray as to render impossible macroeconomic stabilization.[20]

Nove's words of warning should not be dismissed lightly—especially since they overlap so precisely with the imperative conveyed by the legacy of totalitarianism.

CHAPTER 6

Fashioning a
Postcolonial Elite

T he challenges facing Ukraine and the other successor
states are enormous. The task is unprecedented. Never
before have postcolonial elites had to sweep away the
wreckage of totalitarianism and build everything from scratch.
Native elites have been untrained, unskilled, and unprepared for
the tasks of governing countries in all postcolonial settings, but
only the post-Soviet elites must also overcome a seventy-year
totalitarian legacy that did not just distort, in classical colonial
fashion, the polities, societies, economies, and cultures inherited
from pre-Soviet times but actually destroyed them. Indian elites
inherited British political institutions; Algerian elites could draw
on an intact society; even black South Africans are in a compara-
tively better position, since existing white institutions can be
opened to them.

Although Ukrainians are in general highly educated, especially in the sciences and engineering, they lack a genuine political class and, despite having independent status, a functioning
state. They have politicians, they have clerks, and they have
rabble-rousers, but the quality of the first two—if not, alas, of the
third—leaves much to be desired. Still, Ukraine also has one
considerable asset: a clever and competent president, whose Communist past may prove to be the most salient precondition for
Ukraine's success in consolidating its statehood. Just as it took a
Republican president for the United States to open the door to

150   China, it appears that a Communist president was required to claim Ukraine's independence.

THE RISE OF KRAVCHUK

Leonid Makarovych Kravchuk is a paradoxical—some would even say slippery—figure. Until 1989 Kravchuk was head of the Agitation and Propaganda Department (later renamed, in the more modest spirit of glasnost, the Ideology Department) of the Communist Party of Ukraine. His primary job was to disseminate the ideological directives of his bosses in Moscow and Kiev among the party committees in the republic and to oversee their efforts at instilling the "toiling masses" with the proper Communist spirit. Kravchuk's specialty was "counterpropaganda," which he once defined as the "struggle against bourgeois, opportunist, and revisionist ideology." Kravchuk thus spent at least ten years of his life developing strategies for combating the very goals that he has now embraced.

Kravchuk has undergone a breathtaking political transformation, from guardian of the Soviet state to guardian of the Ukrainian state, from supporter of all things Soviet to critic of all things Soviet, from enemy of Ukrainian nationalism to Ukrainian nationalist par excellence. In 1985, Kravchuk put his name to a lavishly produced coffee-table book, *In a Single Family*, which purported to show how fortunate the Ukrainians were to be the "younger brothers" of the Russians within the "family of the Soviet people." Just seven years later, on January 22, 1992, a date Ukrainian nationalists used to celebrate as their Independence Day, that same Kravchuk joined a group of prominent Ukrainian politicians on Kiev's Saint Sophia Square in singing the Ukrainian national anthem, a song that would have earned its singer a stay in Siberia in 1985.

How did this remarkable change come about? Indeed, has it really come about? Or, perhaps, is Kravchuk merely playing at nationalism? Kravchuk himself claims to have undergone a profound ideological metamorphosis in the course of the last few

years: from an apparatchik who swore by the complete works of **151**
Marx and Lenin, which he has apparently read several times, to a
president who now calls George Washington his hero.[1]
Kravchuk's fence-straddling behavior during the failed August
1991 coup attempt, when he neither openly condemned nor
openly greeted the crackdown, suggests that, even as late as that
date, he may have been less then fully committed to the momentous changes that Ukraine had undergone. If so, his sudden
conversion to unconditional independence in the aftermath of the
putsch would appear to have been dictated by political expedience. As a clever politician well versed in the strategies that life
in a Communist apparatus required, Kravchuk, according to this
version, must have sensed that political survival demanded that he
wrap himself in the blue-and-yellow nationalist flag, defend the
nation wholeheartedly, and adopt the nationalist agenda completely. This alone could have saved him from political disaster.

Not surprisingly, many observers, especially in the West,
have doubted that Kravchuk's commitment to independence was
more than tactical. Many have suspected that he was merely
playing for time and that, at the appropriate moment, he would
make another about-face and attempt to incorporate Ukraine into
a renewed union; indeed, this is exactly how extreme nationalists
reacted to the Commonwealth of Independent States, with some
suggesting that Ukraine's membership was tantamount to "national treason." The accusation, however understandable in light
of the Ukrainian party's past history of kowtowing to the central
authorities, missed the point: Kravchuk clearly understood that he
had no future outside an independent Ukraine. Not only was
popular sentiment for secession strong, not only were Russian
policymakers such as Yeltsin and Rutskoi making seemingly irredentist claims on the Crimea and other Ukrainian regions popu-
lated by ethnic Russians, but as September, October, and
November 1991 passed, it also became increasingly clear that even
the Bush administration was ready to accept Ukraine as an independent state. Under conditions like these, Kravchuk would have

152   been a fool not to have understood that his fortunes lay with Ukraine's independence.

Kravchuk and his comrades then mobilized the former party apparatus, which still enjoyed substantial residual influence in the countryside and in the Russian-speaking industrial provinces of eastern and southern Ukraine, for the cause of independence. Although it is highly probable that a majority—perhaps 65 percent of the population—would have voted for independence anyway, the party's authority largely accounts for the fact that those doing so exceeded 90 percent. The party machine did not quite save the day, but it surely made the victory resounding—something that the democrats, with their undeveloped organizations and weak financial base, could not have done.

Kravchuk the Patriarch

Since the referendum Kravchuk has completely adopted the mantle of defender of the Ukrainian state and of the "people of Ukraine." Surprisingly, he has proven masterful at the job. To be sure, Kravchuk, together with the entire postindependence government headed by the former prime minister, Vitold Fokin, had little to say about economic reform throughout 1992. More likely than not, Kravchuk had no clear sense of what should be done about the economy: his degree in Marxist-Leninist political economy did not equip him to understand how actual economies function. Nor could one have expected much more from Fokin, who spent almost twenty years working on the Ukrainian SSR State Planning Committee. It may be more important that Kravchuk has come to play the role of father figure, of the wise and calm patriarch able to heal wounds, to unite the people, and to provide some sense of purpose. Whether or not such talents will suffice in the long run is another question. For the time being, however, Kravchuk is probably the only individual who can project, without necessarily actually possessing, the leadership qualities imputed to Lech Walesa or Václav Havel. As such, Kravchuk is the best that Ukraine can hope for at this stage of its development: an opportunist to be sure, but one whose personal opportunism was also opportune for a population uncertain of its identity, **153** its interests, and its future.

Kravchuk looks especially good compared with his anti-Communist critics. His many years in the party helped smooth the transition to independence in a manner that would have been impossible for his opponents in the presidential race, the most competitive of whom, Vyacheslav Chornovil and Levko Lukyanenko, were former dissidents and well-known nationalists since the 1960s. Kravchuk's past is reassuring to those people with mixed feelings about Ukrainian independence, Ukrainian national identity, or capitalism. Only Kravchuk could have gotten away with a televised speech in mid-January 1991 in which he accused the Moscow leadership of imperial ambitions and great-Russian chauvinism. Coming from a former party apparatchik, his words, "There is a Ukrainian state. There is a people of Ukraine. And they must be defended,"[2] seemed measured and reasonable; coming from Chornovil or Lukyanenko, they would have been considered extremist. While Chornovil and Lukyanenko were the clear favorites of the nationally conscious and/or fully anti-Communist population, Kravchuk could also claim to appeal to large segments of undecided voters, and, due to his skillful appropriation of nationalist rhetoric, symbols, and agenda, to the nationalists as well. Indeed, his election campaign was a masterful political performance, one most Western politicians could envy. He won 62 percent of the vote.

Kravchuk's image and style are key. His television presence is especially noteworthy. He always speaks in measured tones, as if he were a kind but stern high school principal, distinctly, unhurriedly, and rarely with passion. Often he repeats words, phrases, or entire sentences for effect. Evidently, many years of developing the Communist ideological line taught Kravchuk something about the art of public speaking. Even his personal appearance stands out. With his white hair and dark-rimmed glasses, he bears an uncanny resemblance to an owl—impassive, wise, and somewhat comical, but never frightening or threatening.

154   Naturally, he is not without his faults. Although his handling of the Ukrainian army and the Black Sea Fleet must ultimately be considered a policy success for Kiev, it also provoked chauvinist circles in Russia and the Crimea, thereby reducing Yeltsin's maneuverability and thus that of Ukraine as well. Perhaps responding to domestic pressure, Kravchuk has become unnecessarily blunt in his criticism of Russia—criticism that Russian policymakers often deserve, but which still does little to resolve genuine Russo-Ukrainian differences or to improve Ukraine's image in the world. Kravchuk's major flaw, however, is his growing intolerance of domestic criticism. This may even prove to be a fatal flaw, since Kravchuk's domineering position as president has brought him so much authority and decision-making responsibility that vigorous criticism by the media remains one of the few genuine contributions into the policy process by outsiders. Although Kravchuk probably fancies himself the de Gaulle of Ukraine, its postimperial and post-totalitarian legacies threaten to reduce his Gaullist pretensions to risible dimensions and make of him instead Ukraine's Mobutu.

Kravchuk's Transformation

Although Kravchuk's conversion to independence may have been an act of some political expedience, his rethinking of communism and of Ukraine's position within the USSR appears to have been sincere. It began during the first years of Gorbachev's reign and culminated in Kravchuk's election as chairman of the Supreme Soviet of a sovereign Ukraine in mid-1990. Kravchuk's conversion to independence was thus not quite a bolt from the blue but the result of several years' political and ideological realignment.

In 1984 things were quite different. Kravchuk loyally hewed to the party line and could, without any embarrassment, laud the establishment of "political discothèques" in the port city of Mykolaiv, take pride in the fact that over 135,000 people attended courses on such scintillating topics as "Developed Socialism: Problems of Theory and Practice," and betray his aesthetic tastes as unabashedly Brezhnevite:

Literature, the cinema, and theater that expose imperialism and accurately depict the bourgeois way of life play an exceptionally important role in political education. Vitaly Korotich's novel, *The Face of Hatred*, occupies a special place among literary works of this type. This book, based exclusively on documentary material, shows life in America today. The book, which mercilessly exposes the defects in contemporary American society, is relevant today because it gives rise to class feelings and criticism of the inhuman essence of the exploitative way of government. It would be good if our writers wrote many more books like this one.[3]

By 1988, Kravchuk, like Korotich (who, as editor of the Moscow-based magazine *Ogonyok*, was important in promoting glasnost), had changed, even if he had done so by marching in step with Gorbachev's programmatic changes. "Atheist work" should not simply combat religion, but actually interest believers "in our work, our concerns, and our goals in the struggle for socio-economic acceleration."[4] Reflecting the contradictions in Gorbachev's own thinking, Kravchuk recommended that the party "democratize its own agitation and propaganda" and thereby "raise people's social activity" and help resolve the "tasks facing the country at this critical juncture."[5] It was important for all Communists to "learn democracy," Kravchuk noted, and "to remove the gap between the social ideal created by our means of mass information and reality."[6] Kravchuk also supported the party's endorsement of the "development of the independence [*sic*] of Union republics" as part of their "responsibility for the consolidation and development of our multinational state and for the step-by-step perfection of the Soviet federation on the basis of democratic principles."[7]

Although Kravchuk was undergoing a metamorphosis, the obligatory woodenness of his language testifies that he did so within the parameters defined by the party. Even his decision to address the founding congress of Rukh in September 1989 was completely in line with Gorbachev's opening to political opposition. Kravchuk's conciliatory speech was striking less for its substance—for instance, he underlined his opposition to independence—than for its having been made while Volodymyr Shcherbytsky, the hard-line Ukrainian party boss, was still in

156   power. Kravchuk's presentation may have reflected a rift within the Ukrainian party between Shcherbytsky diehards and Gorbachev supporters. This was seemingly confirmed later in September, when a party plenum replaced Shcherbytsky with Volodymyr Ivashko, the party second secretary, responsible for organizational and cadre questions, while promoting Kravchuk to Central Committee secretary. At that point, Ivashko could in all seriousness still claim that

> the main thing for all of us now, in the period of preparations for the 28th CPSU [Communist Party of the Soviet Union] Congress, is to effect a decisive turnabout in the activity of the Party organizations and to strengthen their prestige through real, concrete deeds. Our duty, and I consider this to be extremely important for myself, is to strengthen the ideological and organizational unity of the Party's ranks. Now as never before, it is impermissible to lose the political initiative and drift with the current.[8]

THE TURNING POINT

The year 1990 was a turning point for Kravchuk. On June 4, Ivashko was also appointed chairman of the Ukrainian Supreme Soviet; later in the month, he stepped down as party chief and was replaced by the hard-liner Stanislav Hurenko. Then, just a month later, at the 28th party congress in Moscow, Ivashko abandoned the equivalent of Ukraine's presidency for a job as Gorbachev's second-in-command in the all-Union party. His timing could not have been worse. Rukh was acquiring momentum; the March 1990 elections to the Supreme Soviet had given the democrats a third of the seats and for the first time had confronted the Communist legislature with the popular will; Vilnius had declared independence, and Gorbachev's imposition of an economic blockade on Lithuania was worrisome to all but the most retrograde party members. Russia, whose lead most Ukrainian Communists were used to following, had already declared sovereignty on June 12. So obvious and ill-timed a slap in the face as Ivashko's abandonment of Kiev infuriated even the Communist-dominated Ukrainian legislature, which, taking a cue from the other republics, amazed the world by proclaiming Ukraine's sovereignty on July 16. One

week later, on July 23, Kravchuk became chairman of the Supreme Soviet of an ostensibly sovereign Ukraine.

To everyone's surprise, he became and remained an unconditional supporter of Ukrainian sovereignty—an ambiguous term
that to him may at first have meant only extensive autonomy.
Nevertheless, the concept was sufficiently meaningful for him to
sign a treaty on November 19 with Russian Federation President
Yeltsin; the treaty recognized Ukraine and Russia as sovereign
states that would live in harmony, accept existing borders, and
forswear interference in each other's internal affairs. That
Kravchuk thought of sovereignty in almost nationalist terms became even clearer in the course of 1991, when he repeatedly
insisted that Gorbachev's schemes of renewed union give priority
to the republics, rather than Moscow. Kravchuk may still not have
supported independence, but his own vision of the future of the
USSR appears to have approximated some form of confedera-
tion—a remarkable shift for a former party functionary to have
made.

Why the shift? Opportunism alone does not suffice as an
answer. Clearly, Kravchuk began as a mouthpiece, if not committed supporter, of glasnost and perestroika. As chief of ideology, he
had to follow the Moscow line. By 1989 at the latest, however, he
appears to have become an actual supporter of Gorbachev's new
course. Then, in 1990, he was catapulted into an honorific position, chairman of the Ukrainian Supreme Soviet, under a condition—sovereignty—for which he was probably unprepared. And
it is this position, in combination with the evolving circumstances, that appears to have moved Kravchuk increasingly toward
a nationalist line. A popularly elected parliament with a vocal
nationalist opposition, a power struggle with the reactionary
Hurenko, student strikes in Kiev in the fall of 1990, the Kremlin's
lurch to the right in late 1990, and Gorbachev's obvious inability
to extricate the country from chaos were sufficient incentives for
Kravchuk to defend Ukraine and its sovereignty. Where Kravchuk
was sitting more or less determined where he stood. In this sense,
the August 1991 coup may have been an unwelcome disruption of

158   his routine, but it is hard to believe that Kravchuk could really have hoped for its success: that would have meant rolling back all the authority and prestige he had personally accumulated since 1990. There was surely a substantial element of opportunism in Kravchuk's evolution and conversion to independence, but also an element of genuine ideological rethinking and actual responsiveness to changing political realities. It is likely that while many of Kravchuk's comrades got on the independence bandwagon out of sheer self-interest and opportunism, many also underwent the same transformation as Kravchuk and share a more or less sincere commitment to independence.

Explaining Kravchuk's Success

One question remains: Why has Kravchuk, a party apparatchik from a Brezhnevite mold, been so successful in appropriating the nationalist agenda? Why does his nationalism look so natural? How does he make being president of an independent Ukraine look so easy? The answer, ironically, lies in Kravchuk's many years as counterpropaganda strategist and, perhaps, in his Volhynian roots.

Inured to the intricacies of the Soviet ideological world, Kravchuk was uniquely qualified to understand the complexities of the situation created by perestroika's devastating impact on the Communist way of life. At a time of meaningless symbols and terminological confusion, at a time of such complete uncertainty, Kravchuk's many years of staging Communist verbal pyrotechnics were particularly well suited to guiding him through the political and linguistic maze that had developed since 1987. Kravchuk could make sense of the emerging reality, because he was so well equipped for reading the signals that were emanating from all sectors of the polity and society. He could comprehend all signals because he had spent ten years of his life developing the signals of communism and combating those of nationalism. For Kravchuk to have switched languages in the course of the turbulent events of the last five years was thus easier than it might seem. Kravchuk appears to be a committed nationalist not because he is (although **159** of course he may be) but because he knows how to *sound* like one.

Kravchuk knew the agenda of nationalism as well as the nationalists, somewhat resembling in this regard those KGB officials who, knowing the truth about their country, are reputed to have been among perestroika's staunchest supporters. By contrast, his nationalist and Communist opponents, or for that matter Gorbachev, could read only one set of signals, their own. It may be noteworthy in this regard that Kravchuk's origins are in Volhynia, a region of the western Ukraine and the site of an anti-Nazi nationalist revolt in the early 1940s. Unlike someone from the sovietized parts of the country, say the Donbas, Kravchuk must have heard of the armed nationalist movement, the Organization of Ukrainian Nationalists and the Ukrainian Insurgent Army; he may well have known their language and arguments, and understood their mentality. We may be certain that Kravchuk sincerely rejected nationalism; but unlike Gorbachev, who still has not fully understood that the Soviet Union had a massive nationality problem, Kravchuk must have known that nationalism was a potent, and potentially popular, force with which the Communist regime had to reckon.

UKRAINIAN ELITES

Unlike Kravchuk, who has proved himself a master of post-independence Ukrainian politics, other Ukrainian political figures—typified by the somnolent former prime minister, Fokin—have performed more disappointingly. It is this problem, perhaps more than any other, that threatens to torpedo any serious economic and political reform in the country. There are, of course, exceptions to this rule. Anatoly Zlenko, the foreign minister, is a genuine diplomat, and many of his employees at the foreign ministry have considerable skills, if only because of their knowledge of Western languages and travel abroad. Volodymyr Vasylenko, a professor of international law at Kiev University, a drafter of the constitution, and Ukraine's representative to the EC

160   and NATO, is an outstanding foreign policy adviser who recognized immediately after independence that nuclear weapons were a major liability for Ukraine. Volodymyr Hrynyov, the presidential candidate of the Party of the Democratic Rebirth of Ukraine, has, like many of his colleagues now grouped in the pro-reform "New Ukraine" movement, excellent ideas about economic change and, as a Ukrainian of Russian descent, also takes a level-headed attitude toward Russia. Kravchuk's State Council, a short-lived body of advisers created in February 1992 to permit the president to sidestep the inefficient government, consisted of such talented individuals as Mykola Zhulynsky, a literary critic who introduced Ukraine to the national Communist writer Volodymyr Vynnychenko, and Oleksandr Yemets, also of the Democratic Rebirth party, a young politician touted by many as Ukraine's most likely next president. Even the reactionary Oleksandr Moroz, the dynamic head of the (formerly Communist) Socialist Party, is, unfortunately, no Fokin, though Ukrainian democracy would certainly be safer if he were equally incompetent.

The list could easily be continued, especially if province- and district-level politicians were to be included. Even so, it would still be too short for the needs of a country of Ukraine's size. Worse still, for every competent policymaker there are many, many more screamingly incompetent ones, and even those that are competent are unfamiliar with policymaking, administration, and diplomacy. The problem is most evident in Kiev's choice of ambassadors, who, through no fault of their own, appear to fit mostly in the second category. For instance, the ambassador to the United States, Oleh Bilorus, has no diplomatic experience, having served until recently as the director of Kiev's International Management Institute. Levko Lukyanenko, the former political prisoner and later presidential candidate, has been appointed to Ottawa. Roman Lubkivsky, a writer, is in charge of the Ukrainian embassy in Prague. Although a biologist by profession, Serhii Komisarenko, who represents Ukraine in the United Kingdom, at least served as deputy prime minister since 1989.

The Question of Fokin

Why, then, did Kravchuk not send a powerful signal of the changing times and their changing requirements to the old and new elites by firing the enervated Fokin immediately, in late 1991? Instead, throughout 1992 the president risked alienating the democratic opposition, without which he knows he cannot rule, by stubbornly refusing even to countenance the dismissal of his incompetent protégé and, to make matters worse, by firing his government's lone reformer, Deputy Prime Minister Volodymyr Lanovy, in midyear. Even if Kravchuk initially thought of Fokin as the best man for the job, surely after two years of inactivity, he cannot have believed that his prime minister was getting anything done: the indications to the contrary were obvious. And it does not make sense to argue, as do some of his critics, that Kravchuk is uninterested in reform, if only because his own political survival ultimately depends on it. The most plausible reason for retaining Fokin may in the end be political: as a Ukrainian-speaking Russian who made his party career in the Donbas and the Gosplan (State Planning Commission), Fokin must have been a reassuring presence to Russians, workers, and apparatchiks. And in light of Kravchuk's own lack of a social base, any help he could get from Fokin was surely much appreciated.

Fokin, then, though finally sacrificed on September 30, 1992 (to be replaced by Leonid Kuchma, the former director of the Pivdenmash armaments plant in Dnipropetrovsk, the world's largest, and an industrial manager who succeeded in converting some of the plant's productive capacities to civilian use), illustrates the limits of Kravchuk's authority. However competent Kravchuk may be, he cannot govern without the support, or noninterference, of existing, established elites—and that means, primarily, former apparatchiks as represented by Fokin or Kuchma. Yet Kravchuk will also be unable to govern effectively if he is too dependent on them. Throughout 1992, his resolution of the dilemma was to create parallel structures of power, in particular the shadow cabinet, the State Duma, and to appeal for an alliance with Rukh.

162   That way, presumably, a Fokin or a Kuchma could stay and their constituencies would remain pacified, while actual reform policies could be pursued and the democratic opposition would assume some responsibility for their outcome.

Kravchuk's calculation was sound, but it proved irrelevant in October 1992, when the reform-oriented Kuchma was appointed prime minister as the candidate of both the democrats and the former communists in the parliament, as well as of its increasingly powerful chairman, Ivan Plyushch. Ukraine's catastrophic economic condition had become so self-evident that all parliamentarians could agree that something had to be done. Kuchma appeared to be ideal for the post—as an industrial manager and a member of the pro-reform New Ukraine movement he appealed to all constituencies. Not surprisingly, Kuchma's appointment represented a certain reduction in Kravchuk's authority. The new prime minister insisted that the State Duma be dissolved, and, after receiving six-month emergency powers from parliament, he proceeded to develop an economic reform package of which even the International Monetary Fund expressed approval.

The Former Communists

The poor performance of Ukrainian political elites is understandable. None of the Ukrainian elites was prepared for postindependence realities. Existing administrators and apparatchiks had for years been accustomed to functioning within a colonial and totalitarian system that permitted little personal initiative. Democrats and nationalists had no experience in working within any type of state administration. For years they had acted as oppositionists: their primary task was to mobilize, to inspire, to persuade, to argue in moral terms. Suddenly, both the formerly Communist elites and the new nationalist elites confronted a radically different reality. Colonial administrators began running a state, while former dissidents had to formulate realistic policies instead of mere slogans. In the manner of postcolonial elites everywhere, both groups are having great difficulties in adapting. Even Václav Havel had so much trouble reconciling his roles as critical intellectual

and president that he felt compelled to resign precisely when a   **163**
unified Czechoslovakia needed him most.

The apparatchiks' Communist training has made them particularly ill-suited for the job at hand. Not only must their mindset shift—from colonial administration to independent rule—but, far more significantly, they have to learn virtually everything about how states are run, policies are made, and bureaucracies are organized. Under Soviet rule, republican state bureaucracies, like the central ones, were shapeless, incoherent organizations that were run by party bosses ruling by telephone. Actual organizational rules and regulations were minimal, as party chiefs ran their organizations—much in the manner of mafiosi—more or less at will. Communist bureaucracies were anything but the Weberian organizations designed to do things effectively, dispassionately, and rationally. With the demise of the party, however, the feeble state institutions were suddenly on their own.

The problem goes even deeper. Communist Party recruitment required aspiring candidates to abandon their creative thinking and succumb to the rule of loutish bosses. The party somehow managed to create a system of anti-Darwinian self-selection, according to which the worst and the dimmest were most inclined to join the party or state apparatus. Those with the least initiative and ambition, the conformists, swelled the ranks of the administrative apparatuses. The result is that not only are the current administrators unaccustomed to working like real bureaucrats, but many of them may actually be incapable of learning to do so.

Symptomatic of the problem is Ukraine's almost complete lack of genuine political scientists, who in most countries of the West form a significant recruitment pool for government elites. The study of politics in Ukraine and other former republics was until recently the exclusive preserve of specialists in Marxism-Leninism, which is to say that politics was not studied. As a result, Ukraine probably has no more than fifty specialists in political science. Even if all of them were to join the state apparatus, Ukraine's needs would obviously be far from met.

164   A third problem is that existing ministries are far too small and resource-poor for a country as large as Ukraine. This, too, is not surprising. The subordination of state organs to the party under Soviet rule meant that the state per se remained undeveloped. Now that the party has been suspended, and its apparatus weakened, if not destroyed, the locus of decision-making has shifted to the state, a structure that is not only unprepared, but also too small and too lacking in the elementary tools of administration—such as paper, typewriters, facsimile machines, not to mention computers—to deal with the demands of the times.

Last, the state apparatus is thoroughly corrupt, a feature with origins in the "era of stagnation" under Brezhnev. State employees are poorly paid, lack a professional ethnic, and control access to abundant but unavailable resources—whether material goods or licenses that provide access to such goods—for which citizens are willing to pay money. Under such conditions the temptation to extract bribes is enormous. The secret police is waging a campaign to root out such venal misbehavior, but it is unlikely to succeed. The former KGB is not above pursuing its own material interests, and police action cannot eradicate the reasons for such widespread corruption. The foregoing suggests that the Ukrainian apparatus, like that of every other republic, may be evolving into the type of parasitical bureaucracy that plagues so much of the Third World.

Nationalists and Democrats

Like their counterparts in the existing ministries, the new democratic nationalist elites were utterly unprepared for the policy-making and administrative tasks required to run a state. Ironically, their inadequacies are mirror images of those of the apparatchiks. Naturally, they, too, are untrained for political life; not because they were cogs in the Communist machine, but simply because their political activity was confined to dissent, producing the underground literature known as samizdat, engaging in protests, and so on. Even the last few years of political mobilization centering on Rukh have largely involved organizing demonstrations, marches, human chains, and other mass events, not governing or administering. The new elites were born in struggle; as the Polish and other East European dissident elites discovered, this experi-ence did not teach them skills appropriate to the very different demands of statecraft and nonconfrontational politics.

The democrats in the Ukrainian parliament, for instance, are excellent critics and oppositionists, but they have few concrete or detailed policies of their own to suggest. "Privatization," for instance, is the panacea universally recommended, but how this is to be implemented, in what sequence, and how quickly are all questions that the democrats, despite their integrity and intel-ligence, are largely incapable of answering. Small wonder, then, that the parliament often assumes the appearance of a debating society, with half the people's deputies, those with Communist sympathies, arguing passionately for inaction, while the other half, those with democratic inclinations, argues just as pas-sionately for action of any kind.

A further complication is that many of the new nationalist elites lack the proper temperament to rule states. In contrast to the mediocre apparatchiks, the nationalists often are strong-willed individuals—as they would have had to be in order to become dissidents and survive the concentration camps—who are psycho-logically disinclined to compromise or to maneuver as Kravchuk has. The natural forum for this kind of politician is not a legisla-ture, but a mass meeting. The "Congress of Ukrainians," held in Kiev on January 22–23, 1992, for instance, proved to be the ideal setting for the demagogic sloganeering of nationalists with little sense of political reality and diplomatic niceties. No less depress-ing was the demagoguery evident at Rukh's February 1992 Third Congress, where vehemently opposed factions slugged it out over the issue of working with Kravchuk or of remaining in the opposi-tion, and just barely managed to avert a schism by creating an unworkable triumvirate. Speeches exhorting listeners only to struggle gloriously, while sometimes vaguely reminiscent of the State of the Union messages of American presidents, are not the stuff of serious political discourse.

166   Like the apparatchiks, the new nationalist elites are far too few in number to take the administration of the state into their own hands. And what is perhaps most unfortunate, like the apparatchiks, the new elites appear also to be taking advantage of the perquisites of power. It is not that they are corrupt; quite the contrary, their honesty appears impeccable. But as power holders, they are beginning to take advantage of their positions to acquire access to scarce goods such as housing, food, travel, and especially cars. The popular response is anger. A Kiev taxidriver caught the spirit: "The democrats are sending their children to Canada, while we get Ukrainian language courses and embroidered shirts!"[9] Such behavior is not surprising, but it is especially problematic in a fledgling political system, the legitimacy of which depends almost entirely on the perceived integrity of the new nationalist elites. In this sense, these elites carry a double burden: not only must they provide the initiative without which the state will not embark on reform, but they must also embroil themselves in the politics of a corrupt caste without having any of the corruption rub off on them.

Finally, in contrast to the apparatchiks, the new elites are splintered and splintering. Formerly united in their opposition to Communism and in their pursuit of independence under the aegis of Rukh, the new elites have followed the path of all broad-based coalitions, such as Poland's Solidarity, Czechoslovakia's Civic Forum, and India's Janata Party, and split into a multitude of small, organizationally unsophisticated, and resource-poor parties. In turn, some of these have also split in a pattern uncomfortably reminiscent of 1917–1919, when party fragmentation prevented the formation of stable coalitions and the implementation of effective policies. Eventually, some groups will merge and others will die, but in the meantime the plethora of self-styled parties, while a healthy sign of the emergence of civil society, could produce political deadlock within the parliamentary opposition. Ironically, what may save the democrats is the fact that the Socialist Party, consisting of some 30,000 former Communists, is

currently the largest and best organized political group, which may **167**
compel the anti-Communists to unify in the years ahead.

Thus far, chances of such a development appear slim. The emergence of a seemingly vigorous prime minister further contributed to dissension within the democratic opposition, as it is inclined to fragmentation after the euphoria of independence was replaced with uncertainty over Ukraine's future. The question of allying itself with the president or remaining in the opposition finally split Rukh in mid-1992, with Chornovil leading the oppositionists and Mykhailo Horyn, Ivan Drach, and Larysa Skoryk opting for support. In early August the schism was formalized with the creation of the Congress of National Democratic Forces, a broad-based pro-Kravchuk and anti-Chornovil coalition that hoped to provide Kravchuk with a solid social base and free him from his dependence on the former apparatchiks, thereby undergirding his achievements in state-building while pushing him on to greater economic reforms. Whether the Congress will survive the contradictory forces buffeting Ukraine is, of course, another issue, one that may even be moot in light of Kuchma's support in Parliament and Kravchuk's correspondingly reduced role.

AUTHORITARIAN TEMPTATIONS

In sum, the Ukrainian political class is inadequate, unprepared, and undersized. It resembles the typical postcolonial political elite of a Third World country, while its problems, those bequeathed to it by three hundred years of colonialism, seventy years of totalitarianism, and seven years of Gorbachev, are far greater than those left to the Third World by its imperial rulers. As argued in chapter 2, it is hard to imagine how Ukraine can create a democracy, a market, and a civil society without something resembling a strong and effective state administration that is willing and able to implement the rule of law on which democracy, civil society, and the market must be based. If so, Ukraine's primary task has to be state-building. But how is a state to be built by people who have little notion of what a state and state-building entail? And how are

168   they to build a state under conditions of economic collapse, social unrest, and political discord? The new and old state elites will be tempted to form a coalition, to place the interests of the corrupt and inefficient state they represent above the interests of the society and economy, and to transform the administrative apparatus into a parasitical pseudobureaucracy that is thoroughly incapable of bringing about real change.

In circumstances like these an authoritative president could be enticed to dominate the weak and inefficient state and to become a genuine strongman. Kravchuk is a skilled politician, but he and many in the parliament perceive presidential rule, along the lines of that exercised by Yeltsin, as optimal for the Ukrainian polity. Their rationale is that tough times require tough decisions, which can be made only by someone independent of pressures from society. The logic might be more persuasive in a setting where strong political institutions and effective state institutions already exist, since they would buffer the state and society from undue pressure by the president. Where such institutions do not exist, however, to endow a president with enormous powers— even if, as many legislators suggest, he remains the head of a coalition government of "national accord"—is to create a potentially authoritarian ruler who may be able to transform parliament into a rubber-stamp institution. Under postcolonial conditions a strong presidency is an open invitation to dictatorial rule, no less in Ukraine and Russia than in Congo and Kenya.

If such rule were only able to bring about effective reform, it might, as some argue, in some sense be justified. In Ukraine as in the other republics, this cannot be taken for granted. If the president could form alliances with technocrats and bureaucrats— as did, say, General Augusto Pinochet in Chile—then, perhaps, he could introduce economic reform by authoritarian means. But that is not an option for Kravchuk because Ukraine lacks the professionals he would need to rule without the parliament and parties. The president could turn, and indeed has turned, to popular movements for support, but even if Rukh were eventually to be interested in such an arrangement, it would be unlikely to last for long. The same conclusion holds true for the Congress **169** of National Democratic Forces, which rejected Chornovil's un-compromising opposition to Kravchuk and hoped to provide the president with a firm popular base. Amorphous mass movements are no long-term substitute for institutions.

Moreover, the Ukrainian state, like Russia, has to live amicably with three of the most powerful post-Soviet institutions: the army, the military-industrial complex, and the former KGB. As both Yeltsin and Kravchuk realize, all three interests have to be pacified. Ukraine's proportionally smaller, less experienced, more disorganized, possibly more patriotic, and far poorer army will be immeasurably less threatening than Russia's, but it, too, may be inclined to demand an excessive share of resources and interfere in politics—especially if Ukrainian society unravels and the conflict with Russia escalates. Such conditions would also lend greater importance to the military-industrial complex and the National Security Service, since both institutions can claim an ability to maintain internal stability and to contribute to national security. Ukrainian policymakers will of course hope that the army, military-industrial complex, and SNBU remain committed to civilian rule, but their support will not come cost-free. Kiev will probably have to buy their loyalty at the expense of the economy and society. If so, the forces of repression would form a symbiotic relationship with the state. Unfortunately, such scenarios, which may become commonplace in many of the USSR's successor states, resemble all too closely what has happened in most post-independence states of Africa and Asia.

Preventing Authoritarian Rule

What then, must be done to prevent such developments from occurring in Ukraine? The challenge is three-pronged. First of all, Ukraine needs a genuine state bureaucracy and political elite. Second, its president, even if the most talented politician in the country, should never become too strong. And third, the Ukrainian army has to be kept on a short leash. How are these tasks to be accomplished? Can they in fact be accomplished?

170   Regenerating the state apparatus will require retraining existing apparatchiks, training genuine bureaucrats, getting rid of the deadwood, reducing corruption radically, and attracting the many talented individuals in society at large to government work. Retraining, though a lengthy process, has already begun. The training of competent civil servants is the expressed goal of Kiev's newly established Institute of State Administration and Ukrainian Lyceum, and of the revived Mohyla Academy, an institution originally founded during Ukraine's early-seventeenth-century cultural renaissance. Removing the incompetents is more difficult. Force cannot be employed, while material incentives, such as early retirement, are costly for bankrupt states. Reducing corruption will be virtually impossible so long as state employees remain underpaid and control access to scarce goods. Raising salaries will be a priority, but how the cash-strapped government is supposed to do this without printing karbovantsi or hryvnias and contributing to inflation is hard to imagine. Reducing bureaucratic control of scarce resources will occur only if the economy is privatized and the state withdraws from both economy and society. This, too, will be a lengthy process. Attracting talented individuals will be difficult so long as state service is perceived as corrupt and incompetent and the material gains from private enterprise or racketeering are much greater than those within government service. At present, for example, those Ukrainians most qualified to join the government apparatus, graduates of Kiev University's prestigious Institute of International Relations, also tend to be the most drawn toward business; their language skills and international training make them ideal candidates for Ukraine's emerging entrepreneurial class. The outlook for a rapid regeneration of the state apparatus is, thus, not bright. Although the situation is sure to improve—after all, sooner or later even the most hidebound Communists can learn something about administration—the prospects for a rapid improvement are dim.

The consequences of President Kravchuk's 1992 reorganization of local government illuminated the glaring weakness of central authority. In a conscious imitation of France, Kravchuk

appointed presidential representatives at both province and dis-   **171**
trict levels, hoping in this manner to assert some central control
over the ineffective organs of local rule—the soviets, or councils.
Kravchuk's move made sense as a state- and authority-building
measure, but it also had several undesirable consequences. First, it
reduced local initiative and risk-taking precisely when both were
at a premium. Although the councils and their executive committees traditionally lacked the authority to collect revenues, initiate
major policies, and govern without the constant interference of
the local Communist Party, chaotic economic and political conditions pushed many of them to take matters into their own hands in
1991 and 1992. Direct accountability to the economically dis-
gruntled population forced the councils to respond to popular
needs, while political disarray at the center meant that there was
little to prevent them from taking the lead. The competence of
local elites is not much higher than that of central elites, but
whereas the latter can always "pass the buck" and do nothing, the
former cannot, at least not quite so easily. But after the introduction of prefects, local officials were given a strong incentive to act
only when Kiev told them to do so. One result of this was that
formerly innovative oblasts such as Lviv lost their spirit and
temporarily joined the ranks of the deadbeats.

Second, because of both the lack of competent local administrators and his own reliance on former apparatchiks, Kravchuk
appointed many former soviet chairmen as his representatives. In
essence, as many of his critics charged, nothing changed: the
incompetent and obstructionist Communist old guard is still in
power, but now it is responsible only to Kravchuk, not to local
popular pressures. Finally, Kravchuk's attempt to assert his authority in the provinces may be doomed precisely because the central
Ukrainian state, unlike the postrevolutionary or Napoleonic
French state, is too weak to extend its control over Ukraine's 25
provinces and 479 districts. If so, then ineffectiveness and frustration are probably inevitable.

The issue of local administration dovetails with the ongoing
debate over Ukraine's optimal administrative organization.

172   Should provinces be retained or should larger size *Lands*—after the German example—be introduced to streamline the administration? Should these units be ruled from the center or should they be autonomous? In other words, should the Ukrainian state be centralized or federal? Proponents of the first course, who take France as their model, argue that centralization is imperative because local apparatchiks cannot be trusted and because potential regional separatisms, of Russians in the Crimea or the Donbas, or of Ruthenians wishing to join Slovakia or Hungary in Transcarpathia, can be controlled only by strict central supervision. Proponents of federalism emphasize that Kiev cannot rule so large a territory on its own and that other multinational states have largely utilized federal systems to contain separatism. Both arguments have merit, but so long as the Crimea remains a bone of contention with Russia, and not just with the Russians of the Crimea, it is unlikely that the federalist approach will get a fair hearing.

The President and the Army

Can the president be put in his place? Once again, the task is daunting. The most effective way to curb his powers would be to introduce a mixed parliamentary political system, within which the president is largely symbolic and real power resides in the hands of a prime minister, who can be recalled by the parliament. Such a system does not necessarily result in weak executive rule so long as the prime minister enjoys a majority in the parliament. There is in principle no reason why that should not be the case, especially if electoral rules keep splinter parties out and most of the votes go to two or three major groupings. The example of Poland illustrates exactly what fledgling democracies should not do: permit all parties—twenty-nine in the case of the Polish Sejm—to enter parliament, thereby creating conditions that, sooner or later, necessarily result in deadlock and perhaps authoritarian rule.

Can the Ukrainians move in the desirable direction? Probably not. There are two formidable obstacles. For one thing,

Kravchuk, who is the dominant figure on the Ukrainian scene, **173**
wants to be a strong president. His preferences cannot be ignored.
For another, the absence of an institutionalized party system
means that, despite Kuchma's emergence as a seemingly dynamic
prime minister, effective parliamentary rule is virtually impossible. Debating societies, miniparties, and squabbling grouplets do
not make for stable parliamentary systems. The composition of the
current parliament suggests that Ukraine still has a long way to go
before it can establish effective institutional counterweights to
presidential rule. In theory, therefore, parliamentary systems may
be best for curbing presidents, but as the emergence of strong
presidents in Poland, Czechoslovakia, Lithuania, Russia,
Uzbekistan, Kyrgyzstan, Georgia, and Ukraine suggests, such systems are premised on effective parties, which none of these countries currently has.

The constitution being drafted in Ukraine foresees the establishment of something akin to a French-type political system, with
a strong president and a strong legislature. Ukrainian elites are
aware of the dangers of Kravchuk's inclinations toward authoritarian rule. As one member of the working group on the constitution put it to me, "How do we keep him from becoming a king?"
But they also appreciate that the realities of political life are such
that his domineering presence, like that of Yeltsin in Russia, and
the absence of effective political institutions, make some form of
strong executive rule virtually inevitable.

Can the armed forces be reined in? Ukraine is only in the
process of building its own army and of ridding itself of the formerly
Soviet troops on its territory. Nevertheless, the very fact that the
army has become such an important issue due to Ukraine's fear of
Russia is troubling, even if unavoidable. The army has become
associated too closely with the Ukrainian raîson d'etre, thereby
guaranteeing military concerns an excessively important place in
the life of a supposedly neutral and nonnuclear state. It will
obviously be in the armed forces' interest to have a large army,
consisting, as current plans foresee, of at least 250,000–300,000
soldiers, with sufficient resources to guarantee its members a

174   decent standard of living, and with enough military hardware to ensure combat readiness. And Ukrainian politicians will be hard-pressed not to assign priority to a symbol of statehood, a powerful interest group, and a potential threat to Ukrainian stability. In the absence of outside pressure, then, the army will remain strong and powerful. And if the pressure from Russia does not subside, if talk of border revisions does not end, then even the most staunchly antimilitarist democrats will favor a strong army—and, perhaps, nuclear weapons—as the only bulwark against real or perceived Russian imperialism.

Ukraine, like all the other post-Soviet republics, may be headed toward authoritarian rule by an alliance of a corrupt state, a strongman president, and a powerful military. The prospect is not encouraging. Ukraine's turn to the right would have adverse consequences for stability, democracy, and security in all of Eastern Europe. Is it avoidable? An unconditionally affirmative answer is hard to give. Were Ukraine the only country in such a predicament, then we might expect its neighbors to exert a stabilizing influence on its political system. But its neighbors face similar prospects, and its largest neighbor, Russia, may be most prone to becoming nondemocratic.

This time, the legacy of empire and the legacy of totalitarianism reinforce each other. Elites are weak, resources are minimal, and problems are immense. This characterization applies to all the post-Soviet republics as well as to most of the countries of Central Europe. So they can help themselves only up to a point. Thereafter, countervailing pressure will have to come primarily from without—from outside these countries and outside the region. That can only mean the West.

CONCLUSION

Dilemmas for the West

Although the choices facing Ukraine are depressing, the United States and Western Europe can make a big difference by realizing that they can, indeed, *must* save the day, lest the collapse of the Ukrainian polity and economy drag down in its wake Russia, Poland, Belarus, and Central Europe with unimagined consequences for the political stability of the West. The kind of policies that the West should consider are neither without precedent nor especially unusual. But they do require an appreciation of Ukraine on its own terms and not as a province of Russia or the USSR, and it is this appreciation that is still lacking in most Western debates. Though imperative, overcoming this mind-set will not be easy, for the simple reason that for the last seventy years Ukraine really has been a province not a state, least of all one of Europe's largest. Not surprisingly, American and West European policy has reflected this reality.

WESTERN POLICY TOWARD UKRAINE

The West's attitude toward Eastern Europe in this century provides little support for the view that morality drives policy. In general, the West has traditionally supported the political status quo in Eastern Europe, even when its own proclaimed principles—whether self-determination or human rights—militated against such a position. The current challenge facing the West is

175

176   not to change its approach, but to apply it consistently to the existing status quo, within which Russia, Ukraine, Kazakhstan, and all the other successor states must be given their due. It might be argued that the West's primary goal in Eastern Europe should not be stability, but human rights or some other ethical principle. The argument may be valid for moral reasons, but inasmuch as it is unlikely to sway policymakers and publics, especially when their own well-being is at stake, such reasoning, however laudable, becomes largely irrelevant to actual policymaking.

Consider the time of the Russian Revolution and Civil War, when, despite their avowed devotion to self-determination, the Allied powers—the United States, Great Britain, and France—chose not to recognize the legitimacy of the non-Russian independence movements, except those of the Poles and the Balts, and generally threw their weight behind the counter-revolutionary forces of the White Russians. Despite some minor overtures from France, the Allies ignored the pro-Western Ukrainian People's Republic and thereby ensured its destruction by the Bolsheviks. Western indifference to Ukraine continued throughout the interwar period, as geopolitical realities associated with the rise of Hitler gave priority to the Soviet Union's establishment of diplomatic relations with the United States and admission into the League of Nations in 1934. Stalin's crimes could be, and were, conveniently downplayed or denied, with the classic instances of such shameful behavior being provided by the French statesman Eduard Herriot and the *New York Times* correspondent Walter Duranty during their trips to Ukraine at the height of the Great Famine of 1933. Only Germany, which broke ranks with prevailing Western attitudes in 1922, refused to ignore the non-Russians, but for geopolitical reasons as well. After signing the Treaty of Rapallo that April, Berlin established consulates in Kharkiv (then the Ukrainian capital), Odessa, and Tbilisi, while German scholars and analysts led the world in devoting critical attention to the USSR and Ukraine. Thanks in no small part to the scholarly study of Eastern Europe, *Ostforschung*, Nazi policymakers became

unusually sensitive to the relevance of the Ukrainians to their   **177**
eventual "drive to the East" and quest for *Lebensraum.*

The Priority of Geopolitics

Western attitudes changed somewhat in 1940, when a variety of
countries refused to recognize the Soviet annexation of the Baltic
states. But it was only in the last years of World War II that
Ukrainians and other non-Russians began to attract the West's
explicit attention—not unexpectedly, for exclusively geopolitical
reasons. On the one hand, Stalin's insistence that all Soviet
republics be granted seats in the United Nations produced a
diplomatic tug-of-war that ended with Western acceptance of
Ukraine and Belarus as founding members. On the other hand,
American, British, and West German intelligence services attempted to cultivate the subversive potential of the Ukrainian,
Baltic, and other anti-Communist resistance movements. The
Ukrainians were of particular interest, since they had succeeded in
fielding a fighting force of over 50,000, the Ukrainian Insurgent
Army, which controlled large parts of Western Ukraine until
1946–1947 and inflicted substantial casualties on superior Soviet
forces.

American attitudes toward the Ukrainians assumed clearer
form after the outbreak of Cold War hostilities. As Washington
first toyed with "rollback" and finally settled on "containment,"
some policymakers came to perceive the Ukrainians as a potential
source of Soviet vulnerability. Limited American encouragement
of Ukrainian restiveness—through Radio Liberty (née Radio Liberation) or lukewarm CIA support of émigré groups and guerrilla
movements—continued nonrecognition of the incorporation of
the Baltic states, and the visible brutality of the USSR's domination of its Central European satellites culminated in the passage of
the Captive Nations resolution in the late 1950s.

But that was all. While bridges were assiduously built to
Poles, Hungarians, Yugoslavs, and other Central Europeans,
Western policymakers had only declarative statements to make
regarding Ukrainians and other non-Russians. The one exception

178   was Soviet Jews, who, after the Jackson-Vanik and Stevenson amendments linking Jewish emigration from the USSR to American trade policy were passed in the 1970s, became the beneficiaries of official humanitarian policy measures. In contrast, other groups, as a distinctly geopolitical and not a humanitarian issue, were subordinated to overall United States policy toward the Soviet Union. By the same token, Western policymakers invariably viewed the United Nations representation of Ukraine and Belarus as irremediably bogus and never considered that their symbolic sovereignty could, in appropriate circumstances, be filled with more substantive content. Not surprisingly, when Ukraine's Mission to the United Nations in New York began taking an independent line in 1990–1991, policymakers could not grasp something so seemingly anomalous.

The Non-Russian Resurgence

Ironically, despite attracting little interest, Ukrainians and other non-Russians were nevertheless becoming an important component of the East-West dialogue by virtue of their prominence in discussions on human rights. This development, though unforeseen and probably undesired, was inevitable for two reasons. First, most Soviet political prisoners were Ukrainians, Balts, and Armenians, frequently nationalists; their plight could not be mentioned without noting their ethnic identity. Second, Western verbal commitment to the general cause of human rights necessarily came face to face with two particular rights long since recognized by the international community—emigration and self-determination—which had specific national overtones. Indeed, human rights discourse exposed the inconsistency on which Western attitudes toward non-Russians were based. Just as the right to emigration could not, either logically or morally, be restricted to Soviet Jews, the support of human rights in general had, as United Nations documents insisted, to incorporate national rights. In effect, human rights, as the Soviet government correctly understood, were highly subversive of Soviet stability because they

threatened to depopulate the country and to promote its dismem- **179**
berment.

It was in the period of perestroika that non-Russians finally
intruded on the idyllic world of Western policymakers. By 1990 it
should have been obvious that the USSR was no more. The
republics were clearly running the show, while Gorbachev was
merely running in place. The year 1991 offered even more conclu-
sive evidence of the Soviet state's impotence, as the visibly ner-
vous Mikhail Sergeievich desperately attempted to cobble
together some kind—any kind—of association. He failed, of
course, not just because of the August coup, but because he could
not undo the destruction he himself had wrought.

It took Gorbachev's abdication and the fait accompli of the
December Ukrainian referendum for the West finally to appreciate the reality of independent republics. By early 1992 most of the
countries that mattered had extended diplomatic recognition to
the republics, Russia had occupied the Soviet Union's seat on the
UN's Security Council, and Kazakhstan, Armenia, Azerbaijan,
Moldova, Tajikistan, Turkmenistan, and Uzbekistan had joined
Ukraine, Belarus, Estonia, Latvia, and Lithuania as full-fledged
members of the organization.

WESTERN MISPERCEPTIONS

But old habits die hard. It was evident throughout much of 1992
that Western policymakers still would have preferred the revival of
some form of maximally centralized union. Their unrealistically
optimistic assessment of the Commonwealth of Independent
States and its chances of survival, their continued preference for
dealing almost exclusively with or through Moscow on important
issues, and their willingness to tolerate Russia's expropriation of
Soviet overseas property suggested that the non-Russian successor
states still did not matter. Western attitudes toward Ukraine were
especially disturbing since they revealed an inability to recognize
the dilemmas of a young nation having to come to terms with its

180   former imperial master. Ukrainian behavior vis-à-vis Moscow is hardly above reproach, but it is motivated almost exclusively by fear of a country that until recently Americans, above all, considered an "evil empire." Instead, Ukrainian policies—if, indeed, much of what Kiev does in helter-skelter fashion can be considered such—are all too frequently interpreted by American policymakers and the media as examples of a fanatical and all-consuming nationalism, in contrast to which Russian behavior inevitably appears cool, levelheaded, and even reactive.

Consider the media response to Leonid Kravchuk's decision on March 12, 1992, to halt (as it turned out, temporarily) the removal of tactical nuclear weapons to Russia. In light of Russia's huge nuclear arsenal and ambiguous attitude toward Ukrainian independence, Kravchuk's move was a transparent plea for attention and understanding, and yet the day after his announcement the *New York Times* recommended that the United States use *positive* incentives to induce Russia to disarm, but employ *negative* ones—that is, the threat of "no Western assistance"—toward Ukraine if it "tries to hold onto its arms."[1] The moral is clear: Russia is trustworthy, while Ukraine is not. Plead with the former, get tough with the latter.

The West, evidently, has its own Ukrainian problem, one that it will have to overcome before genuinely rational policies can be formulated. Western elites and publics have grasped the fact of the Soviet Union's demise, but they have yet to appreciate the fact of the Soviet empire's collapse. The end of this empire, as of every empire, means the emergence of new states. These new post-Soviet, non-Russian states have not yet entered and found a proper place in the Western consciousness.

Ukraine exemplifies this problem. Russia must cope with the loss of "southern Russia," of "Little Russia," while the West must understand that a new state, not a south Russian one, has emerged to the north of the Black Sea. The existing Western mind-set leads to the conclusion that developments in Russia are normal, while developments in Ukraine are deviant. The West needs to accept

Ukraine and the other non-Russian successor states for what they **181** are: the genuine states of genuine nations with genuine cultures and histories. A somewhat trivial example illustrates the mentality involved. Apparently, United States Department of State analysts refer to the newly established Central Asian states as the "Stans."[2] Whether or not such a designation is derogatory is beside the point; rather more important is that it suggests that Uzbekistan, Kazakhstan, Kyrgyzstan, Turkmenistan, and Tajikistan are not taken quite as seriously as they should be.

Just as Ukrainians must eventually cease defining themselves in terms of Russia in order to be finally rid of the phobias that haunt them, Western countries should stop defining Ukraine, Belarus, Kazakhstan, and the other non-Russian states in terms only of Russia—as its provinces and appendages, as thorns in its side. Naturally, as the regional great power, Russia will continue to attract the most attention; but Russian importance is surely no grounds for ignoring Lithuania, Ukraine, or Kazakhstan, especially if, as in the case of Ukraine and Kazakhstan, one is dealing with very large states.

UNITED STATES POLICY TOWARD UKRAINE

Recent United States policy toward Ukraine has generally reflected a "Russia only" or "Russia first" mind-set. Until late 1991, Ukraine hardly entered the calculations of American policymakers, who preferred to deal exclusively with Moscow. President Bush, for instance, exhorted Ukrainians to eschew "suicidal nationalism" during his visit to Kiev on August 1—just three weeks before the "suicidal centralism" of the coup plotters and Ukraine's subsequent declaration of independence.

Once confronted with the fait accompli of republican independence, American policy slowly began to shift. On September 27, Ukraine joined the Peace Corps program. Then, several days before the December 1 referendum, President Bush accepted the inevitable and declared that the United States would recognize

182   Ukraine "in a relatively short period of time." Recognition finally came on December 25, and formal diplomatic relations were opened on January 23, 1992. That March, President Bush appointed as ambassador to Kiev his Ukrainian-American deputy press secretary, Roman Popadiuk. Although the choice of Popadiuk was criticized as a White House ploy to appeal to the ethnic vote, it also suggested that the president was serious enough about Ukraine to pick one of his closest advisers for the position.

Whichever interpretation is correct, Popadiuk's appointment did little to bring Ukraine out from Russia's shadow. The fruits of Leonid Kravchuk's visit to Washington, D.C., in May exemplified Ukraine's subsidiary status. Negotiations did result in an agreement conferring most favored nation status on Ukraine and extending Overseas Private Investment Corporation (OPIC) insurance coverage to American firms doing business in Ukraine. And the White House took the opportunity to reiterate its intention of providing $10 million for the establishment of an International Science and Technology Center in Kiev, which would house Ukraine's unemployed nuclear scientists. All these measures were welcome, but they appeared almost insignificant compared with the lavish attention Washington devoted to Russia's nuclear arms, economic ills, and monetary weakness. Symptomatically, only a fraction—no more than several hundred million—of the $24 billion Western aid package to the former USSR was slated for Ukraine and the other non-Russian states, even though their collective needs were surely no smaller than Russia's.

Although policymakers, analysts, and commentators appear to be increasingly cognizant of Ukraine's existence and importance, the level of awareness is still inadequate for dealing with a country that is one of the largest in Europe. The 1992 American presidential election campaign deflected public debate from foreign policy concerns in general, but the underlying problem was, and still is, perceptual. For most policymakers Russia is all that matters; Ukraine remains a secondary concern. This view would be fully defensible on both moral and geopolitical grounds if

Ukraine really did not matter. But, as this book has argued, it **183** does, and greatly so.

Policy Consequences

The problem with giving priority to Russia is that it presents a danger of distortion. Consider that Western reactions to Russian separatism in Moldova and the Crimea have been either non-existent or surprisingly mild. In contrast, Serbian separatism in Croatia and Bosnia-Herzegovina has been condemned universally, even though all these separatisms, as separatisms, are alike, and their consequences—instability, conflict, and violence—either already are or are likely to be identical.

The intellectual privileging of Russia has specific policy consequences as well. At issue is, first of all, the question of whom to help most: Russia or the non-Russian states? Russia or the Central European states? Russia or Ukraine? Few policymakers would be comfortable with so stark a statement of alternatives, but it is not an exaggeration to put the matter in such terms. Since Western resources are limited—both by definition and especially now, at a time of worldwide recession—and the challenges facing all of the successor states are immense, the question of whom to help most is a restatement of a priority that policymakers, business people, and scholars throughout the world appreciate: maximizing utility while minimizing cost. That is, getting the "most bang for the buck."

In general, the Western debate has concluded that Russia should be given priority *now* just as the Soviet Union under Gorbachev was given priority *then*—even when, as in 1989–1990, it was becoming evident that central power in the USSR was rapidly eroding. The argument can be stated as follows: Russia is a nuclear power and will remain one, and Western strategic interests demand that Russia be contained, stabilized, or democratized, so that its threat potential is not realized. Russia is Eastern Europe's largest country, and the fate of reform in the other successor states is dependent on political and economic reform in Russia. Finally,

184   Russia has already taken the plunge and has embarked on reform, and such courage merits support and encouragement.

Although these views are valid, rather more striking than their validity is the degree to which they have swept the field and excluded other arguments from serious consideration.[3] The priority of Russia has become almost an article of faith, and we could not be faulted for suspecting that Western infatuation with Russia is as much at work here as the putative inherent irrefutability of such arguments.

Policy Alternatives

Consider an alternative line of reasoning. That Russia will remain Eastern Europe's only nuclear power is as much a reason to hope that it will become democratic and behave itself as it is cause for alarm. After all, as the inheritor of most of the Soviet Union's military past and as the heir of many tsarist traditions, Russia, it may plausibly be argued, is as likely to continue in their expansionist footsteps as it is to abandon a policy that goes back to Ivan the Terrible. Nuclear weapons may, from this point of view, play as much of an intimidating role in Russia's foreign policy as they did in the Soviet Union's. And rather than expecting a major discontinuity to occur in Russian/Soviet history, would it not be more, or at least equally, realistic to expect that Russia's future behavior will to some degree resemble that of the past? If so, then containing Russia now, as the Soviet Union and tsarist Russia were contained in the past, may be a more realistic policy course for the West to pursue than attempting to integrate it. And if containment is the proper course of action, does that not then mean that priority should be given to its neighbors, who would come to serve as the first line of containment? The current Western debate largely excludes this consideration, which, whatever its merits, is far from absurd.

The evolution of the United States Defense Department's controversial document, the *Defense Planning Guidance for the 1994–99 Fiscal Years*, illustrates this point. An early draft argued, surely not implausibly:

> We continue to recognize that collectively the conventional forces **185**
> of the states formerly comprising the Soviet Union retain the most
> military potential in all of Eurasia; and we do not dismiss the risks to
> stability in Europe from a nationalist backlash in Russia or efforts to
> reincorporate into Russia the newly independent republics of
> Ukraine, Belarus, and possibly others. . . . We must, however, be
> mindful that democratic change in Russia is not irreversible, and
> that despite its current travails, Russia will remain the strongest
> military power in Eurasia and the only power in the world with the
> capacity of destroying the United States.[4]

The final draft expunged these words of warning, and replaced
them with a thoroughly banal sentiment:

> The U.S. has a significant stake in promoting democratic consol-
> idation and peaceful relations between Russia, Ukraine and the
> other republics of the former Soviet Union.[5]

The point is not that the second version is incorrect, but that the
policy debate should focus on both, and not just on the best-case
(or worst-case) scenario. If nothing else, the Kremlin's sale of
advanced military systems to China and Iran suggests that Russia
may still be cause for some Western concern.

Consider also the question of Russia's size as the factor that
gives Russia priority over the other successor states. To be sure,
Russia's presence in Eurasia is so overwhelming as to make the case
for ignoring Russia impossible. But size works both for and against
Russia. After all, the region between Germany and Russia, which
encompasses Poland, Hungary, the Czech Republic, Slovakia,
Ukraine, Belarus, and the Baltics, is also quite large, in terms of
physical size, population, and economic and military strength. If
helping Russia financially means not helping Central Europe as
much as it could or should be helped, will that not in turn subvert
Russian reform, which by the logic of size must also be dependent
on the success of reform in Central Europe, a region that is also
quite large? Moreover, size does not facilitate reform, a point made
in chapter 2. Size may necessitate reform, but it also makes reform
more difficult, more protracted, and more expensive. These two
lines of argument suggest that a plausible case could actually be
made for assigning priority to Central Europe on the rationale
that, first, Western resources are insufficient to have a large

186   impact on reform in a country the size of Russia; second, even limited Western resources may have a substantial impact on reform in smaller countries such as Ukraine, Poland, and Belarus; and, third, the greater likelihood of reform in Central Europe will surely advance reform in Russia. In other words, reforming Central Europe may be a precondition for reform in Russia. Supplement this argument with the first regarding containment and one could conclude that reforming Central Europe is both a strategic and economic priority. If so, then supporting reform in Ukraine above all becomes imperative, since Ukraine is the largest country in Central Europe and Russia's most important counterweight. Just as the argument regarding nuclear weapons can go both ways, so can that concerning size, yet it is remarkable how little the alternative presented above is encountered in public debates.

Finally, consider the case for supporting Russia the most because it has already committed itself to reform. First, reform-minded enthusiasm alone cannot guarantee policy priority. It is hard to imagine the West unconditionally backing, say, Turkmenistan, even if it were to adopt wholesale capitalism tomorrow. Geopolitical importance and economic size generally play a more important role in such policy choices. Second, if the willingness to reform is central, then Poland, the Czech Republic, and Hungary, which have gone much further down that road than has Russia, should be given priority. And last, even if Russia still deserved priority, reform-minded enthusiasm would surely be weak grounds on which to base Western assistance. Enthusiasm comes and goes. If Yeltsin is forced to decelerate reform for the sake of political stability and social peace, as may be the case in the wake of his retreat at the December 1992 session of the Congress of People's Deputies, should the West then abandon him?

The above arguments surely lead to at least one conclusion: the other successor states also matter, and Central Europe in general and Ukraine in particular may matter as much as, and perhaps even more than, Russia. To ignore them—their histories, their problems, their needs, and their perceptions—is a guarantee not of success in Eastern Europe, but of failure. Although policy-

makers may not agree on the right answers, they may be more **187**
likely to agree on the wrong ones—and ignoring Ukraine, Belarus, the "Stans," and Central Europe is as wrong an answer to
the problems of the former Soviet empire as there can be. Zbigniew Brzezinski's advice is well-aimed:

> a recovery program for the Russian economy that does not at the
> same time seek to transform Russia into a post-imperial state could
> prove to be ephemeral. Accordingly any Russian efforts to isolate
> and eventually again to subordinate Ukraine through the mainte-
> nance of a Moscow-controlled outpost in Crimea, for example, or to
> delay the evacuation of Russian troops from the Baltic republics
> should be unambiguously viewed as obstacles to effective financial
> and economic assistance. . . . Above all it is geopolitically essen-
> tial that Ukraine succeed in stabilizing itself as a secure and inde-
> pendent state. . . . Accordingly a critical component of Western
> strategy has to be the deliberate effort—not only economic but also
> political—to consolidate a stable and sovereign Ukraine.[6]

UKRAINIAN SECURITY AND THE WEST

In reorienting their policies Western countries will have to address
the issues that are at the top of the Ukrainian agenda and which
are most amenable to outside direction: security, economic reform, and elite training. The question of security is paramount.
Unless the West provides the militarily impotent non-Russian
states, especially Ukraine, with minimal security assurances, unless it allays their fears of being swallowed up by Russia, they will
have no choice but to give priority to their immediate survival,
with all the deleterious consequences that such concern may have
for peace, economic reform, and democracy. The concern is not
hypothetical, as Foreign Minister Zlenko's address to the UN
General Assembly on September 29, 1992, made clear: "Having
embarked upon the road toward reduction and elimination of
nuclear weapons, we expect strict international guarantees of our
national security against the possible threat or use of force on the
part of any nuclear state [read Russia]. I would like to emphasize
that this is not a rhetorical statement of our newly independent
state."[7] Just how heightened Ukraine's fears are was evident in one
parliamentarian's comparison of transferring nuclear arms to

188   Russia to Kuwait "Surrendering its weapons to Iraq and becoming
an Iraqi protectorate."[8] The very last message the West should
convey to Ukrainians is, as one Western diplomat put it, "Give us
your missiles and go to hell."[9] With incentives like these, Ukraine
may as well go to hell *with* its missiles.

Enhancing Ukrainian security appears rather more formidable a task than it actually is. By according Kiev full membership in
its institutions and including it in its deliberations and procedures,
the West would give Moscow to understand that its former younger
brother possesses special status. Incorporating Ukraine into the
North Atlantic Cooperation Council was a good first step (NATO
Secretary General Manfred Woerner's appreciation of the fact
that Ukraine "is a very peaceful nation" and "is interested in good-
neighborly relations with all its neighbor states" was especially
noteworthy);[10] including it as a full-fledged partner in discussions
of economic stabilization, arms reductions, and the like, assigning
a significant Western diplomatic presence to Kiev, sharing Western intelligence data, continually emphasizing the reality of
Ukrainian independence, and encouraging Ukraine to become a
partner in Western economic and diplomatic ventures would be
useful next steps.

Helping resolve Russo-Ukrainian tensions would be an
equally important signal to both Moscow and Kiev. Ukraine's
insistence that former Soviet forces, on land, air, and sea, be
withdrawn, reduced, or transformed into Ukrainian units is surely
not extreme behavior for a sovereign state. Ukraine's insistence
that the Crimea remain within Ukraine is also no more extreme
than everyday West European or American attitudes toward their
own separatist movements. In other words, although the Ukrainian elites lack diplomatic finesse and political skills, the principles on which their policy preferences are based—reduction of
armed forces and the integrity of existing boundaries—are identical to those enunciated in the West, and, thus, deserving of
Western endorsement.

Moreover, so long as the West remains aloof from the divorce
proceedings between Russia and Ukraine, and appears to favor the

former, tensions between Moscow and Kiev will be unavoidable, **189** armed conflict will be possible, and the West's own interests in a stable East will not be served. The lessons of Bosnia-Herzegovina, where war might have been averted had the West not sent mixed signals to Belgrade, are instructive. In contrast, taking a firm stand on these issues now, suggesting how they should be resolved, proposing mechanisms, and engaging in blatant linkage is no more outlandish than bringing Israelis and Arabs to the negotiating table at Camp David while making clear to both what the preferred outcome is and what the costs of its nonachievement are as well.

In all these respects, the United Nations could play a supportive role, especially if guided by an activist secretary-general, such as Boutros Boutros-Ghali. At the least, the UN can serve as a permanent forum for the regular airing of Russo-Ukrainian misunderstandings. But it can also do much more—by engaging Ukraine and the other republics in its agencies; by continually underlying the reality and sovereignty of all the independent sucessor states; by providing them with some of the information their policymakers need; and, most important perhaps, by contributing to the creation of a culture of compromise and realism in Russo-Ukrainian relations.

Economic Assistance

With regard to economic reform, the West must first come fully to appreciate both the difficulty of introducing market systems and the socially destructive consequences of such a move. The prospect of enormous unemployment is surely unnerving for any government. To insist that Ukrainians and other non-Russians must first embark on destabilizing change before Western aid is forthcoming is thus not very constructive. Since economic transformation is imperative, however, the West must be willing to go out on a limb and assist the Ukrainians *before* as well as *during* their economic reforms. Just as the successor states have no alternative to reform, the West has no alternative to offering massive assis-

190   tance, unless of course the probability of multiple dictatorships east of the Oder-Neisse line is attractive.

The West may have no blank checks to write, but blank checks are precisely what Ukraine and other non-Russian states do not require. What, then, can Western states do for them, especially at a time of worldwide recession? At a minimum, re-scheduling or even forgiving the debt, which will never be repaid anyway, would not be a bad place to start because feverish Russian and Ukrainian efforts to raise capital will only distort economic development. Actively assisting the Ukrainian government in the formulation of realistic monetary and fiscal policies would be useful, too: universities, think tanks, and research institutes may have more to say here than the International Monetary Fund and the World Bank.

Opening West European and American markets to Ukrai-nian goods, and particularly to agricultural products, could also be considered, especially since it would be in the spirit of free trade. Encouraging emigration and instituting a "guest worker" program would not only revive the European Community's labor force and increase the West European tax base, but also reduce unem-ployment in the successor states and provide for a channel of hard currency flows, via remittances. Supporting the Ukrainian hryvnia with the establishment of a hard currency stabilization fund and investing in Ukraine's infrastructure—which could ab-sorb some unemployment while getting the economy moving—might be good ideas. No less critical would be helping all the East European states resolve their energy crisis: persuading Russia to sell its energy resources through a payments union, developing alternative energy sources, and, most important perhaps, modern-izing or scrapping existing atomic energy stations, especially those like the one in Chernobyl near St. Petersburg, Smolensk, and Kursk in western Russia and Ignalina in Lithuania. The nuclear reactors are an enormous environmental hazard, for the East as well as for the West, that the cash-strapped non-Russians or Russians simply cannot deal with on their own.

Training Ukrainian Elites

Last on the list is training and retraining indigenous Ukrainian and other non-Russian (and Russian) elites—the simplest of the three immediate challenges facing the West. Stalin may have exaggerated in his thinking that "cadres decide everything," but he was certainly correct to suggest that quality of personnel matters. Competent elites can improve the quality of Ukrainian policy, of the policymaking process, and of the state bureaucracy—and any difference would be a big difference. They can also forestall diasporization.

Training seminars for intellectuals, administrators, and policymakers and other initiatives of the sort promulgated by the Soros Foundation are invaluable. University exchanges, such as those promoted by the International Research and Exchanges Board, the Netherlands Association for International Affairs, Vienna's Institute for Human Sciences, the EC's European Action Scheme for the Mobility of University Students, the German Academic Exchange Service, and Austria's Bureau for European Educational Cooperation are also critical, as are workshops, conferences, and other such gatherings. Especially important is establishing foreign-language study centers, such as those of the Goethe Institute, since Ukrainian knowledge of Western languages, in particular English and German, is inadequate. Most of these initiatives need not be governmental, though state-sponsored technical assistance, such as training in modern agricultural, industrial, and management techniques, would also be desirable.

Security enhancement, economic stabilization, and competent elites may not suffice to prevent Ukrainian democracy and statehood from breaking down, but they are surely preconditions for their survival. That is to say, secure states with prosperous economies and well-trained administrators should be less inclined to authoritarianism than insecure, poor, and incompetent states. Naturally, verbal pressure should also be exerted and linkage should be pursued, however shamelessly, in order to convey to Ukrainian elites the seriousness with which the West views their

192 commitment to democracy and civil and minority rights. At the same time, however, the West also has a responsibility to realize that such pressure will appear to be only a cruel joke if it also insists that Ukraine square the circle by simultaneously remaining responsive to its people while completely disrupting their lives.

DIVIDING THE BURDEN

The challenges facing the West are, thus, no fewer and no smaller than those already overwhelming the East. Inevitably, therefore, the West's largest and richest representatives will have to take the lead in saving the non-Russians in general and the Ukrainians in particular, both from the Russians and from themselves. Security enhancement will have to become the task of the world's only great power, the United States. Economic assistance will, then, perforce devolve onto the West Europeans, who would be most affected by East European economic and political collapse anyway. The sums involved will be significant, but there is, alas, no alternative. Sooner rather than later, Western Europe should consider including the USSR's westernmost successor states, and especially Ukraine, together with Poland, the Czech Republic, Slovakia, and Hungary, in the European Community. To be sure, their overly rapid inclusion would disrupt the EC, but at least it would provide Western Europe with institutional mechanisms for bailing out and supervising the non-Russians. And besides, since *not* including them may ensure non-Russian economic collapse, the EC would not emerge unscathed in either scenario: the choice, then, is to accept burdens preparedly or to confront them unpreparedly.

Integrating Ukraine, Poland, and other East European states into Europe may necessitate the formation of an East-Central European Commonwealth as a transitional association. Ukraine's Treaty on Friendship and Cooperation with Poland, and the February 16, 1992, agreement on economic cooperation and trade among Ukraine, Poland, Czechoslovakia, and Hungary, are not

only a rational response to the logic of geography and geopolitics, **193**
but also a foretaste of things to come.

An association of formerly Communist states would do well
to have a partner already anchored in the West. In the long run,
Germany may not qualify for the role in light of its own potential
for hegemony and checkered past. (In the short run, of course,
currying German favor, as both Yeltsin and Kravchuk have done
by offering to resettle Germans expelled by Stalin to Kazakhstan,
makes perfect sense.) That leaves only Austria, a rich but
nonthreatening country with the political savvy and economic
know-how for such a sustained leadership role. Not surprisingly,
far-sighted Austrians, such as the Austrian People's Party chairman, Erhard Busek, and the country's most prominent intellectual, Günther Nenning, envision such a *Führungsrolle* for their
country.

THE AUSTRIAN CONNECTION

Austria's business community is already a leading force in the
economies of Poland, the Czech Republic, Slovakia, and Hungary. Expanding into Ukraine and other former republics would be
a challenge for Austrian business, but one for which it is prepared.
Ukraine should be particularly attractive since it offers Austrians
the opportunity to assert themselves in the face of the virtual
certainty that Austria's inclusion in the EC will transform its
economy into an appendage of Germany's. Most obviously,
Ukraine also represents a vast potential market for Austria's consumer goods and a possible source of inexpensive food products as
well as some of the finished goods that account for 70 percent of
Austria's imports. Ukraine's energy resources, raw materials, and
economically strategic position on the Black Sea should also be of
interest to a landlocked country whose imports amount to 40
percent of its Gross Domestic Product.

Austria also has an ace up its sleeve because western
Ukraine's historical, cultural, and economic ties with Hapsburg
Vienna make it a logical beachhead for Austrian business. Lviv is a

194   miniature Vienna, many older Galicians still speak German, the mannerisms of the western Ukrainians are remarkably similar to those of the Viennese, and Western-style entrepreneurship is still alive in Galicia. In other words, Austria has a direct "line" to Ukraine. Incipient Galician capitalists are ideal partners for Austria, both because of the economic opportunities present in western Ukraine, and because they can act as middlemen for investors interested in eastern Ukraine as well. In a word, just as Austria is poised to become a gateway to Central Europe, so could Galicia become the gateway to Ukraine and neighboring republics.

The Austrian connection would also be especially beneficial for Ukraine. Despite obvious differences in size, Austria can offer Ukraine several lessons. The first is that federation, while no panacea for ethnic and regional separatism, is a relatively effective way of coping with that problem. For Ukraine in particular a federal system would have the incalculable advantage of, on the one hand, satisfying the demands of Ruthenians in Transcarpathia and Russians in the Crimea and perhaps the Donbas, while, on the other hand, reducing the salience of their protests by transforming all of Ukraine's provinces into equally empowered administrative federal units.

The second lesson relates to Austria's attitudes toward its own Russia—Germany. Most obviously, the Austrian example suggests that such sentiments need not get in the way of beneficial economic and political relations. Austria pegs its currency to the deutsche mark and most of its trade is with Germany; for almost all of the postwar period, Austria was neutral while Germany was firmly lodged in NATO. Nevertheless, Austrian-German relations are normal, and they can serve as a model for both Ukrainians and Russians.

Austria's other lesson for Ukraine and other post-Communist states is that state intervention, while perhaps no substitute for a vigorous market, can enhance economic prosperity and social stability. Until recently close to 40 percent of Austria's industry was nationalized and economic protectionism was a staple of government policy, while the coordination of the economic interests of labor and capital still remains at the core of Vienna's policy **195** of social *Partnerschaft*. True, Austria's nationalized sectors are currently in trouble; economic protectionism will have to be abandoned when Austria joins the EC; and social coordination may be impossible within the all-European market. But the lesson remains: following the devastation of World War II, Austria's economic policies were critical in raising the country's living standard severalfold and in transforming it into a modern industrial democracy. Austria's experience cannot of course be automatically transplanted to so different and so much larger a country as Ukraine, but it does suggest that pell-mell marketization with no concern for economic balance and social accord may not be the only path for countries desirous of economic growth.

THE END OF CERTAINTY

As Ukraine, Russia, and the other successor states grapple with the complex legacies of empire and totalitarianism, the countries of the West are gradually beginning to realize how difficult dealing with the Soviet Union's collapse will be. The end of the old order does not necessarily mean the dawn of a new peaceful, harmonious one; the end of a historical aberration—totalitarianism—need not mean the end of history; the defeat of communism is not yet the victory of democracy. Like the countries of the East, the countries of the West must resolve several problems for which there are no easy solutions, quick fixes, or simple answers.

Political elites in both East and West must choose between simplicity and complexity, between radical solutions and evolutionary ones. At present, most have apparently opted for the radical approach decried by Karl Popper and Alec Nove. The suddenness and completeness of imperial collapse supports such a solution, as do the political popularity of seeming to take resolute measures, the expedience of choosing policies that place the burden of reform almost entirely on the successor states, and the attractiveness of an uncompromising discourse that suggests that Western confusion is but temporary. Such enthusiasm notwith-

196 standing, radical transformations remain logically impossible and practically counterproductive as a result of the totalitarian legacy.

Seen from this point of view, Ukraine's experience with the legacies of totalitarianism and empire assumes special significance, because it suggests an alternative route to that adopted by Russia, one rather more in tune with the logical consequences of the arguments made in this book. So far, Ukrainian policymakers have been unusually cautious with respect to political, social, and especially economic reform. Wittingly or not, they have seemingly tried to place more or less equal value on a variety of goals: economic prosperity, social peace, and political democracy. Western analysts criticize Kiev for being sluggish, uncommitted, and plodding, but Ukrainian policymakers can respond by pointing to the tentative, if unspectacular, progress that they have made in keeping the economy intact, keeping the Russian speakers mollified, and keeping most of the democrats on their side. Like countries that experience economic modernization relatively late and, thus, are supposed to have the advantage of benefiting from the experience and technology of earlier modernizers, later reformers such as Ukraine may have the advantage of learning from the mistakes of earlier reformers, whether Poland, Czechoslovakia, or Russia. Later reformers may also have to pay a penalty—the disapproval of Western political and economic elites—but, if my analysis is correct, that penalty should be far smaller than that of radicals confronted with political instability, social upheaval, or, as in the case of Czechoslovakia, dismemberment.

What Not to Do

The legacy of totalitarianism can be overcome only by shunning radicalism, recognizing complexity, and introducing piecemeal reforms, first here, then there, continually making adjustments, continually making certain that all the goals identified by policymakers are being pursued to at least some degree, continually avoiding distortions, exaggerations, and egregious mistakes.

The question of multiple goals is central to this approach. In contrast, radicals assign absolute overriding priority to one factor, which they claim determines everything else. For Marx it was **197** class, for Lenin the Bolshevik vanguard. Characteristically, political and social life is reduced to an "epiphenomenon," a derivative of the primary determinants. Evolutionary reformers, however, assign more or less equal priority to economics and politics, and to culture and class. From their point of view, if one cannot conclusively determine what is most important, all factors must be given some (if not equal) consideration. Of course, there is a normative component here as well, one that implies a moral choice. Revolutionaries can ignore other factors because they firmly believe that the factor they favor is the source of all good. Nonradicals view many things as good, and they are uncertain how, if at all, to assign priority. Nonradicals recognize that markets are positive, but they also favor democracy, civil society, social peace, ethnic amity, and so on. They are unwilling to sacrifice them for the sake of the promises that radicals make, both in general and especially in circumstances, as in post-Soviet Eastern Europe, that do not facilitate all-or-nothing solutions in the first place.

Ironically, therefore, the largest contribution the West can make to the reform process in Ukraine, Russia, and other successor states is not financial, military, or political. The best thing the West can do is to stop giving the East *bad advice.* Promoting simplistic solutions in extremely complex situations, encouraging radical change under conditions that negate radical change is a recipe for disaster. If the West is unwilling to soften the blow of Big Bang approaches to political, economic, and social reform, then it should at least desist from advocating such a course and pushing Ukrainians, Russians, and other East Europeans toward a fate they do not deserve. One post-Weimar was surely enough.

NOTES

INTRODUCTION

1. Peter Hole et al., *Ukraine* (Washington, D.C.: International Monetary Fund, 1992), p. 46; *Encyclopedia of Ukraine*, vol. I (Toronto: University of Toronto Press, 1984), pp. 36–37; *Ukraine: A Concise Encyclopaedia*, vol. II (Toronto: University of Toronto Press, 1971), pp. 734, 740.
2. *Ukrains'ka Radians'ka Sotsialistychna Respublika* (Kiev: Holovna Redaktsiia Ukrains'koi Radians'koi Entsyklopedii, 1986), pp. 333–335.
3. *Vsesoiuznaia perepis' naseleniia, 1926* (Moscow: USSR Central Statistical Administration, 1929), vol. 9, table X.
4. Edward Allworth, ed., *Tatars of the Crimea* (Durham: Duke University Press, 1988); Aleksandr M. Nekrich, *The Punished Peoples* (New York: W.W. Norton, 1978).
5. Roman Solchanyk, "Catastrophic Language Situation in Major Ukrainian Cities," *Radio Liberty Research Bulletin*, no. 30, July 29, 1987, RL 286/87, p. 2.
6. Mark B. Tauger, "The 1932 Harvest and the Famine of 1933," *Slavic Review*, vol. 50, no. 1 (Spring 1991), pp. 70–89; Robert Conquest, *The Harvest of Sorrow* (New York: Oxford University Press, 1986); James E. Mace, "Famine and Nationalism in Soviet Ukraine," *Problems of Communism*, vol. 33, no. 3 (May-June 1984), pp. 37–50.
7. Oles' Boiko, "Dyktatura dlia prezydenta," *Post-Postup*, no. 27, 1992, p. 3.
8. Marta Kolomayets, "Kravchuk Threatens Foreign Critics," *The Ukrainian Weekly*, August 30, 1992, p. 1.
9. "Kravchuk to Diaspora: Shut Up or Get Out," *The Ukrainian Weekly*, August 30, 1992, p. 8.
10. Stepan Bandera (1909–1959) was a leading activist in the Organization of Ukrainian Nationalists (OUN) in interwar Poland. Incarcerated by the Nazis in 1941, Bandera spent World War II in the Sachsenhausen concentration camp. After the war, he led the uncompromisingly anti-Soviet and radically right-wing "Banderite" faction of the émigré OUN. In 1959, he was assassinated by a Soviet agent in Munich.

CHAPTER 1

1. For a more extensive discussion of these issues, see Alexander J. Motyl, "From Imperial Decay to Imperial Collapse: The Fall of the Soviet Empire in Comparative Perspective," in Richard L. Rudolph and David F. Good, eds., *Nationalism and Empire* (New York: St. Martin's Press, 1992), pp. 15–43.
2. See my discussion of totalitarianism in Alexander J. Motyl, *Sovietology, Rationality, Nationality: Coming to Grips with Nationalism in the USSR* (New York: Columbia University Press, 1990), pp. 59–71.
3. Ibid., pp. 174–186.
4. Roman Solchanyk, "The Communist Party and the Political Situation in Ukraine: An Interview with Stanislav Hurenko," *Report on the USSR*, December 14, 1990, p. 12.

CHAPTER 2

1. *RFE/RL Daily Report*, no. 199, October 15, 1992, p. 1.
2. Samuel P. Huntington, *The Third Wave: Democratization in the Late Twentieth Century* (Norman, Okla.: University of Oklahoma Press, 1991), pp. 266–267.
3. Louise Uchitelle, "Stealing toward Russian Capitalism," *New York Times*, March 8, 1991, p. 1; Bruce Weber, "Many in Former Soviet Lands Say that Now They Feel Even More Insecure," *New York Times*, April 23, 1992, p. 3.
4. Interview with SNBU Colonel Oleksandr Skipalsky in *Molod' Ukrainy*, October 30, 1991, p. 2.
5. Karl Popper, *The Open Society and Its Enemies*, vol. II (London: Routledge & Kegan Paul, 1945).
6. " 'The Best World We Have Yet Had.' George Urban Interviews Sir Karl Popper," *Report on the USSR*, May 31, 1991, pp. 21–22.
7. "Evrei tozhe skazali 'DA' svobodnoi Ukraine," *Khadashot*, no. 4, p. 1.
8. Ivan Dzyuba, *Internationalism or Russification?* (New York: Monad Press, 1974).
9. Petro Grigorenko, *Memoirs* (New York: W.W. Norton, 1982); Leonid Plyushch, *History's Carnival* (New York: Harcourt Brace Jovanovich, 1977).

CHAPTER 3

1. Alexander J. Motyl, "The End of Sovietology: From Soviet Studies to Post-Soviet Studies," in Alexander J. Motyl, ed., *The Post-Soviet Nations* (New York: Columbia University Press, 1992), pp. 302–316.
2. Yaroslav Hrytsak, "Ukraine: A special case of national identity?," *The Ukrainian Weekly*, January 26, 1992, p. 7.

200 3. See the classic work of political philosophy, Vyacheslav Lypyns'kyi, *Lysty do brativ-khliborobiv* (New York: Bulava, 1954).

4. Speech at a round table on "The Organization of the State and Forms of Administration in Ukraine," Kiev, January 16, 1992.

5. See their conversation in *Ukraina*, no. 46, November 18, 1990, pp. 4–6.

6. Roman Solchanyk, "Ukrainian-Russian Confrontation over the Crimea," *RFE/RL Research Report*, February 21, 1992, p. 29.

7. See Alexander J. Motyl, *The Turn to the Right: The Ideological Origins and Development of Ukrainian Nationalism, 1919–1929* (Boulder, Colo.: East European Monographs, 1980).

CHAPTER 4

1. Leonid Zalizniak, "Stiiki impers'ki stereotypy novykh rosiis'kykh 'demokrativ,'" *Samostiina Ukraina*, February 1992, p. 4.

2. TASS, August 26, 1991.

3. Reuters, January 9, 1992.

4. TASS, December 1, 1991.

5. *Sovetskaia Rossiia*, January 10, 1992, p. 1.

6. Orest Subtelny, *Ukraine: A History* (Toronto: University of Toronto Press, 1988), p. 282.

7. See former Deputy Prime Minister Volodymyr Lanovy's plea for Western understanding, "Come to Kiev. Listen to Ukraine," *New York Times*, April 8, 1992.

8. *The Current Digest of the Post-Soviet Press*, vol. 44, no. 33 (September 16, 1992), p. 24.

9. *RFE/RL Daily Report*, no. 4, January 8, 1993, p. 1.

10. *RFE/RL Daily Report*, no. 194, October 8, 1992, p. 1.

11. *The Current Digest of the Post-Soviet Press*, vol. 44, no. 13 (April 29, 1992), p. 3.

12. Ibid., vol. 44, no. 32 (September 9, 1992), p. 1.

13. Serge Schmemann, "Yeltsin Suggests Russian Regional Role," *New York Times*, March 1, 1993, p. 7.

14. Steven Erlanger, "Ukraine Finds 'Active Independence' Despite Military and Other Obstacles," *New York Times*, September 6, 1992, p. 18.

15. Yaroslav Trofimov, "Foreign Minister Promotes Ukraine's European Role," *The Ukrainian Weekly*, May 31, 1992, p. 3.

CHAPTER 5

1. Keith Bush, "The Disastrous Last Year of the USSR," *RFE/RL Research Report*, vol. 1, no. 12 (March 20, 1992), pp. 34–40; *The Ukrainian Weekly*, November 29, 1992, p. 3; *Ukraine* (Washington, D.C.: International Monetary Fund, 1992), p. 49.

2. *Ukraine: A Concise Encyclopaedia*, vol. II (Toronto: University of Toronto **201**
   Press, 1971), pp. 754, 756, 847.
3. Ibid., p. 765.
4. Ibid., p. 702.
5. Ibid., p. 768.
6. John Tedstrom, "Industrial Conversion in Ukraine: Policies and Prospects,"
   Report on the USSR, August 23, 1991, pp. 13–14.
7. *RFE/RL Daily Report*, no. 201, October 19, 1992, p. 3.
8. John Tedstrom, "The Economic Costs and Benefits of Independence for
   Ukraine," *Report on the USSR*, December 7, 1990, p. 12; *The Current Digest
   of the Post-Soviet Press*, vol. 44, no. 51 (January 20, 1993), p. 28.
9. Nadia Diuk and Adrian Karatnycky, "Ukraine: Europe's New Nation," *The
   World & I*, March 1992, p. 97.
10. Based on conversations with policymakers and officials conducted in Kiev in
    January 1992.
11. David Marples, "Ukraine Declares Moratorium on New Nuclear Reactors,"
    Report on the USSR, October 12, 1990, p. 21.
12. "Newsbriefs on Ukraine," *The Ukrainian Weekly*, February 9, 1992, p. 2.
13. Steven Greenhouse, "Planner Pitches Russia as Land of Opportunity," *New
    York Times*, May 3, 1992, p. 12.
14. See *Ukraine* (Washington, D.C.: International Monetary Fund, 1992).
15. Gabriel Schoenfeld, "Breadbasket Case," *Post-Soviet Prospects*, no. 13, May
    1992, pp. 3–4.
16. See Viktoria-2's advertisement in *Visti z Ukrainy*, no. 13, March 18–25,
    1992. Biznex and Halimport are known to me personally.
17. Richard E. Ericson, "The Classical Soviet-Type Economy: Nature of the
    System and Implications for Reform," *Journal of Economic Perspectives*, vol. 5,
    no. 4 (Fall 1991), pp. 11–27.
18. Ronald I. McKinnon, *The Order of Economic Liberalization* (Baltimore: The
    Johns Hopkins University Press, 1991).
19. Alec Nove, "Economics of the Transition Period," *The Harriman Institute
    Forum*, vol. 5, nos. 11–12 (July–August 1992), p. 8.
20. Ibid., p. 14.

CHAPTER 6

1. *Visti z Ukrainy*, no. 2, January 1992, p. 7.
2. Ukrainian television broadcast of January 9, 1992.
3. *Focus on Ukraine*, vol. 1, no. 2 (February 1985), p. 30.
4. L. M. Kravchuk, "Ateisticheskaia rabota v novykh usloviiakh," *Pod
   znamenem leninizma*, no. 6 (March 1988), p. 14.
5. L.M. Kravchuk, "Zmitsniuiuchy demokratychni zasady," *Komunist Ukrainy*,
   no. 4 (April 1988), p. 38.
6. L.M. Kravchuk, "Deiaki metodolohichni aspekty vykhovannia v umovakh
   perebudovy," *Ukrains'kyi istorychnyi zhurnal*, no. 12 (December 1988), pp.
   10, 14.

202   7. Ibid., p. 16.

8. "Ukraine: Ivashko Replaces Shcherbitsky," *The Current Digest of the Soviet Press*, vol. 41, no. 39 (October 25, 1989), p. 18.

9. Personal conversation in Kiev, January 1992.

CONCLUSION

1. "Nuclear Shocks from Ukraine," *New York Times*, March 14, 1992, p. 24.

2. Personal conversation with State Department analysts.

3. See Melvin Fagen, "Welcome this Change and Support Chernomyrdin," *International Herald Tribune*, December 23, 1992, p. 8. For a view reflective of the current consensus, see Anders Aslund, "Go Faster on Russian Reform," *New York Times*, December 7, 1992, p. 19.

4. "U.S. Strategy Plan Calls for Insuring That No Rivals Develop," *New York Times*, March 8, 1992, p. 14.

5. *Defense Planning Guidance 1994–1999*. See *Wall Street Journal*, June 2, 1992, p. 14.

6. Zbigniew Brzezinski, "The Cold War and Its Aftermath," *Foreign Affairs*, Fall 1992, pp. 31–49.

7. "At the U.N.: Zlenko's Address," *The Ukrainian Weekly*, October 11, 1992, p. 9.

8. *RFE/RL Daily Report*, no. 10, January 18, 1993, p. 5.

9. Serge Schmemann, "Ukraine Finds Nuclear Arms Bring a Measure of Respect," *New York Times*, January 7, 1993, p. 12.

10. Marta Kolomayets, "NATO Invites Ukraine to Join Alliance's Cooperation Council," *The Ukrainian Weekly*, March 1, 1992, p. 12.

Index